MW01226662

MW01226662

THE BEST OF
SINGAPORE
COOKING

Mrs Leong Yee Soo

Marshall Cavendish
Cuisine

All photographs by Yim Chee Peng except those on pages 31, 35, 69, 119, 125, 139, 143, 149, 153, 156, 159, 171, 191, 205, 233 and 239 which are by Mun & Wong Photographers.

First published in 1988
Reprinted 1988, 1989, 1991, 1992, 1994, 1995, 1996, 1998 (twice), 1999, 2001, 2003, 2004, 2008, 2010
This edition with new cover 2013

© 1991 Times Editions Pte Ltd
© 2000 Times Media Private Limited
© 2004 Marshall Cavendish International (Asia) Private Limited

Published by Marshall Cavendish Cuisine
An imprint of Marshall Cavendish International

All rights reserved

No part of this publication may be reproduced, stored in a retrieval system or transmitted, in any form
or by any means, electronic, mechanical, photocopying, recording or otherwise, without the prior permission
of the copyright owner. Request for permission should be addressed to the Publisher,
Marshall Cavendish International (Asia) Private Limited, 1 New Industrial Road, Singapore 536196.
Tel: (65) 6213 9300, fax: (65) 6285 4871. E-mail: genref@sg.marshallcavendish.com
Online bookstore: http://www.marshallcavendish.com

Limits of Liability/Disclaimer of Warranty: The Author and Publisher of this book have used their best efforts
in preparing this book. The Publisher makes no representation or warranties with respect to the contents of this book
and is not responsible for the outcome of any recipe in this book. While the Publisher has reviewed each recipe carefully,
the reader may not always achieve the results desired due to variations in ingredients, cooking temperatures and
individual cooking abilities. The Publisher shall in no event be liable for any loss of profit or any other
commercial damage, including but not limited to special, incidental, consequential, or other damages.

Other Marshall Cavendish Offices:

Marshall Cavendish Corporation, 99 White Plains Road, Tarrytown NY 10591-9001, USA • Marshall Cavendish
International (Thailand) Co Ltd. 253 Asoke, 12th Flr, Sukhumvit 21 Road, Klongtoey Nua, Wattana, Bangkok 10110,
Thailand • Marshall Cavendish (Malaysia) Sdn Bhd, Times Subang, Lot 46, Subang Hi-Tech Industrial Park,
Batu Tiga, 40000 Shah Alam, Selangor Darul Ehsan, Malaysia

Marshall Cavendish is a trademark of Times Publishing Limited

National Library Board, Singapore Cataloguing-in-Publication Data

Leong, Yee Soo.
The best of Singapore cooking / Leong Yee Soo. – Singapore : Marshall Cavendish Cuisine, 2012, c2004.
p. cm.
Includes index.
ISBN : 978-981-4398-58-9

1. Cooking, Singaporean. I. Title.

TX724.5.S55

641.595957 -- dc23   OCN809500058

Printed in Malaysia by Times Offset (M) Sdn Bhd

Foreword

Mrs Leong Yee Soo belonged to the generation of Straits 'nonyas' to whom good cuisine is an article of faith and a personal challenge.

Having spent the major part of her life in thinking, talking, experimenting and teaching food preparation, Mrs Leong felt that she could contribute nothing better to society than to pass on the results of her research and experience. She did regret that the fine art of cooking is fast dying out with women taking up jobs and with instant foods, frozen dinners, snack bars and take-aways so much in evidence.

Realising the role of woman in this nuclear age, Mrs Leong planned her meals with a keen eye on the cost and quality of ingredients, time in preparation, calorie content, food value, etc. She also summoned to her aid modern kitchen equiptment and had so simplified her procedure that dabbling in the kitchen can be a source of fun.

The recipes will speak for themselves. There are household staples that have fortified the Oriental home for generations, meals for large and small groups, young and old, in and out of doors, titbits, snatched meals and feasts for special occasions.

I would recommend this book of tested recipes for every kitchen shelf, for not only is wholesome food conducive to health and happiness, but, like "mother's cooking", it will be affectionately remembered and will go a long way towards fostering goodwill and happy relationships.

Mrs Goh Kok Kee
J.P., M.B.E.

Author's Acknowledgements

My sincere thanks go to Mrs. Rosa Lee, Mrs. Dorothy Norris, Miss Marie Choo, and Miss Patricia Lim who, by their co-operation and inspiring ideas, have made this book possible.

My thanks are due also to Mrs. Dinah Sharif, Miss Iris Kng, Miss Chau Mei Po, Mrs. Irene Oei, and Miss Monica Funk who gave up so much of their precious time in helping me type the recipes.

I would also like to thank all those who have been so helpful in the preparation and arrangement of the food and cakes for the photography sessions.

CONTENTS

Weights & Measures

American measuring spoons are used in this book. All measures are level except when stated. British measuring spoons are slightly bigger in capacity. Use a standard measuring jug for fluid measurement.

Metric equivalents are approximate.

Mass		
1 oz	—	30 g
2 oz	—	55 g
3 oz	—	85 g
4 oz	—	115 g
5 oz	—	140 g
6 oz	—	170 g
7 oz	—	200 g
8 oz	—	225 g
9 oz	—	255 g
10 oz	—	285 g
11 oz	—	310 g
12 oz	—	340 g
13 oz	—	370 g
14 oz	—	395 g
15 oz	—	425 g
16 oz (1 lb)	—	455 g
2 lb	—	905 g
3 lb	—	1.4 kg
4 lb	—	1.8 kg

Capacity		
1 fl oz	—	30 ml
4 fl oz	—	115 ml
8 fl oz	—	225 ml
16 fl oz	—	455 ml

Temperature		
°F	Gas Regulo	°C
225	1	105
250	2	120
275	3	135
300	4	150
325	5	165
350	6	175
375	7	190
400	8	205
425	9	220
450	10	230

Pre-heat oven 15 minutes before use.

Culinary Terms

Bake:
To cook in dry heat, usually in an oven.

Barbecue:
To roast or broil whole such as a pig or fowl, usually on a revolving frame over coals. To cook slices of marinated meat over a coal fire.

Baste:
To pour melted fat, dripping or sauce over roasting food in order to moisten.

Beat:
A quick regular motion that lifts a mixture over and over to make it smooth and to introduce air.

Blanch:
(i) Whiten, i.e., cover with cold water, bring to the boil, strain and remove skins as for almonds.
(ii) To pour boiling water over food then drain and rinse with cold water.

Blend:
Mix to a smooth paste with a little cold or hot liquid.

Boil:
To cook rapidly in liquid over very high heat till bubbles rise continually.

Braise:
To cook meat in fat, then simmer in a covered saucepan or dish with a small amount of water till tender.

Caramelize:
To heat dry sugar or foods containing sugar till light brown.

Dredge:
To sprinkle with flour or sugar.

Fold in:
To mix cake mixture by lifting a part of the batter from the bottom through the rest of the mixture without releasing air bubbles.

Garnish:
To decorate savoury food with sprigs of parsley, sliced lemon wedges, cooked or uncooked vegetables, shallots, grated yolk of egg and cheese, etc.

Glaze:
To brush over pastries, bread, etc. with a liquid such as eggs, milk or water and sugar to improve the appearance.

Grill:
To cook by direct heat on a grill iron or under a red hot grill; used for small tender pieces of meat, fish, etc.

Knead:
To mix by hand or electric dough hook. To press, fold and stretch. Usually applied to dough.

Marinate:
To give flavour to meats, salads, etc. by soaking in a sauce.

Mince:
To chop very finely.

Par-boil:
To boil raw food until partially cooked as for carrots, cauliflower, cabbage, etc.

Roast:
To cook with a little fat in a hot oven. Fat from the baking tin is used to baste the meat or poultry, from time to time.

Score:
To cut very lightly or to mark with lines before cooking. Applied to roast pork, fish, egg plant.

Simmer:
To cook just below boiling point. Small bubbles rise occasionally to the surface of the liquid.

Stew:
To cook slowly until tender in just sufficient liquid to cover the food. A stew may be cooked in a covered saucepan or casserole, on a hot plate or in the oven.

Helpful Hints

Seasoning:

The salt used in these recipes is local fine salt and not the fine table salt. Fine table salt is used mostly in Western cakes where it can be sifted together with the flour. As table salt is finer, it is more saltish than the local fine salt. So measure less salt if you use fine table salt. Use your discretion when seasoning with salt, sugar, chilli, or tamarind; season to your own taste. There is no hard and fast rule for seasoning food. However, for cakes, one must be precise and follow the recipe to get the best results. Msg in recipes refers to monosodium glutamate. As a substitute, chicken stock may be used. Use 1 chicken cube for 1 teaspoon msg.

Oil and fats:

To get the best results, when cooking Chinese dishes especially, use an equal portion of both lard and oil. It gives the dish a special fragrance. In recipes where it is specified that lard is preferable to oil, use lard in order to get its distinct flavour.

For deep-frying, always use either refined deodorised coconut oil, palm cooking oil or corn oil. Do not use olive oil.

Substitutes:

The purplish variety of onion is a good substitute for shallots. If fresh ginger, lemon grass and galangal are not easily available, use the powdered form. It is always advisable to use powdered turmeric. Almonds, cashew nuts, Brazil nuts or macadamia nuts can be used if candlenuts are not available.

Thickening:

Thickening for Chinese dishes means to thicken the gravy so as to coat the food rather than have the gravy running over the serving plate. Corn flour in the recipes refers to tapioca flour sold in the local markets. It is also known as sago flour (refined quality, and not the type used to starch clothes).

Selecting meat, poultry and seafood:
Pork:
Pork should be pink, the fat very white, and the skin thin.

Beef:
Choose meat that is light red and the cross-grain smooth and fine. The same applies to mutton. Do not buy dark-coloured meat with fat that is yellow.

Chicken:
Fresh local chickens have a much better taste and flavour than frozen ones. Frozen chicken is more suitable for roasting, frying or grilling. When buying a local chicken, select one with a white, smooth skin. The tip of the breastbone should be soft and pliable when pressed with the thumb.

Duck:
Select as for chicken. The smaller ones are mostly used for soups and the larger ducks for roasting or braising.

Fish:
When buying fish, first of all make sure that the flesh is firm to the touch. The eyes should be shiny, the gills blood-red and the scales silvery white. Squeezing lemon juice over fish will whiten it and keep it firm when boiling or steaming.

Mix tamarind, salt and some sugar to marinate fish for ½ hour before cooking curries or tamarind dishes.

Prawns:
Fresh prawns are firm to the touch, with shiny shells. The head is attached fast to the body. Avoid buying prawns with heads loosely hanging on.

Cuttlefish:
When cuttlefish is very fresh, the body is well-rounded, firm and shiny. The head is stuck fast to the body and the ink pouch in the stomach is firmly attached.

To fry shallots:

Slice shallots thinly and dip in salt water for a while. Rinse and drain well. Scatter sliced shallots on to absorbent paper to dry or roll up in a tea towel for ½ hour. Heat oil for deep-frying till smoking hot. Add the sliced shallots and stir-fry over high heat till shallots turn light brown. Reduce the heat and keep stirring all the time until the shallots are light golden brown. Remove at once with a wire sieve to drain the oil and scatter on to absorbent paper to cool. Keep in a clean, dry bottle immediately. The shallots keep crisp for months in an airtight bottle.

To fry pounded garlic:

Pound garlic or use an electric mincer to mince the garlic. Place garlic in a wire sieve and immerse in salt water. Drain. Use a thin piece of muslin to squeeze out the water. Heat an iron wok (kuali). Heat oil for deep-frying till smoking hot. Put the garlic in the wok and stir-fry till it turns light brown. Reduce the heat to very low and keep stirring till garlic is light golden brown. Remove at once with a wire sieve and scatter on to absorbent paper. Cool and store as for crispy shallots.

Note:
The crispy shallots and garlic do not retain so much oil when the heat is increased just before removing from wok.

To cook rice:

Wash rice till water runs clear. Use 55 ml (2 fl oz) of water for each 30 g (1 oz) of rice. For 455 g (16 oz) of rice, use between 795-910 ml (28-32 fl oz) water, depending on the quality of the rice. Boil the rice till the water evaporates, leaving steam holes when dry. Reduce heat to low and cook for a further ½ hour. 455 g (16 oz) of rice is sufficient for 8 servings.

To cook meat:

Pork chops should be cooked in moderate heat in a very hot pan or grilled under a hot grill. This will seal in the meat juices. Brown on both sides, turning over twice; lower to medium heat till done, about 15-20 minutes. Cut off the rind and snip the fat in two or three places to prevent bacon from curling during frying.

Fillet steak is the best and most tender of meat cuts; next comes sirloin, scotch, porterhouse, rump and minute steak. Marinating a steak before cooking not only gives it a better flavour but also helps to make it tender. Minute steak, however, is best grilled or fried without marinating.

To cook vegetables:

1. To fry leafy vegetables, separate the leaves from the stalk. The stalks should be placed in the pan together with any other ingredients and cooked first. Stir-fry for a minute or so before adding the leaves.

2. (a) To boil and blanch vegetables, boil a sauce-pan of water over very high heat. When the water is boiling, add some salt, sugar and a tablespoonful of oil.

   (b) Add the stalks, cook for ½ minute and then add the leaves. Cook for another ½ minute. Use a wire ladle to remove the vegetables and drain in a colander.

   (c) Rinse under a running tap and drain well before use.

   (d) Vegetables like long beans and cabbage should be cooked for 5-7 minutes only, to retain their sweetness and crispness.

   (e) When boiling bean sprouts it is important to place them in boiling water for 1 minute. Do not add any oil. Remove and drain with a wire ladle. Transfer to a basin of cold water and soak for 10 minutes or till cold. Spread thinly in a colander till ready for use. The bean sprouts will then keep without 'souring'.

Frying:

1. The pan should be very hot before you pour in the oil; but do not make the oil smoking hot. To get the best results when frying vegetables:-

   (a) Use an iron wok (kuali) as it can take and retain extreme heat, which is most important.

   (b) Add the oil to a smoking hot wok. This prevents food from sticking to the bottom. But overheated fat or oil turns bitter and loses its fine flavour.

2. (a) For deep-frying, the oil must be smoky, that is, when a faint haze of smoke rises from the oil. It is then ready for frying.

   (b) When deep-frying in large quantities, put enough food in the pan and keep the oil boiling all the time.

   (c) Bring the fat back to smoking hot each time you put in food to be fried.

   (d) When frying large pieces of meat or a whole chicken, the heat must be very high for the first 5 minutes to seal in the juices, then lower for the rest of the cooking time so as to give the meat or chicken a nice golden colour as well as to let it be cooked right through.

3. (a) After frying food that is coated with flour or breadcrumbs [this also seals in the meat juices], filter the oil through a wire sieve lined thinly with cotton wool. The oil will come clean of sediments.

   (b) Add more fresh oil to the strained oil for future use.

4. Oil that has been used to deep-fry fish and prawns should be kept separately for future use, i.e., for cooking fish and prawns only.

5. You may clarify hot oil by squeezing some lemon juice on to it but remember to turn off the heat first. Strain and store for future use.

6. Butter will not take intense heat when frying; so put in some oil before the butter.

7. Dust food with seasoned flour before coating with or dipping in batter for frying.

The coconut:

Coconut referred to in all recipes is fresh coconut unless specified. Coconut is used mainly for its rich milky juice so necessary for Asian dishes like curries, sambals and cakes.

Grated white coconut is coconut that is grated after the brown skin has been removed. This form is required for certain nonya kueh.

Use a piece of muslin to squeeze small handfuls of grated coconut so as to get more milk. No 1 milk is got by squeezing the grated coconut without adding water. When water is added to the grated coconut after the first squeeze, the milky liquid extracted is called No 2 milk.

Lemon grass:

Lemon grass gives a pleasant fragrance to cooked dishes. Use lemon rind as a substitute only when this is not available. The fragrance comes from the end of the stalk, about 7 cm (3 in) from the root end. The green outer layer is usually taken off before use. To "bruise" lemon grass, bash with the flat surface of a cleaver or chopper.

Candlenuts:

If unavailable, use almonds, cashew nuts, Brazil nuts or macadamia nuts. Their nutty flavour is the nearest to the candlenut.

Turmeric:

Fresh turmeric is usually used for 'nonya' dishes for its flavour and colour. Oriental dishes, especially curries, need dry turmeric or turmeric powder.

Lard:

The oil extracted from pork fat after it has been fried is called lard. Dice the pork fat before frying. Do not overburn the cubes otherwise the oil extracted will be dark and bitter. Unlike butter or margarine, lard can take intense heat without burning so it is most suitable for food that has to be cooked over high heat.

Screw pine leaves:

These give a special fragrance. There is no substitute. Before tying into a knot, tear lengthwise to get the strongest fragrance.

Hawker Favourites

Char Kway Teow

Fried Spring Chicken

Hae Mee

Ju Her Eng Chye

Kon Loh Mee

Laksa Lemak

Laksa Penang

Loh Kai Yik

Loh Mee

Mee Goreng

Mee Rebus

Mee Siam

Murtabak

Ngoh Hiang

Otak-Otak Panggang

Otak-Otak Puteh

Poh Pia

Satay Chelop

Satay

Yong Tau Fu

Hae Mee

CHAR KWAY TEOW
(FRIED RICE NOODLES)

INGREDIENTS

6 tablespoons water   ⎤
1 teaspoon salt   ⎬ A
½ teaspoon msg   ⎦

Lard for frying
2 teaspoons pounded garlic
310 g (11 oz) bean sprouts, washed and drained
310 g (11 oz) flat rice noodles (kway teow)
2 tablespoons dark soya sauce
4 eggs
Chilli sauce (see recipe)
1 pair of Chinese sausages, sliced thinly and fried
115 g (4 oz) cockles, shelled
55 g (2 oz) chives, cut into 5 cm (2 in) lengths
1–2 tablespoons sweet thick black sauce

METHOD

1. Mix **A** in a bowl.
2. Heat large wok till smoking hot. Put in 4 tablespoons lard and fry garlic till light brown. Add bean sprouts and rice noodles. Sprinkle **A** mixture and dark soya sauce and stir-fry for ½ minute.
3. Push rice noodle mixture to one side of wok. Add 4 tablespoons lard and scramble eggs.
4. Stir in scrambled eggs and mix well with noodles.
5. Pour in chilli sauce, according to taste.
6. Add sausages, and stir-fry for another minute, adding some lard to sides of wok.
7. Leave space in centre of noodles to put in cockles. Cover cockles with mixture, add chives and sweet thick black sauce. Toss for ½ minute and serve on a large serving plate.

Note:
Fry rice noodles in two parts if wok is not large enough. Fry over a very high heat to keep the bean sprouts crunchy.

Lard is preferable to groundnut oil.

Chilli Sauce:
285 g (10 oz) liquidized chilli   ⎤
340 ml (12 fl oz) water   ⎪
1½ tablespoons salt   ⎬ A
1 tablespoon sugar   ⎪
1 teaspoon msg   ⎪
1 teaspoon pepper   ⎦

1 tablespoon lard
1 tablespoon chopped garlic
¾ teaspoon shrimp paste, crumbled

METHOD

1. Heat lard in a small saucepan and fry garlic and shrimp paste till brown.
2. Add **A** and bring to boil.
3. Boil gently for further 5 minutes.
4. Cool and use as required.

Note:
Cool the chilli sauce before pouring it into a plastic container to store in the freezer.

FRIED SPRING CHICKEN

INGREDIENTS

115 g (4 oz) sugar   ⎤
55 ml (2 fl oz) dark soya sauce   ⎪
55 ml (2 fl oz) light soya sauce   ⎪
2 tablespoons wine or sherry   ⎪
6 cloves   ⎪
2 tablespoons honey   ⎬ A
1 teaspoon msg   ⎪
1 teaspoon salt   ⎪
1 teaspoon five-spice powder   ⎪
2.5 cm (1 in) piece cinnamon bark   ⎪
1 teaspoon sesame oil   ⎦

4 spring chickens, whole, each weighing 455 g (1 lb)
Oil for deep-frying

METHOD

1. Mix **A** in a deep saucepan to marinate the chickens for 2 hours.
2. Drain the chickens.
3. Boil marinade for 10 minutes. Put in chickens and boil in 570 ml (20 fl oz) water for another 7 minutes.
4. Drain chickens in a colander.
5. Heat oil in wok till smoky hot. Deep-fry two chickens for 2 minutes. Lower the heat a little and fry till golden brown (about 7–10 minutes).
6. Repeat process with the other two chickens.

Char Kway Teow

HAE MEE
(PRAWN MEE SOUP)

INGREDIENTS

625 g (22 oz) medium-sized prawns
170 g (6 oz) pork fat
2 tablespoons oil

4.5 litres (8 pints) water ⎤
625 g (22 oz) pork ribs, cut into pieces
1 pig's tail, cut into pieces
310 g (11 oz) lean pork
2 teaspoons salt
2 teaspoons sugar
2 teaspoons msg   **A**
1 tablespoon peppercorns
2 tablespoons light soya sauce
2 teaspoons dark soya sauce ⎦

1 tablespoon crispy shallots*
455 g (16 oz) bean sprouts
310 g (11 oz) water convolvulus, cut into long
   pieces
625 g (22 oz) fresh yellow noodles
310 g (11 oz) rice vermicelli, scalded

METHOD

1. Wash and drain prawns. Remove heads and keep aside.
2. Cut pork fat into small cubes and fry in pan till brown. Remove to a bowl.
3. Stir-fry prawn heads with 2 tablespoons oil for five minutes till colour turns red. Set aside in a bowl, for soup.
4. Cook unshelled prawns for 2 minutes in basin with 4.5 litres water. Remove prawns, shell and slice into halves, lengthwise.
5. Return prawn shells to saucepan, add **A** and prawn heads. Cook over a very high heat for 10 minutes. Reduce heat to low and let soup simmer for 1–1½ hours.
6. Strain soup. Return pork ribs and tail to soup.
7. Slice lean pork and set aside.

Garnish:
55 g (2 oz) crispy shallots
   Lard
   Crispy cubed pork fat
   Pepper
5 red chillies, sliced thinly
5 green chillies, sliced thinly
   Light soya sauce

To serve:
1. Boil a saucepan of water.
2. Dip a handful of bean sprouts, water convolvulus, noodles, and rice vermicelli in the boiling water, using a wire-mesh ladle. Drain and place in bowl.
3. Add boiling soup and a few pieces of pork ribs, tail, sliced lean pork and sliced prawns to each bowl.
4. Garnish with crispy shallots, lard-oil and crispy fat cubes. Sprinkle with pepper. Serve with sliced chillies and light soya sauce.

Note:
Only very fresh prawns make a sweet soup.
For crispy shallots, see "Helpful Hints".

(12 servings)

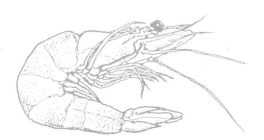

JU HER ENG CHYE
(CUTTLEFISH SALAD)

INGREDIENTS

225 g (8 oz) processed cuttlefish
 55 g (2 oz) processed jellyfish
  6 pieces fried soya bean cakes
285 g (10 oz) young water convolvulus
  2 tablespoons toasted sesame seeds

Sauce Ingredients:
(Mix together)
4-6 tablespoons chilli sauce
  3 tablespoons Hoisin sauce
  1 tablespoon lime juice
  1 tablespoon peanut oil
 ½ teaspoon sesame oil

METHOD

1. Cut cuttlefish into thick slices.

2. Cut processed jellyfish into thin slices.

3. Toast fried soya bean cakes till crispy. Cut into pieces.

4. Blanch water convolvulus for 10 seconds in boiling water with 1 teaspoon each of salt and sugar and 1 tablespoon oil.

5. Scoop out with a wire mesh ladle and drain well. Place on large plate. Arrange cuttlefish, jellyfish shreds and soya bean pieces over vegetables. Sprinkle toasted sesame seeds and pour the chilli sauce mixture over. Serve.

KON LOH MEE
(NOODLES WITH CHAR SIEW)

INGREDIENTS

115 g (4 oz) anchovies	
680 ml(24 fl oz) water	**A**
2 cloves garlic, lightly bashed	
½ thumb-sized piece ginger, lightly bashed	

2-3 tablespoons chilli sauce	
1 tablespoon peanut oil	*sauce*
¼ teaspoon msg	*mixture*
1 tablespoon light soya sauce	*for*
1 teaspoon oyster sauce	*one*
½ teaspoon sesame oil	*serving*
4-6 tablespoons stock	

225 g (8 oz) Chinese mustard greens
  1 teaspoon salt
  1 teaspoon sugar
  8 bundles fresh egg noodles
225 g (8 oz) roast pork strips, sliced finely

METHOD

1. Boil **A** for 1 hour. Strain and keep stock in a bowl.

2. Wash mustard greens, cut into short lengths and blanch in saucepan together with the salt and sugar. Using a wire sieve, remove and immerse in cold water for 5 minutes. Drain.

3. Bring a large saucepan of water to the boil over high heat. Loosen a bundle of noodles and put it into the boiling water. Stir with a wooden chopstick for 1 minute, then scoop it out with a wire-mesh ladle. Immerse in a large basin of cold water for ½ minute. Repeat boiling process for another ¼ minute. Remove and drain.

4. Stir noodles in a bowl of prepared sauce mixture.

5. Transfer to a serving plate, garnish with mustard greens and slices of roast pork. Serve hot. Repeat process with other servings.

(8 servings)

LAKSA LEMAK

INGREDIENTS

1 thumb-sized piece turmeric
½ teacup galangal, sliced
20 dried chillies
5 red chillies
6 candlenuts
2 tablespoons shrimp paste
225 g (8 oz) shallots
1 tablespoon coriander powder or seeds

A

55 g (2 oz) dried prawns, pounded
1 tablespoon sugar
2 tablespoons salt

B

1.2 kg (2½ lb) grated coconut
1 teaspoon salt
1 teaspoon sugar
445 g (1 lb) fresh prawns, for garnishing
225 ml (8 fl.oz) oil
2 stalks lemon grass, bruised
625 g (22 oz) bean sprouts, boiled and drained
1.2 kg (2½ lb) fresh rice vermicelli

METHOD

1. Grind **A** to a fine paste.
2. Squeeze coconut for No. 1 milk. Add 2.7 litres (5 pints) water to coconut and extract No. 2 milk. Set aside.
3. Boil 455 ml (16 fl oz) water with 1 teaspoon salt and 1 teaspoon sugar. Add fresh prawns and cook for about 5–7 minutes.
4. Remove prawns, shell and slice lengthwise. Set aside for garnishing.
5. Return shells to saucepan. Boil for 10 minutes. Strain liquid for stock.
6. Heat oil in aluminium wok. Fry paste (Method 1) and lemon grass till fragrant and the oil comes to the surface.
7. Add No. 2 milk and prawn stock and bring to the boil. Add **B**. Boil for 10 minutes over low heat.
8. Reduce the heat to simmering point. Add No. 1 milk, setting aside 2 tablespoonfuls for the chilli paste. Stir gravy for a minute then remove from heat. Continue stirring to prevent curdling.

CHILLI PASTE:

55 g (2 oz) dried chillies
5 red chillies
1 teaspoon shrimp paste

A

2 teaspoons sugar
1 teaspoon salt
2 tablespoons No. 1 milk

B

2 tablespoons oil
1–2 tablespoons water

METHOD

1. Grind **A** to a fine paste.
2. Heat pan till hot. Heat oil and fry paste till well done and oil comes through.
3. Add 1–2 tablespoons water, stir-fry with **B**.
4. Remove to a bowl.

GARNISH:
Cooked prawns, shelled and sliced lengthwise
8 fish cakes, fried and sliced into thin strips
3 skinned cucumbers, sliced lengthwise (remove soft centre)
55 g (2 oz) polygonum (daun kesom), cut finely

To serve the rice vermicelli:
Place some bean sprouts and rice vermicelli in several bowls. Add hot gravy and garnish with prawns, fish cake, cucumber, polygonum, and chilli paste.

Note:
Transparent bean vermicelli can also be added to the rice vermicelli.

(10 servings)

LAKSA PENANG

INGREDIENTS

455 g (16 oz) shallots
10 stalks lemon grass, thinly sliced
1 thumb-sized piece turmeric
30-40 pieces dried chillies or 4 tablespoons chilli paste **A**
1 tablespoon shrimp paste
1 clove garlic

8 slices dried tamarind
30 stalks polygonum (daun kesom)
2 stalks phaeomaria (bunga kantan) cut into halves **B**
6 heaped tablespoons sugar
2 tablespoons salt

170 g (6 oz) tamarind
4.5 l (10 pt) water
1.2 kg (2½ lb) wolf-herring (Ikan Parang)
2.4 kg (5 lb) fresh coarse rice vermicelli
6 tablespoons prawn paste, mixed with ¾ cup warm water

METHOD

1. Soak tamarind in 455 ml (16 fl oz) water; squeeze and sieve into an enamel saucepan. Repeat process three times with the rest of the water.
2. Grind **A** to a fine paste.
3. Bring tamarind water to the boil with **A** and **B**.
4. Boil for 10 minutes; add the fish and let gravy simmer for 15 minutes till fish is cooked.
5. Remove fish to a plate to cool; remove all bones. Place flaked fish meat in a bowl and set aside.
6. Let the tamarind gravy simmer for 1 hour. Remove the polygonum and phaeomaria.
7. Return the flaked fish to the gravy and bring back to boil.

GARNISH:
1 pineapple, diced
905 g (2 lb) cucumber, thinly shredded without skin and centre
55 g (2 oz) mint leaves
225 g (8 oz) onions, cut into small cubes
15 green chillies, sliced
12 red chillies, sliced
115 g (4 oz) preserved leeks, sliced thinly

To serve:
1. Bring a saucepan of water to a rapid boil. Scald the rice vermicelli and drain in a colander.
2. Place a small handful of scalded rice vermicelli in a medium-sized bowl; pour hot tamarind gravy and some fish over it. Top with garnish, and 1 teaspoon of the thinned prawn paste. Serve.

Note:
Only very fresh fish is suitable for this dish. Dried coarse rice vermicelli can be substituted for fresh. Boil rice vermicelli till soft but not soggy; about 15 minutes. Rinse in cold water and drain.

LOH KAI YIK
(COMBINATION HOT POT)

INGREDIENTS

6 pieces salted bean curd in oil, mashed
4 tablespoons preserved soya beans, pounded   **A**
4 tablespoons sugar
2 tablespoons ginger juice

8 tablespoons sweet red sauce

½ tablespoon salt
2 tablespoons light soya sauce   **B**
1 teaspoon msg

565 g (20 oz) water convolvulus
20 dried bean curd cakes
6 tablespoons lard or oil
8 slices ginger
3 tablespoons pounded garlic
455 g (1 lb) chicken wings
455 g (1 lb) lean streaky pork
455 g (1 lb) pig's skin, cleaned and cut into 10 cm (4 in) squares
455 g (1 lb) pig's small intestines
2 large treated cuttlefish, cut into quarters

METHOD

1. Wash and blanch water convolvulus. Drain and knot each strand.

2. Scald the dried bean curd cakes. Drain and squeeze lightly to remove the oil.

3. Heat lard in wok and fry ginger slices and garlic till light brown. Add **A** and half of the sweet red sauce. Stir-fry over moderate heat till sugar dissolves.

4. Add **B** to 225 ml (8 fl oz) of water. Bring to the boil.

5. Add chicken wings, streaky pork, pig's skin and small intestines. Cook for 20 minutes.

6. Remove chicken wings to a dish.

7. Add another 225 ml (8 fl oz) water and the remaining sweet red sauce.

8. Put in the water convolvulus, dried bean curd cakes and cuttlefish. Boil gently for 5 minutes. Remove to a dish.

9. Let gravy simmer till pork, pig's skin and small intestines are tender. Add hot water to gravy if necessary.

10. Return the chicken wings, water convolvulus, dried bean curd cakes and cuttlefish to the gravy. Let simmer until ready to serve. Put chilli sauce and sweet red sauce in separate saucers to serve with Loh Kai Yik.

Note:
Buy cuttlefish that has been soaked in alkaline water from any market. Pork and chicken livers can be added to this dish.

LOH MEE

INGREDIENTS

250 g (9 oz) small grey prawns, shelled and deveined

200 g (7 oz) squids, cut into thin rings (remove ink bags)

250 g (9 oz) Spanish mackerel (tenggiri papan) cut into thick small pieces

200 g (7 oz) fresh oysters (optional)

A

1 tablespoon light soya sauce
1 teaspoon sugar
1 teaspoon ginger juice

seasoning

600 g (21 oz) fresh flat yellow noodles
400 g (14 oz) bean sprouts, washed and drained
200 g (7 oz) Chinese mustard (chye sim), cut into short lengths
½ teaspoon chopped garlic
½ thumb-sized piece ginger, thinly sliced
3 tablespoons plain flour
600 ml (21 fl oz) prawn stock

3 tablespoons oyster sauce
2 tablespoons top quality Thai sauce
1 tablespoon dark soya sauce
1 teaspoon sesame oil
½ teaspoon pepper
1 teaspoon chicken stock granules

B

Garnish:
3 sprigs coriander leaf (wan swee) cut in short lengths
2 red chillies, seeded, sliced thinly lengthwise
6 tablespoons crispy shallots

METHOD

1. Wash and drain prawn shells and fry with 2 tablespoons oil. Add 1 litre water, bring to boil in wok till stock is reduced by one-third.

2. Marinate **A** in seasoning for ½ hour.

3. Heat 4 tablespoons oil in wok. Fry garlic and sliced ginger till light brown. Add the flour; stir for ½ minute, pour in ½ of prawn stock and **B** and bring to boil. Pour in remaining stock with the seasoned **A** ingredients, cover pan and bring to boil.

4. Remove prawns and fish to one side of pan, put in the chye sim and bean sprouts to cook for ½ minute over high heat, then add in the noodles and cook for approximately 1 minute. Remove noodles to a large serving plate. Spoon gravy over and garnish. Serve hot.

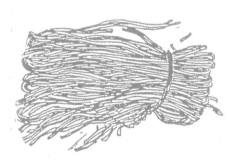

MEE GORENG
(FRIED NOODLES — INDIAN-STYLE)

INGREDIENTS

2–3 tablespoons tomato sauce
1–2 tablespoons light soya sauce
  4 green chillies, sliced
  4 red chillies, sliced
  4 small potatoes; boiled, skinned and cut
    into wedges   **A**

  Oil for frying
  1 onion, sliced finely
  2 tomatoes, cut into wedges
225 g (8 oz) Chinese cabbage cut into 5 cm (2 in)
    lengths
455 g (16 oz) bean sprouts
340 g (12 oz) fresh yellow noodles
  4 eggs
  Light soya sauce
  2 tablespoons crispy shallots★
  6 small local limes, halved

METHOD

1. Heat iron wok till smoky. Put in 2 tablespoons oil, and fry onion slices till soft and transparent.
2. Lightly toss in tomatoes and Chinese cabbage.
3. Add bean sprouts and noodles and stir for 1 minute.
4. Toss in **A** and mix well.
5. Push noodles to one side of wok. Add 2 tablespoons oil and scramble eggs (two at a time) with a sprinkling of light soya sauce. Mix egg and noodles thoroughly.
6. Add paste for noodles (see below) according to taste. Stir mixture over a very high heat for 1 minute. Remove to serving plate.
7. Garnish with crispy shallots, and local limes.

PASTE FOR NOODLES:
225 g (8 oz) onions
 55 g (2 oz) dried chillies
  4 cloves garlic   **A**
  1 tablespoon shrimp paste

  1 tablespoon sugar
  1 teaspoon salt   **B**
  1 teaspoon msg

340 ml (12 fl oz) oil
 55 g (2 oz) dried anchovies

METHOD

1. Grind **A** till fine.
2. Heat 115 ml (4 fl oz) oil in pan; fry anchovies over a moderate heat till crisp. Drain and pound coarsely.
3. In a clean pan, heat remaining oil. Stir in **A** (Method 1) and fry till fragrant and oil comes through. Add **B**. Lower the heat; add the pounded anchovies. Cook for 2–3 minutes, remove to a bowl. Use as required. Store the remainder in a freezer.

Note:
Fry noodles over a very high heat to keep the bean sprouts crunchy and to prevent the noodles from being soggy. Fry in two parts if the wok is not large enough.
★For crispy shallots, see "Helpful Hints".

(8 servings)

MEE REBUS

(BRAISED NOODLES — MALAY STYLE)

INGREDIENTS

18 slices galangal
4 cloves garlic
115 g (4 oz) shallots
14–20 dried chillies
½ thumb-sized piece turmeric
1 teaspoon shrimp paste   **A**

115 g (4 oz) preserved soya beans, pounded
1 teaspoon msg
1–1½ tablespoons salt
2 tablespoons sugar   **B**

115 g (4 oz) boiled sweet potatoes, mashed finely
2 tablespoons flour
2 tablespoons cornflour
225 ml (8 fl oz) water   **C**

1 chicken cube
225 g (½ lb) beef shin, cut into small pieces
225 g (½ lb) small prawns, shelled
115 ml (4 fl oz) oil
680 g (1½ lb) fresh yellow noodles
565 g (1¼ lb) bean sprouts, washed and picked

METHOD

1. Grind **A** to a paste.
2. Boil beef shin and chicken cube in 680 ml (1½ pints) water over a low heat till meat is tender.
3. Fry prawn shells with 1 tablespoon oil for 1 minute. Remove.
4. Bring 900 ml (2 pints) water to boiling point. Add fried shells and let water boil for further 7 minutes. Strain and set aside the stock for gravy.
5. Heat the rest of the oil in wok and fry **A** (Method 1) till it smells fragrant (5–7 minutes). Add **B**. Stir and remove paste.
6. Place the prawns, prawn stock, beef shin and the fried paste in a saucepan. Bring to the boil.
7. Thicken 225 ml (8 fl oz) of this gravy with **C**. Pour it back gradually into the saucepan and stir. Let gravy simmer for 10 minutes.

GARNISH :
8 sprigs Chinese celery, cut into small pieces
4 soya bean cakes, diced and fried
10 green chillies, sliced
6 red chillies, sliced
55 g (2 oz) crispy shallots
12–14 local limes, halved
6 hard-boiled eggs, sliced

To prepare and serve noodles:
1. Scald a handful of noodles and some bean sprouts in boiling water.
2. Using a wire-mesh ladle, drain noodles and bean sprouts and place on plate.
3. Spoon gravy, prawns, and beef over noodles. Garnish. Serve hot.

(10 servings)

MEE SIAM

INGREDIENTS

RICE VERMICELLI:

225 g (8 oz) shallots 50–60 dried chillies 2 tablespoons shrimp paste	**A**

400 ml (14 fl oz) water 1 tablespoon salt 3 tablespoons sugar 1 teaspoon msg	**B**

340 ml (12 fl oz) oil
  3 tablespoons dried prawns, pounded finely
1.2 kg (2½ lb) bean sprouts, washed and drained
625 g (1½ lb) rice vermicelli, soaked in a saucepan of boiling water for ½ minute and drained

METHOD

1. Pound **A** to a fine paste.
2. Heat oil in wok and fry dried prawns for 1 minute. Add paste (**A**) and fry till fragrant and oil comes through. Set aside 3 tablespoonfuls of this fried paste and some oil for the gravy.
3. Add **B** in wok and simmer.
4. Add the bean sprouts and stir-fry for 1 minute. Push bean sprouts to one side of the wok. Add rice vermicelli and stir-fry over a high heat, using a pair of chopsticks. Continue stirring till gravy is absorbed.
5. Mix bean sprouts and rice vermicelli thoroughly. Reduce heat, stir and cook till rice vermicelli is dry and fluffy. Remove to cool on a large tray.

GRAVY:

8 tablespoons preserved soya beans, pounded finely 6 tablespoons sugar 2 onions, sliced thinly 2 walnut-sized tamarind with 225 ml (8 fl oz) water, squeezed and strained 1.8 litres (4 pints) water	**A**

METHOD

1. Mix **A** in saucepan. Stir and bring to boil. Let simmer for ¾ hour.
2. Add 3 tablespoons fried paste and oil. (Rice vermicelli, Step 2). Boil for 5 minutes. Remove from heat. Serve hot.

SPICY PASTE (SAMBAL):

40 g dried chillies or 10 tablespoons chilli paste
  1 teaspoon shrimp paste
  8 tablespoons oil
  1 onion, chopped finely
  1 teaspoon salt
  2 tablespoons sugar
  1 tablespoon tamarind with 125 ml (4 fl oz) water, squeezed and strained

1. Grind dried chillies with shrimp paste till very fine.
2. Heat oil in wok and fry chopped onion till soft and slightly brown. Add chilli paste (Step 1) and fry over a moderate heat till fragrant and oil comes through.
3. Add salt, sugar, and half of the tamarind water. Stir-fry for 1 minute, add the rest of the tamarind water and cook for another 2 minutes, stirring all the time. Remove to a bowl. Serve with the rice vermicelli.

GARNISH:

12 hard-boiled eggs, cut into wedges or sliced
  4 big soya bean cakes, diced and fried
625 g (1 lb 6 oz) medium-sized prawns (shelled and deveined), fried and halved lengthwise
115 g (4 oz) chives cut into 2.5 cm (1 in) lengths
310 g (11 oz) local limes, cut into halves

To serve:
Place rice vermicelli on a large serving plate or on individual dinner plates.

Garnish and serve with the gravy and the spicy paste.

(12 servings)

Mee Siam

MURTABAK
(MEAT CREPES)

INGREDIENTS

455 g (1 lb) plain flour
½ teaspoon pepper
¾ teaspoon baking powder
¾ teaspoon fine salt **A**

    Ghee
4 eggs

METHOD

1. Sift **A** together into a bowl. Add 340 ml (12 fl oz) water, to form a smooth dough. Leave overnight in a covered bowl.

2. Divide dough into 4 equal portions. Roll out thinly on an oiled marble top or formica table top, and spread liberally with ghee. Fold and shape into balls. Cover with a damp cloth. Set aside for ½ hour.

3. Roll out each ball into a thin rectangle. Spread filling in centre of dough. Pat lightly beaten egg over meat. Fold dough over meat to form a rectangle or square and fry in hot ghee till brown on both sides. Serve hot.

FILLING :

605 g (20 oz) minced mutton or veal
¼ teaspoon turmeric powder
½ teaspoon msg
½ teaspoon salt **A**

605 g (20 oz) onions, diced
¼ teaspoon turmeric powder
¼ teaspoon salt
½ teaspoon msg **B**

  2 heaped tablespoons roasted
    coriander seeds
  2 level tablespoons aniseed
20 cardamoms, seeded **C** *pounded finely*

METHOD

1. Fry **A** in a little oil. Remove from pan.

2. Fry **B** in 2 tablespoons oil for 2 minutes. Add **A** and **C**. Mix well and season to taste. Cool on a plate.

NGOH HIANG
(MEAT ROLLS)

INGREDIENTS

1 teaspoon salt
2 teaspoons sugar
1 teaspoon msg
2 teaspoons light soya sauce
1 teaspoon dark soya sauce
1 teaspoon pepper
1 tablespoon lard or oil
1 tablespoon flour
1 rounded teaspoon five-spice powder **A**

455 g (1 lb) minced pork
225 g (½ lb) prawns; shelled, deveined, and
    chopped coarsely
1 onion, chopped finely **B**

  2 dried bean curd wrappers
  2 small eggs
170 g (6 oz) steamed crab meat
Oil for deep-frying

METHOD

1. Cut bean curd wrappers into rectangles, 15 cm × 18 cm (6 in × 7 in).

2. Beat eggs lightly. Add **A**. Mix well.

3. Mix **B** in a large basin. Add the egg mixture and mix thoroughly. Add the steamed crab meat. Mix well.

4. Place a small heap of mixture on each of the wrappers. Roll as for sausages, dampen the open ends with a little flour mixed with water and seal. Steam the rolls for 10 minutes. Cool.

5. Deep-fry rolls in hot fat. Cool before cutting. Serve with cucumber slices.

OTAK OTAK PANGGANG

(SPICY FISH GRILLED IN BANANA LEAVES)

INGREDIENTS

2 onions, weighing 225 g (8 oz) 30 slices galangal (weighing approx. 85 g or 3 oz) 5 candlenuts 25 dried chillies 1 tablespoon shrimp paste 1 thumb-sized piece turmeric	**A**

1.2 kg (2 lb 11 oz) Spanish mackerel
680 g (24 oz) grated coconut (extract 285 ml
    (10 fl oz) No. 1 milk)
2 eggs

3 tablespoons sugar 2 tablespoons salt 1 teaspoon msg 3 tablespoons oil 2 teaspoons roasted coriander	**B**

2 lime leaves, sliced very finely
4 turmeric leaves, sliced very finely
26 banana leaves (22 cm × 20 cm or 10 in × 8 in),
    washed and scalded

METHOD

1. Grind **A** to a fine paste.
2. Bone and fillet the fish. Use a spoon to scrape half of the meat into a bowl. Slice the other half thinly.
3. Pound or mince the scraped fish meat till smooth. Add 170 ml (6 fl oz) water and a pinch of salt. Beat mixture manually till it forms a sticky paste.
4. Add the No. 1 milk. Beat till well-blended. Add the eggs, **A** and **B** and beat till well-blended. Add the sliced fish, lime leaves and turmeric leaves. Mix well into the fish mixture.
5. Place 2 tablespoonfuls of fish mixture in the middle of each banana leaf. Fasten the two ends of the leaf with a stapler or a sharp toothpick.
6. Pre-heat grill. When very hot, place wrapped fish in grill pan, 8 cm (3 in) from the hot grill, for 7–10 minutes on each side.

OTAK OTAK PUTEH

(BAKED FISH PASTE WITH RICH COCONUT CREAM)

INGREDIENTS

¾ tablespoon salt 1½ teaspoons msg 1 teaspoon sugar 1 teaspoon tapioca flour Dash of pepper 1 teaspoon galangal juice	**A**

225 g (8 oz) grated coconut, white
570 g (19 oz) fish meat
2 egg whites, lightly beaten
40 pieces banana leaves (20 × 25 cm)

METHOD

1. Add 4 tablespoons water to coconut and squeeze for milk. Set aside.
2. Stir **A** into coconut milk till dissolved. Set aside.
3. Blend fish meat and coconut mixture in electric food processor to make a fine paste.
4. Remove paste to a large basin and gradually add the egg white. Beat till stiff.
5. Place banana leaf on table. Wet hands and pat spoonful of paste into longish, flat shape on leaf. Fold longer ends of banana leaf over to cover paste. Pin ends with tooth picks. Repeat with remaining paste.
6. Fry packets in iron pan or place under a hot grill until cooked (7–8 minutes).

Note:
To get a fine texture for this dish, use Ikan Parang (Wolf Herring)

POH PIA
(FRESH SPRING ROLLS)

INGREDIENTS

Filling:

905 g (2 lb) streaky pork | **A**
A pinch of salt

8 tablespoons preserved soya beans, pounded
1–1½ tablespoons salt | **B**
8 tablespoons sugar
2 teaspoons msg

455 g (1 lb) small prawns
225 ml (8 fl oz) lard or oil
8 tablespoons pounded garlic (about 30 cloves)

1.8 kg (4 lb) Chinese turnip, shredded
1.8 kg (4 lb) boiled, tender, bamboo shoots, shredded
12 soya bean cakes cut into thin strips and fried

METHOD

To cook filling:

1. Boil **A** with 1 litre (32 fl oz) water for ¾ hour. Remove pork and slice into fine strips. Set aside 455 ml (16 fl oz) of the stock.

2. Shell and devein prawns. Pound prawn shells; add 1 litre water. Strain and set aside liquid.

3. Heat lard in wok and fry garlic till light brown. Add **B**. Stir-fry for 1 minute. Pour in the prawn liquid (Method 2) and bring to boil.

4. Add turnip to cook, then add bamboo shoots and pork stock (Method 1). Boil for ½ hour over moderate heat.

5. Lower heat, add fried soya bean strips and sliced pork. Cook for 1½ hours, stirring occasionally. Add the prawns and cook for a further 10 minutes.

6. Remove filling to an aluminium saucepan. Simmer until ready to serve.

White Skins:

625 g (22 oz) white skins, large, obtainable at markets.

Note:
Keep white skins covered with a damp cloth before serving.

Egg Skins:

285 g (10 oz) flour
A pinch of salt | **A**
3 tablespoons cornflour

10 eggs
680–740 ml (24–26 fl oz) water
85 ml (3 fl oz) oil

To make egg skins:

1. Sieve **A** into a basin.

2. Beat eggs lightly in a bowl. Add water and oil.

3. Add egg mixture to flour and mix evenly.

4. Grease a well-heated omelette pan. Pour enough batter to spread over base of pan thinly, as for a pancake. Cook pancake till sides curl slightly. Turn pancake over on to a flat surface. Repeat process until batter is used up. Pile egg skins on a plate.

Garnish:

8 eggs
A pinch of salt | **A**
3 tablespoons oil

455 g (1 lb) small prawns, shelled and deveined | **B**
A pinch of salt

905 g (2 lb) cucumber, shredded thinly and with centre and skin removed
905 g (2 lb) bean sprouts; picked, washed and scalded
8 bundles of fine Chinese parsley (roots removed), washed and drained
455 g (1 lb) green lettuce, washed and drained
225 g (½ lb) steamed crab meat
2 pairs Chinese sausages, fried and sliced thinly
285 g (10 oz) sweet, thick black sauce
30 cloves garlic, pounded to a fine paste
30 cloves garlic, pounded and fried till crisp
455 g (1 lb) red chillies, pounded to a fine paste

METHOD

1. Beat **A**. Grease pan lightly. Fry egg mixture as for omelette. Fold and slice very thinly. (Grease pan only once.)

2. Fry **B**. Slice prawns lengthwise.

To serve Poh Pia:

1. Place small heaps of cucumber, bean sprouts, Chinese parsley, and lettuce on serving plate.

2. Arrange crab meat, prawns, egg and sausages on separate plate.
3. Place the sweet, thick black sauce, garlic, fried garlic, and pounded chillies in small separate bowls.
4. Arrange the white skins and the egg skins on two separate plates.
5. Place the filling in a deep large bowl.

To roll:
1. Place a white or egg skin on a plate and spread ingredients in this order — a little sweet, thick black sauce, pounded chillies, and pounded garlic.
2. Add a piece of lettuce, a few strands of bean sprouts, shredded cucumber, and a spoonful of filling.

SATAY CHELOP
(STEAMBOAT SATAY)

INGREDIENTS

Gravy:

10 candlenuts	
140 g (5 oz) shallots	
6 cloves garlic	
4 stalks lemon grass, sliced	**A**
4 slices galangal	
30 dried chillies	
1 tablespoon shrimp paste	

625 g (22 oz) roasted peanuts, pounded finely	**B**
900 ml (32 fl oz) water	

225 ml (8 fl oz) oil

115 g (4 oz) sugar	**C**
1 tablespoon salt	

METHOD

1. Grind **A** to a paste.
2. Boil **B** over a low heat for 20 minutes.
3. Heat oil in wok. Fry paste (Method 1) in heated oil till fragrant and oil comes to surface. Add fried paste to peanut sauce. Add **C**, stir and let simmer for 10 minutes. Set aside gravy.

3. Garnish with a few slices of Chinese sausages, egg, prawn, and crab meat. Add a little Chinese parsley, sprinkle a bit of crispy garlic and fold into a neat roll.
4. Cut and serve.

Note:
1. *You need to grease the omelette pan only once as the mixture has sufficient oil.*
2. *Dip shredded Chinese turnip in water to remove the starch. Drain in a colander before cooking.*
3. *Drain gravy from filling before serving.*

(12–15 servings)

INGREDIENTS

225 g (8 oz) pork chop meat, sliced thinly	
225 g (8 oz) cockles	
225 g (8 oz) shelled prawns, halved lengthwise	**A**
225 g (8 oz) pork liver, sliced thinly	
1 treated cuttlefish (obtainable at wet markets)	

685 g (1½ lb) water convolvulus	**B**
455 g (1 lb) bean sprouts, picked	

225 g (8 oz) rice vermicelli

METHOD

1. Scald rice vermicelli for 2 minutes. Drain in colander.
2. Thread **A** on to wooden skewers or satay sticks.
3. Scald **B**. Drain in colander.
4. Add 225 ml (8 fl oz) of peanut gravy to 900 ml (32 fl oz) boiling water in a small saucepan. Let simmer to cook the skewered ingredients.

To serve:
Place small servings of water convolvulus, bean sprouts, and rice vermicelli on a plate. Place the skewered ingredients in the saucepan, letting them simmer till done. Remove cooked food from skewers to the plate of rice vermicelli. Add thick gravy and serve.

(10 servings)

SATAY
(BARBECUED BEEF WITH PEANUT SAUCE)

INGREDIENTS

Meat preparation:

10 shallots	
2 cloves garlic	
¼ thumb-sized piece turmeric or ½ teaspoon turmeric powder	**A**
4 stalks lemon grass, sliced	
2 slices galangal	

2 tablespoons coriander seeds	**B**
2 teaspoons cumin	

1 teaspoon dark soya sauce	
1 teaspoon salt	**C**
4–5 tablespoons sugar	
4 tablespoons oil	

455 g (1 lb) beef, chilled and cut into thin pieces

METHOD

1. Pound **A** to a smooth paste.

2. Fry **B** over low heat for 5 minutes, till fragrant. Pound to a fine powder while still hot.

3. Mix **C** in a bowl and add to pounded paste (Method 1).

4. Rub paste mixture into the beef. Sprinkle the coriander and cumin powder over the beef and mix thoroughly. Marinate beef for 1 hour. Thread seasoned meat on to satay sticks or fine metal skewers. Grill over charcoal fire or under hot grill. Baste with oil and water mixture to keep beef moist.

Peanut Sauce:

15 shallots	
8 cloves garlic	
2 stalks lemon grass, thinly sliced	**A**
20–30 dried chillies, deseeded, or 4–5 tablespoons chilli paste	
4 thin slices galangal	

2 tablespoons salt	
8–10 tablespoons sugar	**B**
4 tablespoons lime juice or 4 tablespoons thick tamarind water	

455 g (16 oz) freshly roasted ground peanuts
225 ml (8 fl oz) oil

METHOD

1. Pound **A** to a fine paste.

2. Boil pounded peanuts with 900 ml (32 fl oz) water over low heat till thick. Stir constantly for about ½ hour. Set aside.

3. Heat oil in wok and fry pounded paste (Method 1) till fragrant and oil seeps through the paste.

4. Add paste to peanut mixture. Add **B**. Boil sauce over a low heat for 5–7 minutes till sugar is dissolved, stirring constantly. Cool peanut sauce and serve separately with barbecued beef and garnish.

Garnish:
2 cucumbers, cut into wedges
2 onions, cut into wedges

Note:
If lemon grass is not available, use 1 teaspoon grated lemon rind.

Satay

YONG TAU FU

INGREDIENTS

(available at market stalls selling fish balls)
20 pieces stuffed triangular white bean curd
10 slices stuffed bitter gourd
60 fish balls
30 pieces stuffed fried spongy bean curd triangles
30 pieces stuffed fried spongy bean curd cubes
10 stuffed green chillies
10 stuffed red chillies

½ cup oil
4 stalks spring onions, chopped coarsely
900 g (2 lb) rice vermicelli
900 g (2 lb) water convolvulus

METHOD

1. Heat ½ cup oil in iron wok. Fry the white bean curd till light brown on all sides. Remove to large tray.

2. Remove rest of oil from wok leaving about 2 tablespoonfuls. Fry bitter gourd over low heat (2 minutes on each side) then add ¼ cup water. Cover wok and cook for 5 minutes. Remove.

3. Cook rice vermicelli for 2–3 minutes in saucepan of boiling water. Remove to a basin of cold water and drain immediately in a colander.

4. Add 1 teaspoon each of salt, sugar and oil to a saucepan of water and bring to a rapid boil. Add water convolvulus and boil rapidly for ½ minute. Pour into a colander and immerse in cold water for 15 minutes. Drain and set aside.

5. Bring soup to the boil. Cook fish balls and remove to a bowl. Add bean curd pieces and boil for 5 minutes; remove to a tray. Boil the green and red chillies with 1 teaspooon oil for 2 minutes. Remove.

Soup:
3.6 litres (7 pints) water
1 thumb-sized piece ginger, bashed
6 cloves garlic, lightly bashed
170 g (6 oz) anchovies, washed and drained
1 chicken cube

Seasoning:
1–2 teaspoons salt
2 teaspoons msg
1 teaspoon sugar

To make soup:
Put some ingredients in a saucepan and bring to the boil togetherr with seasoning. Boil over moderate heat for 1½ hours. Strain and set aside.

To serve:
Bring soup to a boil and boil gently over low heat till ready to serve. Into medium sized bowls put a little rice vermicelli, some water convolvulus and a few pieces each of the *yong tau fu*, fish balls, chilli and bitter gourd. Add boiling soup, garnish with a little spring onion and serve hot with chilli sauce and sweet red sauce.

Note:
Yong tau fu can also be served 'dry' with the soup served in a separate bowl. Sprinkle toasted sesame seeds over each serving and add chilli sauce and sweet red sauce to taste.

(10 servings)

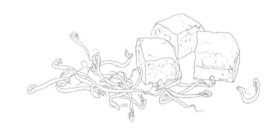

Yong Tau Fu

Nonya Specialities

Assam Gulai

Ayam Buah Keluak

Ayam Goreng Assam

Ayam Kleo

Ayam Merah

Ayam Risa Risa

Ayam Sioh

Ayam Tempra

Babi Assam

Babi Chin

Babi Pong Tay

Buah Paya Masak Titek

Bak Wan Kepiting

Chap Chye Masak Titek

Goreng Ikan Terubok

Hati Babi Bungkus

Ikan Masak Assam Pekat

Itek Tim

Kari Ayam

Pong Tauhu

Satay Babi

Sayor Nanka Masak Lemak

Tauhu Masak Titek

Udang Kuah Pedas Nanas

Udang Kuah Pedas Nanas

ASSAM GULAI
(FISH IN SPICY TAMARIND JUICE)

INGREDIENTS

2 dried tamarind slices
1 tablespoon sugar
A pinch of salt   **A**
Water

3 stalks lemon grass, thinly sliced
½ thumb-sized piece turmeric
20 dried chillies or 2–3 tablespoons
    chilli paste   **B**
20 shallots
2 cloves garlic
1 tablespoon shrimp paste

2 tablespoons sugar
2 teaspoons salt
½ teaspoon msg   **C**
2 stalks phaeomaria (bunga kantan),
    halved lengthwise

1–1½ tablespoons tamarind with 900 ml (2 pints)
    water, squeezed and strained

310 g (11 oz) lady's fingers
625 g (22 oz) prawns or fish head, trimmed and
    washed

METHOD

1. Cut away the stems of the lady's fingers
   before halving them.

2. Boil **A** in a saucepan. Put in the lady's
   fingers and boil till tender (10–15 minutes).
   Drain and set aside.

3. Grind **B** to a fine paste.

4. Heat 115 ml (4 fl oz) oil in wok and fry
   paste till oil bubbles through; stir constantly.

5. Stir in **C** and some of the tamarind water.

6. Cook for 1 minute, then add the rest of the
   tamarind water and bring to boil. Cook for
   further 2 minutes. Do not cover wok.

7. Put in the prawns or fish head and cook till
   done. Finally, add the lady's fingers.

Note:
To choose young and tender lady's fingers, bend the ends to see if
they snap easily. Those that do not break easily are tough and
stringy.

AYAM BUAH KELUAK
(CHICKEN IN BLACK NUT CURRY)

INGREDIENTS

30 Indonesian black nuts
    Pinch of salt
½ teaspoon sugar
1 chicken, 1.4 kg (3 lb), cut into pieces
1 teaspoon salt
1 teaspoon msg
340 g (12 oz) *garam assam* paste*, thawed

570 g (20 oz) pork ribs, cut into pieces

85 g (3 oz) tamarind soaked in 170 ml
    (6 fl oz) water, squeezed and strained
1–1½ level teaspoons salt   **A**
1 teaspoon msg
905 ml (32 fl oz) water

METHOD

1. Soak nuts in cold water for ½ hour. Brush
   nuts to remove sandy particles. Crack where
   nut is smooth and remove meat. Add a
   pinch of salt and ½ teaspoon sugar and
   pound together to form a firm, smooth
   paste, then refill shells.

2. Season chicken with 1 teaspoon salt and
   1 teaspoon msg and leave for ½ hour.

3. Place the thawed *garam assam* paste in an
   enamel pan with **A** and bring to the boil
   over high heat. Add pork ribs and boil for
   5 minutes. Reduce heat to moderate and
   cook for ½ hour. Add the nuts and then the
   chicken and continue cooking for another
   ½ hour or till chicken is tender, stirring
   occasionally.

4. Serve with white rice.

*See page 185.

Ayam Buah Keluak

AYAM GORENG ASSAM
(FRIED TAMARIND CHICKEN)

INGREDIENTS

Marinade Ingredients:

3 tablespoons tamarind pulp (light coloured)	
1½ teaspoons salt	
3 teaspoons fine sugar	
1 teaspoon msg, optional	**A**
1 teaspoon pepper	
2 teaspoons light soya sauce	
8 tablespoons water	

1.2 kg (2½ lb) whole chicken, cut into 4 pieces
Oil for deep frying

METHOD

1. Combine **A** in a bowl. Stir till well mixed.

2. Wash chicken pieces and wipe with kitchen towel till very dry.

3. Prick chicken with fork to allow marinade to soak in. Leave to marinate for ¾ hour.

4. Heat an aluminium kuali till hot. Pour in approximately 570 ml (20 fl oz) of oil and heat till very hot. Add chicken pieces, bring down heat to moderate and fry till light brown, dry and crispy on both sides. Turn heat to low if chicken browns too quickly.

Note:
To prevent chicken being greasy, keep oil at boiling point.

AYAM KLEO
(CHICKEN IN RICH SPICY GRAVY)

INGREDIENTS

1.2 kg (2½ lb) chicken, cut into 4 pieces
625 g (22 oz) grated coconut with 435 ml (14 fl oz) water, squeezed and strained

4 dried chillies	
2 red chillies	
1 stalk lemon grass, thinly sliced	
6 candlenuts	
1 thumb-sized piece ginger	**A**
¼ thumb-sized piece turmeric	
3 cloves garlic	
15 shallots	

1 teaspoon salt	
1 teaspoon msg	**B**
2 tablespoons water	

1 teaspoon salt	
½ teaspoon msg	
1 slice dried tamarind	**C**
5 lime leaves	
2 stalks lemon grass, lightly bashed	

METHOD

1. Grind **A** to a fine paste.

2. Marinate the chicken in **B** and 2 tablespoonfuls of the paste for ½ hour.

3. Set grill to hot. Grill the marinated chicken till brown on both sides (10 minutes for each side).

4. Mix the rest of the paste with the coconut milk and **C**, in a saucepan. Put in the chicken and mix well. Cook over a moderate heat for 15 minutes. Reduce heat and let chicken simmer till tender. Cook until the gravy is thick and oil comes up to the surface.

Ayam Kleo

AYAM MERAH
(CHICKEN IN RED SPICY SAUCE)

INGREDIENTS

10 daun limau purot
2 stalks lemon grass, bashed **A**

10 candlenuts
¼ thumb-sized piece ginger
2 tablespoons chilli powder
10 red chillies, seeded   **B** *ground to a fine paste*
10 red chilli padi
1 clove garlic
1 teaspoon shrimp paste
55 g (2 oz) shallots

1.2 kg (2½ lb) chicken, cut into big pieces
455 g (1 lb) grated coconut
4 tablespoons oil
30 g (1 oz) tamarind, squeezed in 115 ml (4 fl oz) water, strained

METHOD

1. Marinate chicken with 1 tablespoon sugar and 1 teaspoon each of salt and msg for ½ hour.

2. Squeeze coconut for No. 1 milk; set aside. Add 285 ml (10 fl oz) water to squeezed coconut and squeeze again for No. 2 milk. Set aside.

3. Grease a roasting pan with 2 tablespoons oil. Rub chicken pieces with another 2 tablespoons oil and roast chicken in a hot oven till lightly brown. Repeat for other side. Remove from oven and set aside.

4. Heat an aluminium pan. Combine No. 2 milk, **A** and **B**, and boil over medium heat for 10 minutes, adding 1 tablespoon salt and ½ teaspoon msg.

5. Add roasted chicken, pan juices and tamarind water. Boil for another 10 minutes.

6. Pour in No. 1 milk, reduce heat to low and simmer uncovered for 10–12 minutes or till chicken is tender. Remove from heat. Serve hot or cold.

AYAM RISA RISA
(CHICKEN IN SPICY COCONUT SAUCE)

INGREDIENTS

1.6 kg (3½ lb) chicken, cut into big pieces
455 g (1 lb) grated coconut, white
155 ml (6 fl oz) oil

6 cloves garlic
½ thumb-sized piece ginger
6 slices galangal
2 stalks lemon grass
½ thumb-sized piece turmeric or ½ teaspoon turmeric powder   **A** *ground to a fine paste*
20 dried chillies or 2–3 tablespoons chilli powder

4 daun limau purot, sliced thinly
10 candlenuts, pounded finely
2 tablespoons lime or lemon juice
115 g (4 oz) shallots, sliced thinly and fried till light brown

METHOD

1. Season chicken pieces with 1 teaspoon each of salt, sugar and msg. Set aside.

2. Squeeze coconut for approximately 230 ml (8 fl oz) No. 1 milk. Add 170 ml (6 fl oz) water to same coconut and squeeze again for No. 2 milk.

3. Heat an aluminium saucepan with 115 ml oil to fry **A** with the daun limau purot till fragrant and oil seeps through. Add candlenut paste and stir-fry for ½ minute. Put in chicken pieces, 1 teaspoon each of salt and msg, 2 teaspoons sugar and No. 2 milk. Cook over moderately high heat for 10 minutes; stir to prevent burning.

4. Add ½ of No. 1 milk and lime juice. Stir and cook uncovered over moderate heat for 10 minutes or till chicken is tender and gravy begins to thicken. Reduce heat to low, add in remaining No. 1 milk and allow to simmer for another 5 minutes till gravy is thick, moist and oily. Stir in fried shallots. Remove from heat. Serve hot or cold.

AYAM SIOH
(CHICKEN IN THICK SPICY
TAMARIND JUICE)

INGREDIENTS

3 tablespoons coriander powder, roasted 10 tablespoons sugar 1 tablespoon salt 2 tablespoons dark soya sauce 1 heaped teaspoon pepper 170 g (6 oz) shallots, pounded finely	**A**

1.6 kg (3½ lb) chicken, quartered
2 tablespoons salt
225 g (8 oz) tamarind
    Oil

METHOD

1. Wash chicken in water mixed with salt. Drain.

2. Soak tamarind in 340 ml (12 fl oz) water and squeeze into deep bowl. Strain and add **A**. Stir well.

3. Add chicken pieces. Cover and leave to marinate overnight or at least for 10 hours.

4. Transfer chicken and marinade to heavy-bottomed aluminium saucepan and cook for 20 minutes over moderate heat.

5. Reduce heat to low and cook for another 20–30 minutes or till chicken is very tender. Remove from heat and cool before frying chicken pieces in oil. Serve hot or cold.

AYAM TEMPRA
(SPICY CHICKEN)

INGREDIENTS

1 teaspoon salt 1 teaspoon msg	**A**

1 tablespoon dark soya sauce 1 tablespoon sugar ½ teaspoon salt ½ teaspoon msg 2 teaspoons lime juice 225 ml (8 fl oz) water	**B**

905 g (2 lb) chicken, cut into pieces
8 green chillies
6 red chillies
5 tablespoons oil
225 g (8 oz) onions, cut into rings

METHOD

1. Marinate the chicken in **A** for ½ hour.

2. Slice the chillies slantwise, thickly.

3. Mix **B** in bowl.

4. Heat iron wok. When very hot, heat 4 tablespoons oil and fry onions and chillies for ½ minute.

5. Add the marinated chicken and stir-fry over high heat till cooked (7 minutes). Add **B** (Method 3) and cook for another 5 minutes.

6. Lower the heat, cover wok and cook gently for 20 minutes or till chicken is tender.

7. Remove lid, add the last tablespoon of oil, stir well and serve hot or cold.

BABI ASSAM
(PORK BRAISED IN TAMARIND SAUCE)

INGREDIENTS

4 candlenuts
90 g (3 oz) shallots   A *pounded finely*
1 tablespoon shrimp paste

Seasoning:
½ teaspoon salt
1 chicken cube   B
2 tablespoons sugar

4 tablespoons oil
2 tablespoons preserved salted soya beans, pounded

570 g (20 oz) belly pork, cut into thick strips
30 g (1 oz) tamarind, squeezed in 285 ml (10 fl oz) water, strained

8 green chillies, slit halfway lengthwise
6 red chillies, slit halfway lengthwise

METHOD

1. Heat oil in kuali and fry **A** till fragrant and light brown. Add salted preserved soya bean paste, seasoning (**B**) and stir over low heat for short while.

2. Put in pork with ⅓ of tamarind juice. When pork begins to change colour add in red and green chillies and the remaining tamarind juice. Bring to boil, reduce heat and simmer till pork is tender (approx. ¾–1 hour). While cooking, add a little water if gravy is too thick. Serve hot.

BABI CHIN
(BRAISED PORK IN DARK SOYA SAUCE)

INGREDIENTS

115 g (4 oz) shallots, pounded coarsely
30 g (1 oz) garlic, pounded coarsely   A
1 thumb-sized piece cinnamon bark

Seasoning:
2 tablespoons sugar
1 teaspoon salt   B
2 teaspoons dark soya sauce

1.4 kg (3 lb) shoulder pork (with skin)
2 lengths sugarcane, 30 cm long

1 tablespoon coriander powder
3 tablespoons preserved salted soya beans, pounded finely

85 g (3 oz) Chinese mushrooms
455 g (1 lb) boiled bamboo shoots, cut into thick wedges

METHOD

1. Wash and cut meat into 4 cm (1½ in.) cubes.

2. Remove skin of sugarcane, cut into two lengthwise and cut again into 8 cm (3 in.) lengths.

3. Heat oil in non-stick wok. Fry **A** till brown, add preserved salted soya beans, coriander powder and seasoning (**B**). Stir-fry for 2 minutes, add 425 ml (15 fl oz) water and sugarcane and bring to boil.

4. Increase heat to high and put in pork pieces. Cook till sauce is almost dry, stirring occasionally. Add in another 425 ml water and stir till gravy starts to boil. Keep boiling for 5 minutes.

5. Put in the mushrooms and bamboo shoots. Reduce heat to low, cover pan and allow to simmer till pork is tender. Stir from time to time to prevent burning. Add a little water if gravy becomes too thick while cooking. Serve hot.

Babi Chin

BABI PONG TAY
(STEWED PORK)

INGREDIENTS

115 g (4 oz) shallots, pounded coarsely
  4 pieces garlic, pounded coarsely   **A**
  8 cm (3 in) piece cinnamon bark

  2 tablespoons preserved soya beans,
    pounded
  1 tablespoon sugar   **B**
  1 teaspoon salt
  1 teaspoon dark soya sauce

625 g (1 lb 6 oz) pig's trotters
625 g (1 lb 6 oz) shoulder of pork
  6 tablespoons cooking oil

METHOD

1. Cut meat into pieces.
2. Heat oil in wok and fry **A** till brown. Add **B** and stir-fry for ½ minute.
3. Put in meat. Add 150 ml (5 fl oz) water and cook over high heat, stirring occasionally till almost dry (½ hour).
4. Pour in 305 ml (11 fl oz) water and bring to a rapid boil for 5 minutes. Transfer the stewed pork to a heavy-bottomed aluminium saucepan, cover and let simmer for 1–1½ hours or till meat is tender. Serve hot or cold.

Note:
This is an ideal picnic dish eaten with French loaf. Add more hot water when meat is tender, for more gravy.

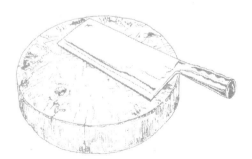

BUAH PAYA MASAK TITEK
(PAPAYA SOUP)

INGREDIENTS

  3 candlenuts
  1 tablespoon shrimp paste
85 g (3 oz) shallots   **A**
  1 red chilli
  1 tablespoon peppercorns or 1 tablespoon
    pepper powder

Seasoning:
  1 teaspoon salt
  2 teaspoons sugar   **B**
  1 chicken cube

  1 green papaya, approximately 905 g (2 lb)
340 g (12 oz) small fresh prawns
900 ml (30 fl oz) water
  55 g (2 oz) dried prawns, pounded finely
225 g (8 oz) salt fish bones, cut into small pieces
  1 handful basil leaves (daun kemangi)

METHOD

1. Grind **A** to a fine paste.
2. Skin papaya and cut into small pieces.
3. Shell fresh prawns and reserve shells. Rub prawns with a little salt and sugar; fry shells in 1 tablespoon oil, then pound and boil in 900 ml (30 fl oz) water for 5 minutes. Strain and keep prawn stock.
4. Combine dried prawns, paste **A**, salt fish bones and seasoning (**B**) in the stock. Bring to boil in an enamel saucepan. Put in papaya pieces and boil over moderately hot fire till tender. Add prawns and cook for 2–3 minutes. Remove from heat and serve hot.

To serve:
Dish papaya itek into a large bowl. Place basil leaves over and sprinkle a tablespoon of lard. Serve boiling hot.

BAK WAN KEPITING

(MINCED PORK WITH CRAB AND
BAMBOO SHOOT SOUP)

INGREDIENTS

1 tablespoon lard or oil
1 tablespoon chopped garlic, browned
1 teaspoon salt
Dash of pepper
1 teaspoon msg   **A**
1 egg
½ teaspoon sugar
1 tablespoon light soya sauce

115 g (4 oz) steamed crab meat
55 g (2 oz) boiled bamboo shoots,   **B**
   shredded very finely

455 g (1 lb) minced pork
115 g (4 oz) fish paste

Ingredients for soup:

2 tablespoons lard or oil
1 teaspoon garlic, chopped finely
250 g (9 oz) boiled bamboo shoots, thinly shredded
1 chicken cube
1 level teaspoon salt
1 teaspoon msg

METHOD

1. Mix minced pork, fish paste and **A** in large bowl. Add **B** and mix well. Set aside.

2. Heat 2 tablespoons lard in an aluminium saucepan. Fry 1 teaspoon garlic till lightly browned. Add finely shredded bamboo shoots and fry for short while. Pour in 2.5 litres (5 **pints**) water and chicken cube and bring to boil.

3. Take spoonfuls of meat and form balls the size of walnuts. Bring soup to rapid boil and put in meatballs. When meatballs float to surface, test one to see if cooked. Dish into serving bowl and serve hot.

CHAP CHYE MASAK TITEK
(STEWED VEGETABLES, NONYA STYLE)

INGREDIENTS

120 g (4 oz) shallots
  4 candlenuts
  1 red chilli
  2 tablespoons shrimp paste } *pound together*

250 g (9 oz) belly pork, to boil in 500 ml (17 fl oz) water
250 g (9 oz) medium-sized grey prawns
  30 g (1 oz) cloud ear fungus (bok nee), soaked in warm water
  60 g (2 oz) golden needles (kim chiam)
  30 g (1 oz) transparent vermicelli, soaked in boiling water
  60 g (2 oz) soya bean strips (foo chok)
  6 tablespoons oil
10 sweet bean curd strips (thim chok)

  2 tablespoons preserved salted soya bean, pounded

600 g (21 oz) cabbage, cut into pieces
  60 g (2 oz) Chinese mushrooms, soaked in hot water

Seasoning:
1¼ teaspoons salt
  1 teaspoon msg
  2 teaspoons sugar

METHOD

1. Add ¼ teaspoon salt in 500 ml (17 fl oz) water and boil belly pork in it for 20 minutes. When done, cut into thin slices and set aside. Keep stock.

2. Shell prawns and devein. Pound shells finely, stir in 250 ml (9 fl oz) water and strain. Set aside.

3. Wash cloud ear fungus thoroughly to remove grit. Cut away rough patch at base and set aside.

4. Cut off hard tops of golden needles and wash in water; drain. Cut transparent vermicelli into short lengths. Soak soya bean strips in cold water for 10 minutes. Drain.

To cook stew:
1. Heat an iron or non-stick wok. Add oil and fry sweet bean curd strips over low heat till they blister and turn light brown. Remove immediately.

2. In the same pan, fry the paste over moderate heat till oil bubbles through and is fragrant. Add preserved bean paste and seasoning and stir fry for 2 minutes. Then add prawns and prawn stock and bring to boil. Put in cabbage, cook over high heat for 5 minutes, then pour in pork stock and remaining ingredients. Continue cooking for another 15–20 minutes or till cabbage is tender. Serve hot.

GORENG IKAN TERUBOK
(FISH IN SCREW PINE LEAVES)

INGREDIENTS

905 g (2 lb) herring, whole or cut into two pieces
  1 teaspoon salt
  6 screw pine leaves
225 ml (8 fl oz) oil

METHOD

1. Wash the fish, rub it with the salt and leave to marinate for ½ hour.

2. Wrap the screw pine leaves round the fish.

3. Heat oil in an iron wok and fry fish till crisp and brown on both sides.

4. Remove the screw pine leaves and place the fish on a plate. Pour the hot oil over and serve hot.

Note:
Do not scale the fish. The fish should be fried over a moderately high heat so that it is thoroughly cooked and the scales are crisp. Sprinkle some water whilst frying before covering the pan. The steam from the water will hasten the cooking.

HATI BABI BUNGKUS
(MEAT AND LIVER BALLS)

INGREDIENTS

3 tablespoons sugar
1 teaspoon salt
2 tablespoons dark soya sauce   **A**
2 tablespoons vinegar

4 tablespoons oil
15 shallots, pounded very finely

310 g (11 oz) minced pork
310 g (11 oz) pork liver, boiled, and diced very finely
2 teaspoons pepper
2 tablespoons roasted coriander powder
455 g (1 lb) pork membrane, cleaned and cut into 15 cm (6 in) squares

METHOD

1. Heat oil in pan and fry pounded shallots till light brown. Reduce the heat to low.

2. Add **A**. Stir-fry for ½ minute. Remove pan from heat.

3. Mix minced pork and liver with fried ingredients. Sprinkle pepper and coriander powder. Knead well to mix thoroughly.

4. Form walnut-size balls from meat mixture. Place on tray.

5. Wrap each meat ball tightly with a small piece of pork membrane. Overlap the membrane two or three times to prevent the meat from bursting out of the wrapper while being fried.

To fry meat balls:
1. Heat a flat-bottomed frying pan, half-filled with oil.

2. Fry meat balls (sealed end downwards) over moderate heat till brown.

Note:
1. *Boil liver till it is half-cooked. It will then bind with the minced meat and not crumble easily.*

2. *Do not buy pig's membrane that has been kept overnight.*

3. *Wash membrane with water and remove all dirt and bristle.*

4. *Squeeze membrane lightly to drain excess water.*

IKAN MASAK ASSAM PEKAT
(FISH IN TAMARIND JUICE)

INGREDIENTS

Thumb-sized piece fresh turmeric or 1 teaspoon turmeric powder
2 tablespoons shrimp paste   **A**
8 shallots, weighing approximately 55 g (2 oz)

1 teaspoon sugar
½ teaspoon salt
Walnut-sized piece tamarind, seeded   **B**
½ cup water

625 g (1 lb 5 oz) spotted Spanish mackerel

Seasoning:
6 tablespoons sugar
1½ teaspoons salt

6 red chillies, slit lengthwise
6 green chillies, slit lengthwise
1 teaspoon lard or oil

METHOD

1. Grind or blend **A** to a very fine paste.

2. Scale and wash fish. Remove bones and cut fish into 2.5 cm (1 in) cubes.

3. Marinate fish with **B** for ½ hour. Drain in a colander.

4. Pour tamarind juice into an enamel saucepan and boil gently for 15 minutes with the seasoning and **A**.

5. Put fish, red and green chillies into the saucepan and cook for 5–7 minutes or till fish is cooked.

6. Stir in the lard and remove from heat. Serve hot or cold.

ITEK TIM
(SALTED CHINESE MUSTARD DUCK SOUP)

INGREDIENTS

4 dried tamarind slices
2 thick slices ginger   **A**
4 salted plums

625 g (1½ lb) pig's foreleg, cut into pieces
½ tablespoon brandy
2 teaspoons salt   **B**
1 teaspoon msg

565 g (20 oz) preserved salted Chinese mustard
1 duck, cut into four pieces
1 tablespoon brandy

METHOD

1. Cut the salted mustard into big pieces and soak in water for ½ hour. Drain.

2. Season the duck with brandy.

3. Boil 3.6 litres (7 pints) water. Add the duck, salted mustard and **A**. When the water re-boils, add **B**.

4. Let the soup boil rapidly for 10 minutes. Lower the heat and let simmer till the meat is tender (about 1–1½ hours).

Note:
You may add four tomatoes (quartered) during the last 10 minutes of cooking time.

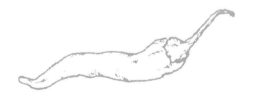

KARI AYAM
(CHICKEN CURRY)

INGREDIENTS

85 g (3 oz) shallots
3 cloves garlic
½ thumb-sized piece ginger, thinly sliced   **A**
1 teaspoon shrimp paste

1 chicken approx. 1.6 kg (3½ lb), cut into pieces
455 g (1 lb) grated coconut (white)

1 sprig curry leaves
5 tablespoons corn oil or refined oil
55 g (2 oz) curry powder for cooking
30 g (1 oz) curry powder for marinating chicken

METHOD

1. Season chicken pieces with 1 level teaspoon each of salt, sugar and msg and the curry powder for ½ hour.

2. Squeeze coconut for first milk. Set aside, add 570 ml (20 fl oz) water to coconut and squeeze for second milk. Set aside.

3. Grind **A** to a rough paste. Heat oil in an aluminium wok. Fry paste till oil bubbles through, and mixture turns light brown.

4. Add in the curry powder, curry leaves with ½ of the first milk. Stir till oil bubbles through and turns reddish. Add in the rest of the first milk, and bring to the boil, continually stirring to prevent burning at bottom.

5. Put in seasoned chicken pieces and stir well with the paste **A** mixture. Cook over moderate heat stirring occasionally.

6. Reduce heat to low, put lid on saucepan and simmer for 20 to 25 minutes or till chicken is tender. Add in some of the second milk to get desired thickness for the gravy — thinner gravy if eaten with bread and thicker gravy for rice. Simmer again for 5 to 7 minutes. Remove from heat. Serve hot or cold.

PONG TAUHU

(BEAN CURD WITH MEAT BALL SOUP)

INGREDIENTS

625 g (1 lb 6 oz) prawns
4 small soya bean cakes **A**

1 tablespoon salt
1 teaspoon msg
1 egg
1 teaspoon dark soya sauce
4 tablespoons oil **B**
1 tablespoon fried crispy garlic
1 teaspoon pepper

1 tablespoon preserved brown
soya beans, pounded **C**
1 teaspoon sugar

1–1½ teaspoons salt
1 teaspoon msg **D**

625 g (1 lb 6 oz) young bamboo shoots, boiled
310 g (11 oz) streaky pork
625 g (1 lb 6 oz) minced pork
2 tablespoons finely chopped spring onions
1 teaspoon pounded garlic

METHOD

1. Shell and devein prawns. Wash, drain and fry the shells. Pound the fried shells and mix with 1.4 litres (48 fl oz) water. Strain and set aside prawn stock.

2. Mince **A** together to fine mixture.

3. Cut bamboo shoots into fine strips.

4. Boil streaky pork with 900 ml (32 fl oz) water. Cut into fine strips. Set aside pork stock.

5. Mix **B** in bowl. Add **A**, minced pork and spring onions. Grease hands and roll mixture into walnut-sized balls. Place the meat balls on a tray.

6. Heat 2 tablespoons lard or oil and fry garlic till light brown. Add **C**. Stir-fry for 1 minute. Add bamboo shoots and stir. Add prawn and pork stock. Season soup with **D**. Boil for 15 minutes.

7. Add meat balls and pork strips to boiling soup. Boil gently till meat balls float to the surface. Keep boiling for 5–7 minutes. Remove from the heat.

SATAY BABI

(GRILLED OR FRIED SPICY PORK SLICES)

INGREDIENTS

4 stalks lemon grass, thinly sliced
4 red chillies, seeded
10 dried chillies, seeded
4 candlenuts **A**
1 teaspoon shrimp paste
15 shallots

1 teaspoon salt
½ teaspoon msg
½ teaspoon pepper **B**
2 teaspoons sugar
3 tablespoons oil

225 g (8 oz) grated coconut
680 g (1 lb 8 oz) pork, cut into 1½ cm (½ in) thick slices
85 ml (3 fl oz) oil

METHOD

1. Extract No. 1 milk from coconut.

2. Grind **A** to a fine paste.

3. Mix with **B** and No. 1 milk to season pork. Marinate for 1 hour.

4. Thread the meat on to wooden or metal skewers. Brush with oil and place under a pre-heated hot grill until cooked.

Peanut sauce and garnish:
Please see page 28.

Pineapple sauce:
1 small ripe pineapple

1. Cut skin off pineapple and ensure "eyes" are removed.

2. Scrape into a bowl leaving out the hard core.

3. Drain off excess juice and serve the pulp on top of peanut sauce, or separately.

Note
The marinated meat can also be fried over a high heat in an iron wok (kuali) till almost dry and the oil comes through. Chicken can be used instead of pork.

SAYOR NANKA MASAK LEMAK

(JACKFRUIT AND CHICKEN IN RICH SPICY COCONUT GRAVY)

INGREDIENTS

115 g (4 oz) shallots or onions
  2 cloves garlic
  2 candlenuts
  6 pieces galangal, sliced thinly
  1 stalk lemon grass, sliced thinly   **A**
10 dried chillies
  1 teaspoon shrimp paste
  ¼ thumb-sized piece ginger
  ½ thumb-sized piece turmeric or
     ¾ teaspoon turmeric powder

680 g (1½ lb) young jackfruit
  1 tablespoon salt
565 g (20 oz) grated coconut, white
  1 tablespoon coriander seeds, roasted and pounded finely
  4 tablespoons oil
680 g (1½ lb) small whole chicken, cut into small pieces

Seasoning:
  2 teaspoons sugar
  2 teaspoons salt
  1 teaspoon msg
  ½ teaspoon pepper

  1 turmeric leaf
  6 daun limau purot

METHOD

1. Cut the jackfruit into small pieces. Put in a saucepan with enough water to cover the jackfruit. Boil with 1 tablespoon salt for 20–25 minutes or till jackfruit is tender. Drain jackfruit in a colander and set aside.

2. Squeeze coconut for No. 1 milk. Set aside. Add 565 ml (20 fl oz) water to coconut and squeeze for No. 2 milk. Set aside.

3. Roast the coriander seeds in a frying pan till fragrant. Pound till fine while still hot. Set aside.

4. Heat 4 tablespoons oil in wok and fry the paste **A** over moderate heat for 2 minutes. Add roasted coriander, chicken pieces, seasoning and ¼ of No. 1 milk. Keep stirring for 2 minutes until oil appears on surface and mixture is fragrant.

5. Add in turmeric leaf and daun limau purot. Then add No. 2 milk and jackfruit. Cook over moderate heat for ½ hour or till chicken is tender.

6. Pour in the remaining No. 1 milk. Stir well, reduce heat and simmer for 5–7 minutes. Remove from heat. Serve hot or cold.

TAUHU MASAK TITEK
(SPICY SOFT BEAN CURD AND SALT FISH SOUP)

INGREDIENTS

455 g (1 lb) minced pork
455 g (1 lb) fresh prawns, minced
½ teaspoon salt
½ teaspoon sugar
½ teaspoon msg   **A**
1 teaspoon light soya sauce
  Dash of pepper
1 tablespoon lard or oil

Ingredients for spicy paste:
55 g (2 oz) shallots
4 candlenuts
1 fresh red chilli, seeded   **B** *Ground finely*
1 tablespoon shrimp paste
¼ teaspoon pepper

1 piece soft bean curd, cut into 24 pieces
115 g (4 oz) Penang salt fish bones, cut into pieces

Seasoning for stock:
1 teaspoon salt
1 teaspoon msg or 1 chicken cube

4 stalks Chinese celery, chopped

METHOD

1. Wash salt fish bones and drain.

2. Wash and drain prawn shells; fry in 1 tablespoon oil till cooked. Boil shells in 905 ml (2 pints) water for 10 minutes adding stock seasoning. Set aside stock after straining.

3. Mix **A** in a large bowl and blend well by hand. Make small candlenut-sized balls and set aside.

4. Heat 3 tablespoons of oil in an aluminium saucepan till very hot. Fry spicy paste **B** till fragrant. Pour in prawn stock, salt fish bones and bring to boil. Put meat balls in to cook till well done. Add soft bean curd pieces, cook for 10 minutes and remove from heat.

5. Remove to serving bowl and garnish with Chinese celery.

UDANG KUAH PEDAS NANAS
(PRAWNS IN PINEAPPLE GRAVY)

INGREDIENTS

14 slices galangal
½ thumb-sized piece turmeric
115 g (4 oz) shallots   **A**
3 red chillies
1 tablespoon shrimp paste

900 ml (32 fl oz) water
1 tablespoon salt
1 tablespoon sugar   **B**
1 pineapple, cut into thin pieces
2 dried tamarind slices

625 g (1 lb 6 oz) king prawns, washed and trimmed
Sprigs of basil leaves

METHOD

1. Pound **A** in the given order to a fine paste.

2. Transfer the paste to an enamel saucepan. Add **B** and mix well. Boil over a moderate heat for 10 minutes.

3. Add the prawns, cook uncovered for 2 minutes. Remove from heat. Garnish with basil leaves. Serve hot.

Note:
The gravy can be boiled first. Add the prawns to cook just before serving so that the prawns will be sweet and more tasty.

Porridge and Rice

Kai Chok

Chicken Rice

Flavoured Chicken Rice

Fried Rice

Nasi Kuning

Nasi Lemak Kuning

Nasi Briani Ayam

Nasi Pilau

Nasi Ulam

Pineapple Rice

Steamed Glutinous Rice

Kai Chok

KAI CHOK
(CHICKEN CONGEE — HONG KONG STYLE)

INGREDIENTS

2.8 litres (6 pints) water
1 teaspoon salt   **A**
1 teaspoon msg
2 tablespoons peppercorn

795 g (1¾ lb) chicken
1 tablespoon light soya sauce
1 teaspoon sesame oil
170 g (6 oz) No. 1 Thai fragrant rice
1.7 litres (4 pints) water
½ teaspoon salt
1 tablespoon oil

3 tablespoons glutinous rice powder
225 ml (8 fl oz) water   *thickening*

1 oz young ginger, shredded very
  finely
2 stalks spring onions, cut finely   *garnishing*
  Dash of pepper
  Chinese crullers, sliced

METHOD

1. Boil **A** in a saucepan. Add chicken and boil rapidly for 5 minutes, reduce heat, cover pan and simmer chicken for 30 minutes.

2. Remove chicken and immerse in a basin of cold water for 5 minutes. Debone chicken and set aside. Put bones back in saucepan to simmer with the chicken stock for 1½ hours.

3. Strain chicken stock into another saucepan adding boiling water, if necessary, so that it measures 2.2 litres (4 pints).

4. Cut chicken meat into small cubes and mix with 1 tablespoon light soya sauce and 1 teaspoon sesame oil. Put in a bowl, cover and set aside.

5. While chicken is being cooked, boil rice with the salt and oil in a fairly large saucepan till porridge is thick and smooth, stirring occasionally to prevent burning.

6. Pour in the chicken stock, stir till well blended and bring to boil. Mix thickening and pour gradually into the porridge, stirring all the time. Simmer for 5 minutes before serving.

To serve:
Put some chicken into individual bowls, add the boiling porridge and garnish with shredded ginger, spring onions and a dash of pepper. Top with Chinese crullers and serve hot.

Note
Pressure cooker can also be used to cook the porridge.

Cooking time depends on each brand, approximate time 20–30 minutes. Remove the lid of cooker to check if porridge is smooth. Add some hot water if porridge is too thick. Cover lid and cook for further 5–7 minutes.

To make Chee Yiok Chok (pork congee), use instant seasoned minced pork instead of chicken and put in to boil with the congee. Sliced liver can be added if desired.

(10 servings)

INSTANT SEASONED MINCED PORK

INGREDIENTS

1 teaspoon sugar
1 teaspoon sesame oil
1 teaspoon light soya sauce   **A**
1 teaspoon msg
1 tablespoon corn flour

455 g (1 lb) minced pork
3 tablespoons *twa tow chye* (salted radish), finely chopped

METHOD

1. Place minced pork and *twa tow chye* in a large bowl.

2. Mix **A** with the minced pork and stir by hand till well blended.

Note
Pack meat mixture into plastic bag if storing in freezer.
To use frozen meat, chop off one chunk and leave to thaw before putting into soup. Form into balls while cold and set aside. Return rest of meat to freezer immediately.

CHICKEN RICE

INGREDIENTS

CHICKEN:

6–8 cloves garlic, bashed lightly
  2 thumb-sized pieces ginger, bashed lightly | **A**
  4 stalks spring onions, tied into a knot

1.6 kg (3½ lb) whole chicken

GARNISH:

2 cucumbers, sliced
4 tomatoes, sliced
2 sprigs Chinese parsley, cut into pieces

METHOD

To boil the chicken:

1. Wash chicken and rub some salt over it. Stuff chicken with **A**.
2. Boil 2.1 litres (4 pints) water with 1 teaspoon salt rapidly over high heat.
3. Add chicken, leaving saucepan uncovered. When water re-boils, cook for further 2 minutes then reduce the heat to very low, cover and let simmer for 25–30 minutes. (Do not remove lid throughout cooking time).
4. Set aside 995 ml (35 fl oz) chicken stock for the rice. Remove chicken immediately to immerse in a basin of cold water for 5 minutes.
5. Transfer chicken to a large plate and brush it immediately with oil. Remove stuffing.
6. Allow chicken to cool before cutting it into pieces. Arrange on a serving plate.
7. Garnish. Serve with chilli sauce and ginger sauce.

RICE:

625 g (22 oz) Thai No. 1 rice
115 ml (4 fl oz) lard or oil
995 ml (35 fl oz) chicken stock (Method 4)
  2 teaspoons salt
  1 teaspoon msg
  6 screw pine leaves, tied into a knot

1. Wash rice until water runs clear. Drain.
2. Heat pan. Fry rice in heated lard for 2 minutes. Put the chicken stock, salt and msg in a saucepan. Add the fried rice and screw pine leaves. Boil over moderate heat till all the stock is absorbed.
3. Reduce heat to low and cook for a further 15 minutes. Rake rice with a fork and serve hot.

GINGER SAUCE:

55 ml (2 fl oz) chicken stock
½ teaspoon salt
½ teaspoon msg | **A**
½ teaspoon sugar

2 thumb-sized pieces ginger

1. Slice ginger thinly and pound till fine.
2. Mix **A** in a bowl and add the pounded ginger.

CHILLI SAUCE:

10–12 red chillies
  ½ teaspoon salt
  55 ml (2 fl oz) warm water
  2–3 tablespoons lime juice

1. Scald chillies. Remove stems and pound chillies coarsely with ½ teaspoon salt.
2. Remove to a bowl and mix with warm water and lime juice.

Note:
When cooking 625 g–1.2 kg (22-43 oz) rice, use an electric rice cooker. When rice is cooked, wipe water from under the lid of cooker to prevent rice getting soggy.

(8 servings)

FLAVOURED CHICKEN RICE

INGREDIENTS

1 teaspoon salt
1 teaspoon msg   **A**
1 teaspoon dark soya sauce

1 thumb-sized piece of ginger,
  shredded finely
3 cloves garlic, thinly sliced   **B**
4 shallots, thinly sliced

2 tablespoons light soya sauce
1 teaspoon dark soya sauce
1 teaspoon msg
1 teaspoon salt   **C**
1 tablespoon sesame oil
1 chicken cube, mashed
¼ teaspoon pepper

905 g (2 lb) deboned chicken, cut into pieces

115 ml (4 fl oz) lard or oil

4 dried Chinese mushrooms, soaked and sliced
  thinly
625 g (22 oz) No. 1 Thai rice, washed and drained

935 ml (33 fl oz) boiling water
2 pairs Chinese sausages, fried and cut into 4 cm
  (1½ in) pieces
Chinese parsley

METHOD

1. Marinate the chicken in **A** for ½ hour.
2. Heat 2 tablespoons oil in hot pan and fry chicken till brown on all sides. Set aside.
3. Heat lard in wok and fry **B** till light brown. Add the mushrooms and stir-fry for 1 minute. Add the rice and fry till oil is absorbed.
4. Mix **C** in a bowl. Add to rice together with 935 ml (33 fl oz) boiling water. Cook till rice is quite dry.
5. Place the fried sausages and the fried chicken pieces on the rice. Allow to cook for ½ hour over a low heat. Serve hot.

FRIED RICE

INGREDIENTS

6 tablespoons water
1 teaspoon salt
1 teaspoon msg   **A**
1 tablespoon light soya sauce
¼ teaspoon pepper

4 tablespoons lard or oil
4 eggs, lightly beaten with a pinch of salt
2 tablespoons chopped onions
85 g (3 oz) small shelled prawns
455 g (16 oz) cold cooked rice
115 g (¼ lb) roast pork, diced
4 tablespoons chopped spring onions

METHOD

1. Heat 2 tablespoons lard in wok and scramble beaten eggs. Remove and set aside.
2. Heat rest of the lard and fry onions till transparent. Stir-fry prawns, followed by rice.
3. Mix **A** in a bowl and add to the rice, stir-frying all ingredients.
4. Add the scrambled eggs and roast pork. Continue to stir-fry over a high heat. Finally add the spring onions. Serve fried rice hot, in a large dish.

NASI KUNING
(YELLOW RICE)

INGREDIENTS

625 g (22 oz) briani rice
  2 tablespoons oil

1 teaspoon pounded ginger 4 cloves garlic 6 shallots, thinly sliced	**A**
8 cm (3 in) piece cinnamon bark 8 cardamons, lightly bashed 8 cloves	**B**

115 g (4 oz) ghee or butter
½ teaspoon turmeric powder
  blended with 1 tablespoon
  lime juice
	C

995 ml (35 fl oz) boiling water

1 teaspoon msg 1 rounded teaspoon salt 1 chicken cube 55 g (2 oz) almonds, chopped 115 g (4 oz) sultanas	**D**

METHOD

1. Wash the rice and drain it in a colander.
2. Heat an iron wok (kuali). Heat the oil and brown **A** in the given order.
3. Add **B** and stir-fry. Add **C**.
4. Add the rice and stir-fry till the oil is absorbed.
5. Remove the rice to a saucepan or an electric rice cooker. Pour in the boiling water and season with **D**. Boil with the lid on over a moderate heat till the rice has absorbed all the water. Reduce the heat to low and cook for about 15 minutes. Spoon the cooked rice on to a large platter. Garnish with a sprinkling of fried almonds and sultanas.

To fry the almonds and sultanas:
1. Place 3 tablespoons oil in a heated pan to stir-fry the chopped almonds till light brown, over a low heat. Drain on absorbent paper. Store in a bottle.
2. In the same oil, fry the sultanas for 2 minutes. Drain and cool on absorbent paper.

NASI LEMAK KUNING
(SPICY YELLOW RICE)

INGREDIENTS

30 g (1 oz) SANTAN instant coconut cream
  powder
1½ teaspoons salt
  1 cube chicken stock
  6 tablespoons oil
  2 stalks lemon grass, bashed
100 g (3 oz) shallots/onions, thinly sliced
  1 thumb-sized cinnamon stick
500 g (18 oz) long grain rice
1½ level teaspoons turmeric powder
  1 tablespoon lime juice
  4 screw pine leaves, tied into a knot

METHOD

1. Dissolve SANTAN powder in 720 mls (25 fl oz) water and strain into a saucepan. Stir in salt and chicken stock. Allow to heat over very low fire till mixture comes to a boil. Set aside.
2. Heat oil in the wok, fry lemon grass till fragrant and light brown. Add in cinnamon and shallots/onions, continue to stir fry till brown. Pour in rice, turmeric powder, lime juice and stir till evenly mixed. Remove from heat.
3. Transfer rice mixture into the rice cooker and pour in the hot SANTAN mixture and screw pine leaves. Leave rice to cook till dry and grainy.
4. Wipe steam from underlid to prevent rice from getting wet and soggy.
5. Transfer rice onto a large serving plate. Garnish with sliced egg omelette, fine chilli strips and crispy shallots.

One 30 g packet of SANTAN powder is equivalent to 1 lb white grated coconut.

NASI BRIANI AYAM

(GHEE RICE WITH MILD SPICY CHICKEN)

INGREDIENTS

1 thumb-sized piece ginger
3 cloves garlic
4 green chillies
A

1 handful mint leaves
2 stalks coriander with roots, rinsed
2 tomatoes, cut in eighths
2 tablespoons tomato puree
B

Seasoning:
2 teaspoons salt
2 teaspoons msg
1 teaspoon sugar

1.6 (3½ lb) chicken quartered
225 g (8 oz) ghee or 112 g (4 oz) butter with 112 ml (4 fl oz) oil
1 teaspoon dry chilli powder mixed to a paste with water
1 level teaspoon garam masala (see recipe)
170 ml (6 fl oz) evaporated milk mixed with 1 tablespoon lemon juice and 112 ml (4 fl oz) water
285 g (10 oz) shallots, thinly sliced

METHOD

1. Marinate chicken pieces with 1 level tablespoon salt and 1 teaspoon msg for 1 hour.

2. Heat a large saucepan with half of the ghee. Fry the shallots till golden brown. Set aside.

3. Fry **A** till fragrant. Add chilli paste and garam masala, then add in **B**, seasoning and ½ of the milk mixture. Stir-fry till oil bubbles through.

4. Put in chicken pieces, fried shallots, remaining milk and oil. Cook over high heat for 10 minutes.

5. Reduce heat to low and cook gently till chicken is tender. Drain chicken, keeping oil to cook the briani rice.

To Cook Rice :

1 teaspoon chopped ginger
1 tablespoon chopped garlic
4 shallots, thinly sliced
C

5 cm (2 in) cinnamon bark
8 cardamoms, lightly bashed
6 cloves
D

600 g (21 oz) Basmati (long grain) rice, washed and drained
55 g (2 oz) ghee

Seasoning:
1 teaspoon msg or 1 chicken cube
1½ teaspoons salt
1.1 litres (40 fl oz) boiling water

Colouring for Rice :
Mix 1 teaspoon yellow food colouring with ¼ teaspoon Rose essence and 4 tablespoons water.

1. Heat wok with 55 g (2 oz) ghee to fry **C** till lightly browned, add in **D** and stir-fry for ½ minute. Add in the remaining oil and the rice. Stir in pan till oil is absorbed into rice.

2. Pour in the boiling water and the seasoning. Cook rice in an electric rice-cooker till dry and fluffy. Do not stir while cooking.

3. Remove lid and sprinkle the yellow colouring mixture over rice. Continue to cook for another 10 minutes. Remove from heat. Loosen rice, mixing colours evenly. Serve hot with chicken.

GARAM MASALA

(GROUND MIXED SPICES)

115 g (4 oz) coriander seeds, washed and dried
55 g (2 oz) cumin seeds, washed and dried
2 tablespoons black pepper
1 tablespoon white pepper
3 teaspoons cardamom seeds
30 g (1 oz) cinnamon bark, broken into small pieces
2 teaspoons cloves
3 nutmegs

1. Spread the ingredients in a large aluminium tray. Heat under a warm grill till fragrant and very lightly browned — do not allow to darken. Grind mixture, while still warm, in a coffee grinder till very fine. Keep in an air-tight bottle and store in fridge.

Nasi Briani Ayam

NASI PILAU
(BUTTERED RICE WITH ROAST CHICKEN)

INGREDIENTS

Seasoning:

1 teaspoon salt
1 teaspoon msg
1 teaspoon pepper
1 teaspoon brandy   **A**
1 teaspoon sugar
1 tablespoon ginger juice
1 tablespoon light soya sauce

625 g (22 oz) No. 1 Thai rice   **B**
1 litre (32 fl oz) water

1.4 kg (3 lb) chicken, whole
170 g (6 oz) butter
115 ml (4 fl oz) water

1 handful raisins, fried
30 almonds, sliced and fried
6 slices cooked ham, cut into pieces and rolled
A few lettuce leaves
1 cucumber, sliced

METHOD

1. Mix **A** in a bowl.
2. Marinate chicken, both inside and out, using 1 tablespoon of the seasoning. Leave for an hour.
3. Heat roasting pan. Grease chicken with half of the butter and place it in heated pan. Add water to the leftover marinade, mix well and pour into the roasting pan. Roast chicken for ½ hour till brown. Reduce the heat to moderate and continue roasting till the chicken is cooked (¾–1 hour).
4. Debone and cut the chicken into serving portions. Set aside. Leave the juices in the pan.
5. Cook **B** in a rice cooker.
6. Rake rice with a fork, add the rest of the butter, pan juices and mix well.
7. Dish the rice onto a large serving plate. Scatter the raisins and almonds over it. Arrange the chicken and rolled ham on top. Decorate border of the dish with lettuce and cucumber.

NASI ULAM

INGREDIENTS

455 g (1 lb) small prawns, shelled
225 g (½ lb) wolf herring (ikan parang), remove centre bone
170 g (6 oz) grated coconut, white
55 g (2 oz) long beans
1 cucumber
905 g (2 lb) cooked rice (cooled)
1 tablespoon light soya sauce
6 lime leaves, sliced very thinly
2 turmeric leaves, sliced very thinly
55 g (2 oz) dried shrimps, optional
Cooking oil
Salt

METHOD

1. Fry prawns with a pinch of salt.
2. Season fish with salt and fry with oil till cooked. Break fish into small pieces and place under grill for 10 minutes or till dry.
3. Add a pinch of salt to the coconut and fry in an iron wok over low heat till light brown, stirring all the time. Cool.
4. Scald and cut long beans into very fine pieces.
5. Skin cucumber, remove soft centre and cut into tiny cubes.

To serve:
1. Place the cooled rice in a large bowl.
2. Sprinkle ½ teaspoon fine salt and 1 tablespoon light soya sauce, and mix well.
3. Add the prepared ingredients, together with the lime leaves, turmeric leaves and dried shrimps. Stir with two wooden spoons till well mixed. Serve cold.

(8 servings)

PINEAPPLE RICE

INGREDIENTS

55 g (2 oz) shallots or onions, sliced finely
2 cloves garlic, sliced finely   **A**
2 cm (¾ in) cinnamon stick

1 teaspoon curry powder
¾ teaspoon turmeric powder
1 teaspoon msg or 1 chicken cube, crushed   **B**
2 level teaspoons salt
1 tablespoon lemon juice

3 tablespoons oil
55 g (2 oz) dried prawns, pounded coarsely
55 g (2 oz) ham, cut into small squares
225 g (8 oz) pineapple cubes (from can)
2 tablespoons butter

560 g fragrant (20 oz) Thai rice, washed and
   drained
170 ml (6 fl oz) pineapple juice (from can)
   Boiling water
4 pandan leaves, knotted

METHOD

1. Pour 3 tablespoons oil in a heated wok. When hot, fry dried prawns and ham till brown. Remove to a plate. In the same wok, fry pineapple cubes for 5 minutes till light brown. Remove to a plate.

2. Add butter to wok and fry **A** till light brown. Add **B** and stir. Put rice in and keep stirring till oil is absorbed. Pour in pineapple juice and stir for 1 minute.

3. Transfer rice into an electric rice cooker. Add enough boiling water and pandan leaves. When rice is cooked, allow rice to rest in cooker to dry for ½ hour. Loosen rice with fork and reheat briefly. Serve hot in cut-out pineapple.

STEAMED GLUTINOUS RICE

INGREDIENTS

1 piece dried streaky pork★
6 dried Chinese mushrooms, soaked   **A**
2 pairs Chinese sausages

1 teaspoon ginger   **B**
1 teaspoon garlic

310 g (11 oz) pork bones
680 ml (24 fl oz) water   **C**
¼ teaspoon salt
1 teaspoon peppercorns

2 teaspoons dark soya sauce
1 teaspoon msg   **D**
1 teaspoon sesame oil

4 tablespoons lard
10 shallots, thinly sliced
625 g (22 oz) glutinous rice, washed, soaked overnight and drained

METHOD

1. Dice **A** and chop **B**.

2. Boil **C** and let it simmer gently until the stock is reduced by half (approximately 1 hour). Strain.

3. Heat lard in wok and fry chopped ingredients and shallots till brown. Add diced ingredients and stir-fry for 1 minute. Add the glutinous rice and mix it thoroughly with the fried mixture. Pour in the stock. Season with **D** and stir-fry for a moment.

4. Reduce heat to very low. Cover wok and cook for a further 5 minutes till the stock is absorbed.

5. Remove cooked glutinous rice and press it down firmly into small bowls. Place the bowls in a steamer and steam for 20 minutes. Serve hot.

★This is the seasoned, dried variety imported from China.

Noodles

Birthday Noodles, Nonya Style

Crispy Noodles with Prawns

Beef Kway Teow

Fried Noodles

Hokien Mee

Kai See Ho Fun

Nonya Mahmee

Teochew Kway Teow

Birthday Noodles, Nonya Style

BIRTHDAY NOODLES NONYA STYLE

INGREDIENTS

285 g (10 oz) belly pork
285 g (10 oz) small prawns, shelled and deveined
  (keep shells)
285 g (10 oz) big prawns, shelled and deveined
  (keep shells), minced finely
175 g (6 oz) fish paste (available from wet markets)
  1 tablespoon tapioca flour
2–3 drops red food colouring
225 g (8 oz) fine rice vermicelli (mee suah)★
  1 litre (32 fl oz) oil
  5 tablespoons lard
  1 tablespoon pounded garlic
  1 tablespoon preserved soya bean paste, pounded

Garnish:
30 g (1 oz) coriander leaves, cut into short lengths
30 g (1 oz) spring onions, cut into 1 cm (½ in.)
  lengths
  3 tablespoons crispy shallots

METHOD

1. Boil belly pork with 1 teaspoon msg in 1 litre (32 fl oz) water. Keep stock.

2. Marinate whole prawns with ¼ teaspoon each of salt and sugar. Set aside.

3. Fry all the prawn shells in 2 tablespoons oil till well cooked. Put shells in a saucepan, add 1 litre water and boil for 20 minutes. Strain stock and set aside.

4. Put minced prawns in a large bowl. Add fish paste and sprinkle in ¾ teaspoon fine salt, 1 teaspoon msg, 1 tablespoon tapioca flour and 2–3 drops red food colouring. Rub paste with palm of hand in a circular motion for 2 minutes. Sprinkle 3 tablespoons water and rub again till paste becomes sticky. Take fistfuls and throw against side of bowl (10–15 times) to smoothen paste.

5. Take fistfuls of paste to squeeze through thumb and first finger to make balls, then leave in cold water for 30 minutes.

6. Slice belly pork thinly and cut into thin strips. Pour prawn and pork stock into saucepan and bring to a boil. Drop in the prawn-and-fish balls till they rise to the surface. Scoop out and keep stock.

To cook noodles:

1. Loosen fine rice vermicelli for deep frying. Heat 1 litre oil in a wok till hot. Oil is ready when a piece of noodle put in for testing rises to the surface. Fry each skein of noodles separately till light brown, turning once. Set aside.

2. Heat lard in a hot aluminium or iron wok and fry garlic till light brown. Add 1 tablespoon sugar and preserved soya bean paste. Stir-fry till oil seeps through. Add 2 cups of reserved stock, whole prawns, shredded pork and prawn-and-fish balls. Cook for 2 minutes and scoop out prawns, pork and prawn-and-fish balls, leaving gravy.

3. Pour in remaining stock and bring to a boil. Reduce heat to low, put in fried vermicelli and stir well with chopsticks. Season to taste after vermicelli softens in gravy.

4. Dish vermicelli onto a large serving plate. Return the prawns, pork and prawn-and-fish balls to boil gently. When ready, pour over vermicelli. Sprinkle with pepper and garnish. Serve immediately.

Note:
This is a traditional nonya dish served only on birthdays. Instead of making tiny prawn-and-fish balls, the mixture can be made into square patties and boiled in the prawn stock. When cooled, cut into small cubes.

★The best fine rice vermicelli is made in China. They are available in boxes and are packed in skeins tied with red strings. No seasoning is added to the gravy because the vermicelli is quite salty. Season gravy to taste only after vermicelli has been introduced.

See Page 123 for Nonya Salad to complement Noodles.

CRISPY NOODLES WITH PRAWNS

INGREDIENTS

605 g (21 oz) big prawns
¼ teaspoon msg
1 teaspoon ginger
1 chicken cube
2 tablespoons oil
1 packet dry egg noodles (200 g)
　Oil for deep frying
4 tablespoons lard
6 slices ginger
1 teaspoon pounded garlic
4 dry Chinese mushrooms, soaked and sliced
285 g (10 oz) Chinese mustard greens, cut into 3 cm
　(1½ in) lengths
455 ml (16 fl oz) chicken stock, or 455 ml hot water
　with 1 chicken cube for gravy

Seasoning:
1 tablespoon light soya sauce
1 tablespoon oyster sauce
½ teaspoon sugar
1 teaspoon msg
¼ teaspoon salt
½ teaspoon sesame oil

　A *mixed in a bowl*

2 tablespoons corn flour
4 tablespoons water

　B *thickening*

METHOD

Shell prawns leaving tails; devein and marinate with ¼ teaspoon msg and 1 teaspoon ginger.

To prepare crispy noodles:
1. Bring 565 ml (20 fl oz) water to boil with one chicken cube and 2 tablespoons oil. Put in noodles and cook till noodles separate and become soft (approximately 3–4 minutes). Immerse noodles in cold water and drain immediately in a steel colander. Allow to cool and dry for ½ hour before frying.
2. When wok is heated, pour in oil. When very hot, put in the noodles, a little each time and fry till crispy and light brown. Scoop out with wire ladle onto absorbent paper. Keep the noodles warm.

3. Heat 3 tablespoons lard in wok and fry ginger and garlic till light brown. Add mushrooms and mustard stalks and stir-fry for a short while. Add mustard leaves, chicken stock and seasoning and bring to boil.
4. Arrange prawns over the leaves, cover pan and cook over high heat for 2 minutes. Remove lid, gradually add in thickening, stirring constantly. Lower heat and when gravy boils, add last tablespoon of lard.
5. Transfer crispy noodles to a serving plate and immediately pour sauce over. Serve hot.

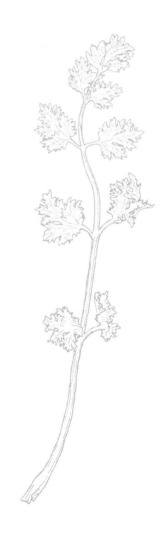

BEEF KWAY TEOW

INGREDIENTS

455 g (1 lb) beef tripe, scalded
455 g (1 lb) beef ribs
905 g (2 lb) beef shin or brisket, whole   }
  1 tablespoon salt
  1 teaspoon msg
  1 teaspoon dark soya sauce   **A**
  1 teaspoon peppercorns
  4 cloves
  2 thick slices galangal
  1 tablespoon grated palm sugar

  1 tablespoon Bovril (optional)
565 g (20 oz) bean sprouts
905 g (2 lb) flat rice noodles
115 g (4 oz) salted Chinese mustard, cut into thin
    pieces
  6 sprigs Chinese celery, cut into pieces

METHOD

1. Bring 2.7 litres (5 pints) water to a rapid boil in saucepan. Add **A**. Boil rapidly for 20 minutes.
2. Reduce heat and let simmer till meat and tripe are tender. Add Bovril to taste.
3. Remove tripe and meat from the soup and cut into small pieces.

To serve:
Boil water to scald bean sprouts. Drain. Immerse noodles in the boiling water for a moment and drain. Place a small handful of bean sprouts and noodles in a bowl, add some meat and tripe. Add boiling soup and garnish with salted Chinese mustard and Chinese celery. Serve hot with chilli sauce and pounded galangal.

Note:
Remove meat when tender and leave tripe to simmer till soft.
For pounded galangal, skin two thumb-sized pieces. Slice thinly and pound till fine.

(15 servings)

FRIED NOODLES

INGREDIENTS

1 packet dried egg noodles   }
1 chicken cube   **A**
1 tablespoon lard

1 tablespoon oyster sauce
½ teaspoon salt
2 tablespoons light soya sauce
1 teaspoon sesame oil   **B**
½ teaspoon pepper
1 teaspoon msg
½ teaspoon sugar
115 ml (4 fl oz) hot water

225 g (8 oz) lettuce, cut into strips   }
2–3 chillies, seeded and cut into long thin   **C**
    strips

  6 eggs, lightly beaten with a pinch of salt
  1 teaspoon pounded garlic
112 g (¼ lb) small, cooked prawns, shelled
455 g (16 oz) bean sprouts, washed and picked
225 g (½ lb) roast pork, shredded finely

METHOD

1. Boil 900 ml (32 fl oz) water in a saucepan. Add **A**. Boil for 5–7 minutes or till noodles separate. Immerse in cold water. Drain in a colander.
2. Heat a little oil and scramble eggs in heated wok. Remove to a dish.
3. In the same wok, add 2 tablespoons lard. Fry garlic till light brown. Add prawns and stir-fry for ½ minute.
4. Add bean sprouts, noodles, eggs and roast pork.
5. Toss mixture in wok. Mix **B** in a bowl, then pour over and around the noodle mixture. Stir-fry and cook for 2 minutes.
6. Remove noodles to a large serving plate. Garnish with **C** and serve.

HOKIEN MEE

INGREDIENTS

455 ml (16 fl oz) water ⎤
  1 teaspoon salt   **A**
  2 teaspoons msg ⎦

  4 eggs ⎤
625 g (22 oz) bean sprouts, picked and
  washed
625 g (22 oz) fresh yellow noodles
  2 teaspoons pounded garlic   **B**
  2 tablespoons light soya sauce
 55 g (2 oz) chives, cut into 3 cm lengths ⎦

  4 limes, halved ⎤
  4 red chillies, sliced thinly **C**

310 g (11 oz) medium size prawns
310 g (11 oz) cuttlefish (remove the centre bone and
  ink bag)
310 g (11 oz) streaky pork
  Lard for frying

METHOD

To make the stock:
1. Remove prawn heads. Wash and drain. Fry heads in 1 tablespoon oil for 1 minute. Remove from pan and pound. Mix with 225 ml water. Strain and set liquid aside.

2. Boil **A** in saucepan.

3. Put in cuttlefish to boil for 2 minutes. Remove and cut cylindrically. Set aside.

4. Cook prawns in the same stock. Remove and shell, leaving tails on. Set aside.

5. Cook streaky pork in stock till done (about 15 minutes). Set aside to cool. Slice pork into thin strips. Set aside.

6. Pour the prawn liquid (Method 1) into the stock and continue boiling till liquid is reduced to 455 ml (16 fl oz). Strain.

To fry the noodles:
1. Halve **B** and the cooked prawns, pork and cuttlefish to fry in two separate lots.

2. Heat a large iron wok. When very hot, heat 2 tablespoons lard to fry one lot. Add eggs to scramble, then add bean sprouts and noodles. Add 1 tablespoonful of stock to noodles, stir-fry and cover.

3. Remove lid, put prawns, pork and cuttlefish over noodle mixture. Cover and cook for a further 2 minutes. Remove lid and stir-fry noodle mixture evenly over a high heat for a short while.

4. Push aside noodle mixture. Add another 2 tablespoons lard to fry the garlic till light brown. Add light soya sauce and a ladleful of stock. Stir in noodle mixture and mix evenly.

5. Lastly, add chives and stir. Remove to a plate, garnish with **C** and serve hot.

6. Repeat process with the other half of the ingredients.

Note
Use lard to fry as it gives a better flavour and aroma than ordinary cooking oil. Frying should be done over a high heat throughout to prevent the noodles from becoming soggy and to keep the bean sprouts crunchy.

(6 servings)

KAI SEE HO FUN
(FLAT RICE NOODLES WITH BRAISED CHICKEN)

INGREDIENTS

55 g (2 oz) ginger, lightly bashed
6 cloves garlic, lightly bashed **A**
3 stalks spring onion, tied into a knot

Lard or oil for frying

Seasoning:
1 teaspoon msg
4 tablespoons light soya sauce
1 teaspoon dark soya sauce
1 teaspoon sesame oil **B**
½ teaspoon pepper
½–1 teaspoon salt
455 ml (16 fl oz) water

Thickening:
1½ tablespoons corn flour
115 ml (4 fl oz) water **C** *mixed in a bowl*
1 tablespoon lard
1 teaspoon sesame oil

1.14 kg (2½ lb) chicken
1 tablespoon pounded rock sugar
455 g (1 lb) Chinese mustard greens, cut into 5 cm (2 in) lengths
1 tablespoon sugar
1 teaspoon salt
1 tablespoon oil
905 g (2 lb) flat rice noodles
8 tablespoons crispy shallots★ (optional)

METHOD

To braise chicken:
1. Wash chicken and season both inside and outside with salt. Drain. Stuff chicken with **A**.
2. Heat 4 tablespoons lard or oil in an iron wok. Add pounded rock sugar and fry till sugar turns light brown. Pour in the seasoning **B**, stir and bring to the boil.
3. Put in chicken, increase heat to high, spoon gravy all over chicken and cook till chicken is nicely browned. Boil for 15 minutes. Reduce heat to medium, cover pan and simmer for 30–40 minutes or till chicken is well done. Add a little water if necessary during cooking. Remove chicken to cool.
4. Remove stuffing, debone and reserve bones and set aside meat.
5. Pour gravy into a saucepan. Add 830 ml (30 fl oz) hot water, and chicken bones and simmer for 1 hour. Stir in the thickening **C**, cook for 1 minute and remove from heat.
6. Bring 2.3 litres (80 fl oz) water to the boil. Put in the vegetable stalks to boil for ½ minute. Add the leaves, sprinkle 1 tablespoon sugar, 1 teaspoon salt and 1 tablespoon oil into saucepan. Stir and continue boiling over high heat for another ½ minute. Drain in a colander. Place colander in an enamel basin and put under running water till vegetable is well cooled. Drain and set aside till ready to serve.

To serve flat rice noodles:
1. Cut chicken into bite-sized pieces.
2. Heat gravy till almost boiling point.
3. Divide noodles into 8 portions.
4. Bring 3.4 litres (7 pints) water in a saucepan to a rapid boil. Put one portion of the noodles into the saucepan and boil for 10 seconds only. Scoop and drain noodles with a wire mesh ladle and remove to a bowl. Sprinkle 1 teaspoon of light soya sauce and a few drops of sesame oil. Stir with chopsticks and remove to a plate.
5. Place some vegetables and a few pieces of chicken over noodles, pour hot gravy over and serve. Repeat process for the other seven portions.

Note:
Garnish with crispy shallots just before serving.

Choose the broad and smooth, very white and light-textured noodles for this recipe.

★See "Helpful Hints".

NONYA MAHMEE

INGREDIENTS

1 tablespoon preserved soya beans, pounded
½ teaspoon salt
1 teaspoon msg **A**
½ teaspoon pepper
1 teaspoon sugar

170 g (6 oz) water convolvulus, cut into short lengths
625 g (22 oz) bean sprouts, washed and picked **B**
625 g (22 oz) fresh yellow noodles

1 cucumber, without skin and centre, shredded very finely into 4 cm lengths
2 eggs, fried into thin omelettes and finely shredded
3 tablespoons fried crispy shallots **C**
3 red chillies, slit, seeded and shredded as for cucumber
Dash of pepper
1 bundle coriander leaves

170 g (6 oz) streaky pork

310 g (11 oz) small prawns
4 tablespoons lard or oil
1 tablespoon pounded garlic

METHOD

1. Boil the streaky pork in 455 ml (16 fl oz) water and ¼ teaspoon salt for 20 minutes. Set aside the stock and cut the boiled pork into thin strips.

2. Shell the prawns. Wash and drain shells in colander and pound coarsely, adding 455 ml (16 fl oz) water. Stir and strain liquid into a bowl.

3. Heat lard in wok and fry pounded garlic till light brown. Add and stir-fry **A** for 1 minute.

4. Pour in the prawn liquid and pork stock and bring to the boil. Add prawns and streaky pork. Cook for 1 minute.

5. Add **B** to the boiled mixture. Stir-fry for 2–3 minutes over high heat to cook the noodles.

6. Dish on to a large plate and garnish with **C**. Serve hot.

TEOCHEW KWAY TEOW
(FLAT RICE NOODLES IN SOUP)

INGREDIENTS

Seasoning: (A)
½ teaspoon sugar, ¼ teaspoon salt, 1 teaspoon light soya sauce

3.4 litres (6 pints) water
1½ tablespoons salt
2 teaspoons msg **B**
1 tablespoon peppercorns
605 g (21 oz) pork bones

Cooked prawns
Cooked fish balls
4 fish cakes, fried and sliced thinly *garnishing*
4 tablespoons *tung chye*
Chinese celery
Spring onions

605 g (21 oz) medium-sized prawns
40 small fish balls
115 g (4 oz) minced pork, mixed with 4 tablespoons water and ½ teaspoon msg
605 g (21 oz) flat rice noodles
605 g (21 oz) bean sprouts, wash and picked
4 cloves garlic, chopped and fried to a light brown with 8 tablespoons lard or oil
8 fresh red chillies, sliced thinly and mixed with 8 tablespoons fish soya sauce

METHOD

1. Shell prawns leaving the tail unshelled. Slit prawns half-way lengthwise and remove dark veins. Season with **A**.

2. Bring **B** to a fast boil in a saucepan for ½ hour. Remove froth as it floats to the surface. Add another 455 ml (16 fl oz) water and bring it to the boil again over high heat. Remove froth as it rises and continue boiling for 1 hour over moderate heat. Add prawn shells and continue boiling for another hour.

3. Strain stock into a saucepan. Cook prawns. Set aside. Put in fish balls.

4. Scoop out fish balls as they rise.

5. Dish a portion of noodles and bean sprouts (blanched) into a bowl, add soup, garlic oil, top with garnishing and serve with chillies.

Claypot Dishes

Beef Shin With Mixed Vegetables

Braised Beef Brisket

Chicken

Fish Head

Seafood

Tofu and Crab Meat

Tofu with Pork and Prawns

Fish Head in Clay Pot

BEEF SHIN WITH MIXED VEGETABLES

INGREDIENTS

455 g (1 lb) beef shin, sliced thickly
55 g (2 oz) golden needles (kim chiam)
55 g (2 oz) cloud ear fungus (wan yee)
10 slices young ginger
2 cloves garlic, sliced
4 pieces Chinese mushrooms, soaked and sliced thinly
1 carrot, parboiled and flower cut
55 g (2 oz) canned bamboo shoots, flower cut
10 dried red dates, pips removed and soaked
2 soya bean strips (tow kee), cut into small pieces
1 can asparagus tips
55 g (2 oz) spring onion, cut into 4 cm (1½ in) lengths

Seasoning A:
½ teaspoon bicarbonate of soda
2 teaspoons light soya sauce
2 tablespoons oil
1 tablespoon peppercorns

Seasoning B:
(Mix together)
2 teaspoons sugar
½ teaspoon salt
1 teaspoon msg
1 crumbled chicken stock cube
1 teaspoon sesame oil

Thickening:
Mix together 2 tablespoons tapioca flour with 3 tablespoons water

METHOD

1. Stir-fry beef with 2 tablespoons oil over high heat till beef changes colour; add in 455 ml (16 fl oz) boiling water and seasoning **A**. Cook over low heat till beef is tender. Drain beef and keep stock.

2. Cut off hard tips of golden needles and tie each piece into a knot.

3. Soak cloud ear fungus in boiling water for 5 minutes. Rub well in cold water to remove sandy particles and cut off hard tips.

4. Heat an iron wok, add in 3 tablespoons lard or oil to fry the sliced ginger, garlic and mushrooms till lightly browned. Add in the carrots, bamboo shoots, red dates and tow kee. Stir-fry for 1 minute. Add seasoning **B**,

beef stock and bring to the boil.

5. Transfer cooked mixture to a large clay pot, place beef shin and asparagus over and return to heat to cook for 20 minutes over moderate heat. Add spring onions.

6. Add thickening, stir well to thicken and stir in 1 tablespoon lard. Serve hot.

BRAISED BEEF BRISKET

INGREDIENTS

680 g (1½ lb) beef brisket, cut into thick slices

570 ml (20 fl oz) water 2 tablespoons dark soya sauce 2 tablespoons light soya sauce 1 teaspoon msg 1 teaspoon sugar 2 teaspoons vinegar 1 teaspoon pepper	**A** *mixed in a bowl*

2 tablespoons oil

3 cloves garlic, bashed 2 segments star anise 4 shallots, bashed 4 slices ginger 2 thick slices galangal 2 stalks lemon grass, bashed	**B**

455 g (1 lb) lettuce, cut into big pieces

METHOD

1. Marinate beef in **A** for ½ hour.

2. Heat oil in clay pot till very hot. Add **B** and stir-fry for 2 minutes. Add the beef and marinade and bring to the boil over high heat. Boil for 10 minutes. Reduce heat, cover and simmer for 1½–2 hours or till beef is tender. Arrange lettuce on a serving plate and add beef just before serving.

CHICKEN

INGREDIENTS

905 g (2 lb) chicken, cut into 4 pieces

½ teaspoon salt
1 teaspoon sugar | A
½ teaspoon pepper

Oil
2 tablespoons lard

2 cloves garlic, bashed
4 slices ginger | B
4 shallots, bashed

55 g (2 oz) boiled bamboo shoots
55 g (2 oz) sliced carrots
170 g (6 oz) canned button mushrooms | C
6 Chinese mushrooms
225 g (½ lb) long Chinese cabbage

905 ml (1½ pints) water
1 chicken cube
2 tablespoons light soya sauce
1 teaspoon dark soya sauce
½ teaspoon sesame oil | D
1 tablespoon oyster sauce
1 tablespoon A1 sauce
¼ teaspoon pepper
1 teaspoon msg
½ teaspoon sugar

1 level tablespoon corn flour | E
4 tablespoons water

METHOD

1. Season chicken with **A** and set aside for ½ hour.

2. Heat oil in pan to brown chicken on all sides. Remove to a dish.

3. Heat lard in a fairly large clay pot. Brown **B**. Add **C** and stir-fry for 2 minutes over high heat. Pour in **D** and bring to the boil. Put chicken in pot, cover and cook over a high heat for 10 minutes. Reduce heat and simmer for 30 minutes or till chicken is tender. Remove lid. Stir in **E** and serve.

FISH HEAD

INGREDIENTS

1 large threadfin fish head, cut into big pieces
1 tablespoon ginger juice
1 tablespoon light soya sauce
1 soft soya bean cake, cut into pieces
2 tablespoons oil
3 tablespoons lard
4 slices ginger
4 cloves garlic, lightly bashed

55 g (2 oz) boiled bamboo shoots, cut into slices
55 g (2 oz) sliced carrots | A
4 Chinese mushrooms, soaked and cut into pieces
225 g (½ lb) long Chinese cabbage

905 ml (1½ pints) water with 1 chicken cube for stock
½ teaspoon salt
½ teaspoon sugar | B
1 teaspoon msg   *mixed together*
3 teaspoons light soya sauce
1 tablespoon oyster sauce
Dash of pepper

115 g (4 oz) roast pork, cut into small pieces
2 stalks spring onions, cut into short lengths

METHOD

1. Season fish head with ginger juice and light soya sauce and set aside for ½ hour.

2. Fry soya bean cake in a non-stick wok with 2 tablespoons oil till lightly browned. Remove to a plate.

3. Heat 1 tablespoon lard and brown the fish head on all sides. Set aside. Pour in the rest of the lard; brown the ginger and garlic. Add **A**, stir-fry for 2 minutes, add **B** and bring to the boil. Transfer to a clay pot. Add the roast pork, fish head and the fried soya bean cake. Cover and cook over moderate heat for 20 minutes. Add the spring onions and serve hot.

SEAFOOD

INGREDIENTS

Stock:
455 g (1 lb) pork bones or chicken pieces
  1 tablespoon peppercorns
  1 soft soya bean cake, cut into pieces
  2 tablespoons oil
170 g (6 oz) threadfin
170 g (6 oz) medium-sized prawns
  Oil
  1 cup boiling water

½ teaspoon msg
¼ teaspoon salt
1 teaspoon ginger juice **A**
1 tablespoon oil

  2 tablespoons lard
  1 clove garlic, chopped
  4 slices ginger
4–6 Chinese mushrooms, or
    10–12 button mushrooms
 55 g (2 oz) canned bamboo shoots, sliced
225 g (8 oz) pak choy, cut into pieces
 ½ carrot, cut into small pieces

Seasoning:
 1 teaspoon salt
 1 teaspoon msg
½ teaspoon sugar
 1 tablespoon oyster sauce
 1 chicken cube

20 fish balls
  Few slices of canned abalone (optional)
  2 stalks spring onions, cut into short lengths

METHOD

1. Boil pork bones or chicken with 1.7 litres (3 pints) water and 1 tablespoon peppercorns for 2 hours till stock is reduced by one-third.

2. Lightly brown the soya bean cake in a non-stick pan with 2 tablespoons oil. Set aside.

3. Slice the threadfin fairly thickly. Shell prawns leaving tail unshelled. Slit back of prawns and remove dark veins. Wash shells and fry them in a little oil till they turn colour and smell fragrant. Pour in 1 cup boiling water and simmer for ½ hour. Strain and keep stock.

4. Season fish and prawns with **A**.

5. Heat 2 tablespoons lard or oil in a large clay pot. Fry the ginger and garlic till light brown. Fry the mushrooms and the rest of the vegetables for 2 minutes over a high heat. Add the prawn and chicken or pork stock and seasoning; bring it to a fast boil for 5 minutes. Cover and continue boiling for 15 minutes over a moderate heat.

6. When vegetables are tender, add the prawns, soya bean cake, fish and fish balls. Continue to simmer for 5–7 minutes or till prawns and fish are cooked. Add more boiling water to clay pot if stock evaporates too much. Lastly add abalone. Garnish with short lengths of spring onions before serving.

TOFU AND CRAB MEAT

INGREDIENTS

115 g (4 oz) crab meat from 1.2 kg (42 oz) crabs
  1 chicken breast, minced finely
  1 teaspoon light soya sauce
115 ml (4 fl oz) water

225 g (½ lb) chicken and 1 chicken
  cube for stock
  1 tablespoon peppercorns   **A**
½ teaspoon salt
  1 teaspoon msg

  1 soft soya bean cake

Seasoning:
1 teaspoon salt, 1 teaspoon msg, dash of pepper,
2 tablespoons light soya sauce

1 small can creamed corn
2 eggs, lightly beaten

Thickening:
1½ tablespoons corn flour
 55 ml (2 fl oz) water

  2 tablespoons finely cut spring onions
  1 tablespoon lard (optional)

METHOD

1. Steam crabs whole, for 20 minutes. Remove and immerse in cold water. Drain. Remove meat and keep in refrigerator.

2. Combine minced chicken with 1 teaspoon light soya sauce and 115 ml water. Set aside.

3. Boil **A** in a clay pot over moderately high heat for ½ hour. Reduce heat and simmer for 1½ hours. Strain.

4. Chop soya bean cake into very fine pieces. Set aside.

5. Return stock to clay pot, add seasoning and bring it to the boil. Mix ½ cup stock with the minced chicken and add together with soya bean cake. Stir and bring to the boil. Add the corn, crab meat and beaten egg. Stir in the thickening. Add the tablespoon of lard and sprinkle spring onions.

TOFU WITH PORK AND PRAWNS

INGREDIENTS

  1 soft soya bean cake, 10 cm × 10 cm × 3 cm
    (4 in × 4 in × 1¼ in), cut into small squares
  Oil
15 medium-sized prawns
  2 tablespoons oil or lard
  2 cloves garlic, bashed
  3 shallots, bashed
  3 slices ginger

  55 g (2 oz) boiled bamboo shoots, sliced
    into thin pieces
15 button mushrooms   **A**
  4 dried mushrooms, soaked and
    quartered
1 or 2 fresh cuttlefish, cleaned and sliced

285 g (10 oz) *peck chye*, white longish type
55–85 g (2–3 oz) roast pork

710 ml (25 fl oz) boiling water
  1 chicken cube
  2 teaspoons light soya sauce   **B**
  1 teaspoon oyster sauce
  1 teaspoon msg
½ teaspoon sesame oil

  1 teaspoon tapioca flour
  3 tablespoons water

  2 stalks spring onions cut into 3.5 cm lengths

METHOD

1. Soak soya bean cake in salted water for 10 minutes and drain. Heat an iron wok, add ½ cup oil and fry soya bean cake. Remove and set aside.

2. Remove shells from prawns. Heat clay pot and put in 2 tablespoons oil to fry the garlic, shallots and ginger till lightly browned. Add **A**, stir-fry over high heat for a minute, add the *peck chye* and roast pork and stir-fry for another minute.

3. Add **B**, bring to the boil and boil over moderately high heat for 5 minutes.

4. Add soya bean cake and prawns to cook for a while. Add thickening, and lastly the spring onions. Serve hot.

Soups

Bak Kut Teh
Chicken and Corn
Chicken Macaroni
Hot and Sour
Shark's Fin Soup
Sop Kambing
Soto Ayam
Thom Yam Soup

Thom Yam Soup

BAK KUT TEH
(SPICY SPARERIB CONSOMME)

INGREDIENTS

625 g (1 lb 6 oz) pork sparerib, cut into small pieces

½ teaspoon pepper | **A**
½ teaspoon salt

3 tablespoons lard
1 tablespoon sugar

2 cloves garlic, bashed
1 teaspoon preserved brown soya beans, | **B**
   pounded

2 segments star anise
2.5 cm (1 in) piece cinnamon bark
1 teaspoon peppercorns
1 teaspoon salt | **C**
1 teaspoon msg
1 teaspoon dark soya sauce
1.4 litres (3 pints) boiling water

1 tablespoon crispy shallots*
  Crispy Chinese crullers, sliced

METHOD

1. Marinate sparerib in **A** for ½ hour.

2. Heat pan till very hot. Add 2 tablespoons lard and fry sparerib till well-browned. Remove to a dish.

3. In a clean pan, heat 1 tablespoon lard and caramelize the sugar till light brown. Add **B**. Stir-fry for ½ minute, then add the fried sparerib and **C**.

4. Let the consomme boil rapidly for 10 minutes, reduce the heat and let simmer for a further 1½–1¾ hours or till the meat is tender. Remove excess oil from the surface before serving.

5. Serve hot with cruller slices.

*See "Helpful Hints".

CHICKEN AND CORN

INGREDIENTS

1.2 kg (2½ lb) chicken

1.4 litres (3 pints) water
1 teaspoon salt | **A**
1 teaspoon peppercorns

2 eggs, beaten with 2 tablespoons water
½ teaspoon salt
1 teaspoon msg | **B**
1 teaspoon light soya sauce

1 big can of creamed corn

4 tablespoons cornflour
1 tablespoon plain flour | **C**
115 ml (4 fl oz) water

METHOD

1. Cut the chicken into large pieces.

2. Mince the chicken breast and mix with 4 tablespoons water. Set aside.

3. Boil **A** in a saucepan. Add the cut chicken pieces, and let soup simmer for 1½ hours. Boil until three-quarters of the soup is left. Strain into another saucepan.

4. Add 225 ml (8 fl oz) soup to the minced chicken. Mix well.

5. Bring the rest of the soup to the boil rapidly. Add **B**, stirring slowly till the egg mixture floats to the top. Add the corn and the minced chicken and bring to the boil. Reduce heat, blend **C** in a bowl and stir it in gradually.

6. Remove from the heat and serve in large bowl.

CHICKEN MACARONI

INGREDIENTS

1 teaspoon salt
1.2 kg (2½ lb) chicken, whole

3.7 litres (8 pints) water
1 tablespoon peppercorns
2 teaspoons salt   **A**
2 teaspoons msg
1 teaspoon sugar

2 tablespoons light soya sauce
1 teaspoon msg   **B**
½ teaspoon sesame oil

225 g (8 oz) macaroni, boiled and drained

4 tablespoons crispy shallots*
1 bunch coriander leaves   **C**
1 cup croutons
Dash of pepper

METHOD

1. Rub 1 teaspoon salt over chicken. Marinate for ½ hour.

2. Boil **A**.

3. Put in the chicken and bring to rapid boil for 5 minutes. Cover the saucepan and let simmer for 40 minutes.

4. Remove and immerse chicken in cold water for 10 minutes. Debone the chicken and return the bones to the soup. Let soup simmer for 2 hours till it is reduced by one-third. Strain into another saucepan.

5. Shred or dice the chicken.

6. Mix **B** in a bowl. Add 4 tablespoons soup. Add the chicken and mix well.

To serve:
Place the macaroni in a large bowl and arrange the chicken on top. Add boiling soup and garnish with **C**.

*See "Helpful Hints".

HOT AND SOUR

INGREDIENTS

115 g (4 oz) pork fillet, shredded
1 tablespoon tapioca flour
905 g (2 lbs) chicken, quartered
1 teaspoon peppercorns

4 dried Chinese mushrooms, soaked,
  shredded
1 small carrot, parboiled, shredded thinly   **A**
115 g (4 oz) bamboo shoots, shredded thinly
55 g (2 oz) ham, shredded thinly

Seasoning:
1 teaspoon salt
1 teaspoon msg
1 tablespoon light soya sauce
2 tablespoons Thai fish sauce
1 teaspoon sugar
2 tablespoons vinegar
2 tablespoons tapioca flour in 1 cup water

55 g (2 oz) cooked crab meat
2 eggs beaten with 2 tablespoons water
1 tablespoon lard
½ teaspoon sesame oil
2 tablespoons spring onions, chopped coarsely

METHOD

1. Marinate shredded pork with a pinch each of salt, msg, sugar and 1 tablespoon tapioca flour with 1 tablespoon water. Set aside.

2. To make stock, boil chicken in 1.5 litres (3 pints) water with 1 teaspoon peppercorns and ½ teaspoon salt. Boil rapidly for 10 minutes, removing froth as it rises. Add 1 cup cold water and continue boiling over moderate heat, uncovered, till stock is reduced by half. Strain stock. Take chicken drumsticks only and shred into thick pieces. Set aside.

3. Bring chicken stock in a saucepan to a boil. Add **A** and pork and boil for 3 minutes. Pour in seasoning gradually and stir till stock reboils. Add crab meat. Pour in slowly the beaten eggs, lard and sesame oil and stir gently. Add chicken meat and remove from heat as soon as it comes to a boil. Pour into a large soup bowl, sprinkle with spring onions and dust with pepper. Serve hot.

SHARK'S FIN SOUP

INGREDIENTS

905 g (2 lb) small chicken, cut into
    four pieces
1.4 litres (2½ pints) water   **A**
1 teaspoon peppercorns

1 tablespoon oyster sauce
1 tablespoon light soya sauce
1 teaspoon msg   **B**
1 teaspoon sherry or wine
Dash of pepper

225 g (½ lb) steamed crab meat
115 g (¼ lb) prepared softened shark's fins   **C**
    (already soaked in alkaline water)

2 eggs, beaten with 2 tablespoons water

5 tablespoons cornflour
55 ml (2 fl oz) water   **D**

2 tablespoons lard

METHOD

1. Boil **A**. Simmer till stock is reduced by
   one-third (1–1½ hours). Strain into another
   saucepan. Return chicken stock to the boil.

2. Mix **B** in a bowl. Add to the stock with **C**.
   Bring to the boil. Add beaten eggs, stirring
   gently till they rise to the surface.

3. Blend **D** and pour gradually into the soup,
   stirring all the time to prevent curdling.
   Lastly, stir in the lard. Serve hot.

Note:
You can buy softened shark's fins at certain supermarkets.

SOP KAMBING
(MUTTON SOUP)

INGREDIENTS

285 g (10 oz) shallots
55 g (2 oz) garlic
115 g (4 oz) ginger   **A**
½ piece nutmeg

2 teaspoons pepper
1 teaspoon turmeric powder
1 teaspoon cumin powder   **B**
2 tablespoons coriander powder

2 pairs sheep's trotters, cut into short lengths
1.8 kg (4 lb) mutton ribs, cut into pieces

3.6 litres (7 pints) water
10 cm (4 in) piece cinnamon bark
20 cardamom seeds, bashed   **C**
1 cluster star anise

2 tablespoons salt
1–2 teaspoons msg
½ teaspoon bicarbonate of soda

6 tablespoons plain flour
2 tablespoons quick cooking oats,
    pounded finely   **D**
225 ml (8 fl oz) water

½ cup crispy shallots
15 sprigs Chinese celery, cut into pieces   **E**

METHOD

1. Pound **A** to a fine paste. Add **B** and mix
   thoroughly in a large bowl. Marinate ribs in
   mixture for ½ hour.

2. Boil **C**. Add the marinated ribs and season
   with salt and msg. Boil rapidly for
   20 minutes. Reduce the heat and let simmer
   for 1½–2 hours or till the meat is tender.

3. Boil the trotters in a small saucepan with
   455 ml (16 fl oz) soup and the bicarbonate
   of soda. Let simmer till trotters are tender.

4. Pour the soup and trotters back into the
   saucepan of ribs. Mix and bring to the boil.

5. Blend **D** in a bowl and pour gradually into
   the soup. Stir till well-blended.

6. Let simmer until ready to serve. Serve hot.

7. Serve in individual soup bowls and garnish
   with **E**.

SOTO AYAM
(INDONESIAN CHICKEN SOUP)

INGREDIENTS

1.2 kg (2½ lb) chicken, whole, including liver and
    gizzard
1 teaspoon salt
1 tablespoon oil

8 shallots, chopped coarsely 2 cloves garlic, bashed 1 teaspoon peppercorns ½ thumb-sized piece fresh turmeric 4 candlenuts, lightly bashed 1 thumb-sized piece ginger, lightly bashed 3 stalks lemon grass, bruised	**A**
2–3 teaspoons salt 2 teaspoons msg 3.5 litres (7 pints) water	**B**
1–2 tablespoons chilli padi, pounded finely 4 tablespoons dark soya sauce 1 teaspoon sugar	**C**

4 hard-boiled eggs, shelled and diced
225 g (8 oz) boiled potatoes, diced
30 g (1 oz) bean vermicelli, soaked in hot water

4 sprigs Chinese celery, cut into pieces 2 stalks spring onions, cut into pieces ½ cup crispy shallots 8 local lemons, cut into wedges	**D**

METHOD

1. Wash the chicken and rub in 1 teaspoon salt. Set aside.

2. Heat oil in a pan and fry **A** over a high heat for ½ minute. Set aside.

3. Boil **B** in a saucepan. Put in **A**, the chicken, liver and gizzard.

4. Cover the pan and let simmer for ¾ hour. Remove the chicken, liver and gizzard to a basin of cold water for 10 minutes to cool.

5. Debone chicken. Dice and put the meat aside. Return bones to the stock. Boil gently for 1½ hours. Strain stock and leave to simmer till ready to serve.

6. Mix **C** together in a bowl.

To serve:
Place a little of the diced ingredients and the bean vermicelli in individual soup bowls. Add boiling soup and garnish with **D**. Add **C** sauce with a squeeze of local lemon to taste. Serve hot.

THOM YAM SOUP
(HOT SOUP, THAI-STYLE)

INGREDIENTS

500 g (17 oz) medium-sized prawns
400 g (14 oz) fish meat, cut into cubes
200 g (7 oz) cuttlefish, cleaned and cut into small
    pieces
2 blue-flower crabs, cleaned and cut into small
    pieces
1 small can sliced button mushrooms

Ingredients for Stock:
3 stalks lemon grass, cut into thick slices,
    slantwise
3 green chillies, each cut into two
10 green chilli padi, bashed lightly
10 red chilli padi, bashed lightly
2 stalks coriander, washed and left whole
1 onion or 6 shallots, sliced thinly
6–8 tablespoons green lime juice (from limau nipis)
8 daun limau purot

Seasoning:
2–3 tablespoons Thai soya sauce
1 tablespoon sugar
1 tablespoon msg

METHOD

1. Cut whiskers from prawns and soak in 2 tablespoons sugar, rinse before cooking.

2. Marinate fish meat in 1 tablespoon Thai soya sauce.

3. Marinate cuttlefish with 1 tablespoon sugar.

4. Combine ingredients for stock in an enamel saucepan with 855 ml (2 pints) water and bring to the boil. Boil gently for 10 minutes. Put in the crabs, prawns, fish and cook till stock boils. Boil for 2–3 minutes, lastly add in the seasoning, sliced mushrooms and the cuttlefish, boil for ½ a minute and remove from heat. Serve immediately.

Pork and Mutton

Barbecued Spareribs

Braised Pork with Crunchy Black Fungus

Braised Pork in Soya Sauce, Buns for Braised Pork

Roast Pork Strips (Char Siew)

Sweet and Sour Pork Ribs

Braised Mutton Ribs

Mutton in Tomato Curry

Braised Pork with Crunchy Black Fungus

BARBECUED SPARERIBS

INGREDIENTS

2 tablespoons tomato sauce
2 tablespoons sugar
1 tablespoon sweet chilli sauce
1 tablespoon sherry or brandy
2 tablespoons light soya sauce   **A**
½ tablespoon lime juice
1 tablespoon msg
1 teaspoon pepper

905 g (2 lb) pork spareribs, cut into pieces
4 tablespoons lard
4 cucumbers, sliced

METHOD

1. Mix **A** in a bowl.

2. Wash sparerib pieces. Drain and dry with a tea towel.

3. Marinate spareribs in **A** (Method 1) for 4 hours. Thread the pieces on to skewers. (Set aside marinade in a bowl for basting.)

4. Line baking tray or grill pan with foil to collect the juices and dripping for basting.

5. Heat grill or oven, 230°C (450°F) or Regulo 9–10. When very hot, brush sparerib pieces with lard. Grill or bake for 10 minutes. Turn over once to brown the other side. Reduce the heat to 150°C (300°F) or Regulo 4 and cook for another 15–20 minutes. Mix the dripping with the marinade. Baste and grill till well done. Serve hot or cold with cucumber slices.

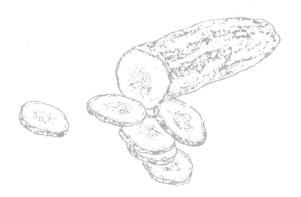

BRAISED PORK WITH CRUNCHY BLACK FUNGUS

INGREDIENTS

1.6 kg (3½ lb) pork belly
30 g (1 oz) black fungus (mok yee)
2 eggs lightly beaten
5 tablespoons plain flour
6 cloves garlic, cut into 2–3 pieces
3 pieces salted preserved bean curds (mashed)

Seasoning:
2 tablespoons light soya sauce
2 tablespoons dark soya sauce
2 tablespoons sugar
½ teaspoon pepper
2 level teaspoons five-spice powder

METHOD

1. Wash and cut pork into 4 cm (1½ in) squares; drain.

2. Soak black fungus in boiling water for 20 minutes. Remove the gritty hard bits.

3. Place pork pieces in a large mixing bowl, add in beaten eggs, seasoning mixture and rub into the pork. Add in the flour and mix well. Leave to marinate for half an hour.

4. Heat oil for deep frying. Put in one-quarter of the pork pieces to fry till pork turns golden brown. Scoop pork to a heavy bottom saucepan. Leave oil in pan to be really heated before frying each batch of the seasoned pork.

5. In a clean wok, heat 3 tablespoons oil. Fry garlic, add mashed bean curd, stir for a moment then put in 4 tablespoons water to cook for 1 minute. Add in 24 fl oz water and allow to boil.

6. Pour the gravy sauce over the pork in saucepan. Sprinkle 2 teaspoons sugar and 2 teaspoons dark soy sauce, add the black fungus and cook over moderately high heat for 10 minutes. Reduce heat, and simmer for ¾–1 hour or till pork is tender. Add hot water if gravy evaporates before pork becomes tender. Serve hot.

BRAISED PORK IN SOYA SAUCE

INGREDIENTS

1 tablespoon dark soya sauce
1 teaspoon honey
½ teaspoon five-spice powder | **A**

2 tablespoons lard

2 cloves garlic, pounded finely
4 shallots, pounded finely
3 segments star anise
1 tablespoon sugar | **B**

2 tablespoons dark soya sauce
1 teaspoon msg
1 teaspoon salt | **C**

905 g (2 lb) pork, with skin and some fat
225 ml (8 fl oz) water

METHOD

1. Marinate the whole piece of pork in **A** for ½ hour.
2. Heat lard in an aluminium wok, then fry **B** till light brown.
3. Reduce heat to moderate. Add the marinated pork and cook till brown on all sides. Add **C** and half of the water. Cover and cook for 10 minutes.
4. Remove lid, turn pork over and continue boiling gently till sauce is thick and oily.
5. Add rest of the water and bring to the boil, stirring constantly to prevent the sauce from sticking to bottom of wok.
6. Remove meat and sauce to a heavy-bottomed saucepan. Cover and let simmer till meat is tender (1–1¼ hours). Add a little water if sauce thickens before meat is tender. Leave to cool. Slice pork and add hot sauce. Serve hot with buns.

BUNS FOR BRAISED PORK

INGREDIENTS

1½ tablespoons fresh yeast
1 teaspoon sugar
2 tablespoons lukewarm water
½ tablespoon salt
3 tablespoons lard or oil | **A**

8 tablespoons castor sugar
225 ml (8 fl oz) lukewarm water | **B**

565 g (20 oz) flour, slightly warmed under a low grill
Small pieces of greaseproof paper
Flour for dusting

METHOD

1. Dissolve **A** in a bowl and let stand for 5 minutes.
2. Place flour in a mixing bowl. Pour yeast mixture **A** in centre. Add **B** (dissolved in a bowl).
3. Stir flour gradually to form a smooth dough.
4. Knead dough on a floured board (or use an electric dough hook) till smooth and glossy. Dough should not stick to hands or bowl. Place dough in a greased bowl. Cover with a damp cloth and leave dough to rise in a warm place till double its bulk.
5. Turn dough on to a floured board. Divide it into four portions. Roll each portion and cut it into equal pieces (each the size of a hen's egg).
6. Flatten each piece with a rolling pin and shape into a flat ball, 0.5 cm thick × 7 cm diameter. Brush half of each lightly with oil. Fold into two and place on a piece of greaseproof paper.
7. Space buns apart on trays. Cover with a dry cloth and leave to rise in a warm place for 15–20 minutes.
8. Steam buns over rapidly boiling water for 7–10 minutes.

ROAST PORK STRIPS
(CHAR SIEW)

INGREDIENTS

1 tablespoon salt
7 tablespoons sugar
1 tablespoon light soya sauce
1 tablespoon sherry or wine
2 tablespoons msg
Orange food colouring
4 tablespoons water
} **A**

905 g (2 lb) pork, cut into thick strips
3 tablespoons lard

METHOD

1. Mix **A** in a bowl to marinate pork for 6–8 hours.

2. Thread pork on to skewers. Brush lard over pork.

3 Pre-heat grill till very hot. Grease rack with lard. Grill pork on both sides till brown. Reduce heat and cook the pork till well done. Baste pork from time to time while grilling.

Note:
Line grill pan with foil to collect the dripping for basting. Serve with sliced cucumber.

SWEET AND SOUR PORK RIBS

Marinade:
¼ teaspoon salt
¼ teaspoon sugar
1 teaspoon msg
1 teaspoon ginger juice
2 teaspoons light soya sauce
1 small egg, beaten with 1 tablespoon cornflour
} **A**

455 g (1 lb) tender pork ribs, cut into 3 cm (1 in) pieces
Salt water
115 g (4 oz) cornflour
Oil for deep-frying

METHOD

1. Wash pork ribs in salt water and drain.

2. Mix **A** in a bowl. Marinate ribs for ½ hour.

3. Roll the marinated ribs in cornflour. Leave to stand for 10 minutes.

4. Deep-fry ribs and drain.

5. Arrange on a serving dish to serve with sweet and sour sauce.

Sauce:
170 ml (6 fl oz) water
1 tablespoon cornflour
} **A**

¼ teaspoon salt
¼ teaspoon msg
3 tablespoons sugar
5 tablespoons tomato ketchup
1 teaspoon sesame oil
1 teaspoon soya sauce
3 tablespoons vinegar
} **B**

2 Chinese mushrooms, soaked and shredded
1 onion, quartered
2 small tomatoes, quartered
2 red chillies, seeded and sliced thickly
} **C**

1 cucumber
2 tablespoons lard
2 stalks spring onions, cut into 5 cm (2 in) lengths

METHOD

1. Skin the cucumber and cut it lengthwise into quarters. Remove the soft centre and cut into fairly thick pieces, slantwise.

2. Blend **A** and **B** in separate bowls.

3. Pour lard in a hot pan and stir-fry **C** for a minute over a high heat. Lower the heat. Add **A** and **B** (Method 2) and stir mixture till it boils.

4. Add the cucumber and spring onions. Remove from heat.

5. Pour sauce over the fried ribs just before serving. Serve hot.

Note:
Green peppers and pineapple can also be added to this dish. Put them in to cook with the other vegetables.

BRAISED MUTTON RIBS

INGREDIENTS

1 tablespoon wine or sherry
1 tablespoon light soya sauce
2 teaspoons dark soya sauce
2 teaspoons sugar } **A**

1 tablespoon oyster sauce
1 teaspoon sugar
2 teaspoons msg
1 tablespoon dark soya sauce
1 tablespoon light soya sauce } **B**

1 tablespoon cornflour
4 tablespoons water
1 teaspoon lard } **C**

565 g (1¼ lb) mutton ribs, cut into pieces
Oil
2 tablespoons lard

170 g (6 oz) boiled tender bamboo shoots, cut into wedges
170 g (6 oz) young tender ginger, cut into wedges
10 Chinese mushrooms, with stems removed, soaked in hot water and drained before use } **D**

1 tablespoon wine or sherry

METHOD

1. Marinate ribs for ½ hour in **A**.

2. Mix **B** and **C** in separate bowls.

3. Deep-fry ribs in hot smoking oil for 3 minutes. Remove and immerse fried ribs in a basin of ice-cold water. Discard the flakes of floating fat and place ribs in a dish.

4. Heat wok (kuali). When very hot, add the lard and stir-fry **D** for 1 minute. Add the ribs. Sprinkle the wine and stir-fry for another minute.

5. Pour in **B** (Method 2) and 225 ml (8 fl oz) water. Cook over a low heat till ribs are tender and gravy is thick and almost dry. Remove ribs to a dish.

6. Add **C** (Method 2), stir-fry and return ribs to cook for ½ minute. Place on a plate and serve immediately.

MUTTON IN TOMATO CURRY

INGREDIENTS

2 tablespoons ginger juice
1 teaspoon salt
1 teaspoon msg
2 tablespoons curry powder
4 tablespoons water
1 tablespoon oil } **A**

2 cloves garlic, thinly sliced
10 cardamoms, bashed
8 cloves
1 thumb-sized piece cinnamon bark } **B**

1 teaspoon salt
1 teaspoon msg
2 teaspoons sugar } **C**

905 g (2 lb) mutton chops, cut into pieces
4 tablespoons ghee or 2 tablespoons butter and 2 tablespoons oil
2 onions, thinly sliced
2 tablespoons tomato ketchup
2 tablespoons tomato purée
6 tablespoons curry powder, mixed to a paste with 8 tablespoons water
2 teaspoons lime juice
1 small can evaporated milk

METHOD

1. Marinate chops in **A** for ½ hour.

2. Heat wok. Add ghee to brown **B**. Add sliced onions and fry till fragrant (5 minutes). Stir in the tomato ketchup and purée.

3. Add curry paste and fry over a moderate heat till oil seeps through. Add 225 ml (8 fl oz) water and **C** and stir-fry for 5 minutes. Add the lime juice.

4. Add marinated chops, half of the evaporated milk, and another 225 ml water. Cook over a high heat for 15 minutes, stirring occasionally. Let meat simmer till tender (about ¾ hour).

5. Add the remaining evaporated milk, stir and continue simmering for another 10 minutes. Serve hot.

Beef

Beef Curry

Dry Beef Curry

Beef Brisket

Beef Braised in Dark Soya Sauce

Beef with Celery

Chinese Beef Steak

Fillet Steak

Ox Tail Stew

Dry Beef Curry

BEEF CURRY

INGREDIENTS

1 thumb-sized piece ginger 2 green chillies 4 cloves garlic	A
8 tablespoons curry powder 225 ml (8 fl oz) water 2 onions, thinly sliced	B
20 shallots, thinly sliced 5 cloves 6 cardamoms, bashed 1 thumb-sized piece cinnamon bark	C

1 teaspoon salt
1 teaspoon msg
905 g (2 lb) beef (rump steak), cut into pieces
4 tablespoons ghee or oil
115 g (4 oz) grated coconut with 455 ml (16 fl oz) water, squeezed and strained

1 teaspoon salt 1 teaspoon msg 4 sprigs mint leaves, picked 2 sprigs Chinese parsley, cut finely 4 tomatoes, quartered	D

METHOD

1. Pound **A** finely. Add salt and msg and marinate beef for ½ hour.

2. Mix **B** in a bowl.

3. Heat ghee in wok and fry **C** till light brown. Add the marinated beef, stir-fry for 5 minutes, then add 285 ml (10 fl oz) water. Boil gently till meat is tender, adding more water if necessary. Cook till almost dry.

4. Add **B** (Method 2), stir-fry over a low heat for 5 minutes with one-third of the coconut milk. Add **D** and the rest of the coconut milk. Let curry simmer for 15 minutes, stirring occasionally.

5. Remove from heat. Serve hot or cold.

Note:
New potatoes can be added to the curry. Add them to cook with the mint, Chinese parsley and tomatoes.

DRY BEEF CURRY

INGREDIENTS

285 g (10 oz) grated coconut
455 g (1 lb) beef (rump steak) cut into thick slices

1 clove garlic, pounded finely 4 slices ginger, pounded finely ½ teaspoon salt 1 teaspoon msg 1 teaspoon sugar 1 tablespoon curry powder	A

55 ml (2 fl oz) oil
55 g (2 oz) shallots or onions, thinly sliced
2 tablespoons tomato sauce
3 tablespoons curry powder mixed to a paste with a little water

Seasoning:
¾–1 teaspoon salt
1 teaspoon sugar
1 teaspoon msg

METHOD

1. Squeeze grated coconut for No. 1 milk. Set aside. Add 455 ml (16 fl oz) water to the grated coconut and squeeze for No. 2 milk. Set aside.

2. Season beef with **A** and leave for ½ hour.

3. Heat oil in non-stick saucepan or heavy-bottomed aluminium saucepan. When hot, fry the sliced shallots till lightly browned. Add the seasoned beef and fry till beef changes colour. Add tomato sauce and stir for a short while. Add ½ of the No. 2 milk, cover pan and cook over moderate heat for ¾ hour, stirring occasionally.

4. Mix the curry powder paste with the No. 1 milk and the rest of the No. 2 milk. Pour into saucepan, add seasoning and simmer till meat becomes tender and gravy starts to thicken (about ½–¾ hour). Add a few spoonfuls of water if mixture becomes dry before meat is tender.

BEEF BRISKET

INGREDIENTS

1 tablespoon ginger juice
2 tablespoons light soya sauce
3 tablespoons dark soya sauce **A**
1 teaspoon pepper
1 teaspoon msg

1 tablespoon sugar
½ teaspoon msg
¼ teaspoon salt **B**
1½–2 tablespoons vinegar

1 tablespoon cornflour
3 tablespoons water **C**

1 tablespoon sugar
6 slices ginger **D**

8 cloves garlic, lightly bashed
10 shallots, cut into halves **E**

2 segments star anise
1 stalk lemon grass, bruised **F**
2.5 cm (1 in) piece cinnamon bark

905 g (2 lb) beef brisket, cut into pieces
2 tablespoons lard or oil

METHOD

1. Marinate beef in **A** for 1 hour.

2. Mix **B** and **C** in separate bowls.

3. Heat lard in a hot saucepan to brown **D**. Add **E** and fry for 1 minute. Add **F**, marinated beef and **B** (Method 2). Stir-fry and cook over a high heat for 10 minutes. Add 285 ml (10 fl oz) water, and let it boil for 10 minutes.

4. Transfer dish to an earthen clay pot. Bring back to heat and simmer till meat is tender, (about 1½–2 hours).

5. Thicken gravy with **C** (Method 2) and stir well.

To serve:
Place whole pieces of lettuce on a large serving plate. Arrange beef on lettuce and serve hot.

BEEF BRAISED IN DARK SOYA SAUCE

INGREDIENTS

1 tablespoon dark soya sauce
1½ tablespoons sugar **A**
1 tablespoon oil

2 tablespoons lard or oil

2 slices ginger
1 clove garlic, sliced thinly
1 onion, sliced thinly
1 tablespoon sugar **B**
5 cm (2 in) piece cinnamon bark
2 segments star anise

½ teaspoon salt
1 tablespoon sugar
1 teaspoon msg
2 tablespoons dark soya sauce **C**
1 teaspoon peppercorns

905 g (2 lb) rump steak

METHOD

1. Marinate beef in **A** for 1 hour.

2. Heat lard in a heavy-bottomed saucepan. Brown **B**. Add the marinated beef. Increase heat; brown beef on all sides to seal in the juices. Add **C** and 115 ml (4 fl oz) water. Cook for 10 minutes. Add another 115 ml water and boil for another 10 minutes.

3. Reduce heat, cover pan and simmer till beef is tender (about 1½–2 hours), turning beef over once in the pan. Add more water if necessary.

Note:
When beef is tender, remove the lid and increase heat to high to thicken the sauce. Cool for a while before slicing the beef. Heat gravy and pour over meat before serving.

BEEF WITH CELERY

INGREDIENTS

Marinade:

1 tablespoon light soya sauce
1 teaspoon dark soya sauce
1 teaspoon msg
1 teaspoon sugar
1 teaspoon vinegar
1 egg white, beaten lightly

A

Gravy:

3 teaspoons tapioca or cornflour
6 tablespoons water
1 tablespoon light soya sauce
1 tablespoon sherry
1 tablespoon oyster sauce

B *mixed in bowl*

455 g (1 lb) fillet or rump steak
6 stalks celery
6 slices ginger
1 tablespoon chopped garlic
2 stalks spring onions, cut into 2½ cm (1 in) lengths

METHOD

1. Slice meat into 2½ cm (1 in) strips. Let beef stand in marinade **A** for 1 hour.

2. Cut celery diagonally and boil rapidly in salted water for ½ minute. Drain and rinse in cold water. Set aside.

3. Heat wok. Add 2 tablespoons oil and when hot, cook the beef in two portions. Remove and set aside.

4. In a clean pan, heat 2 tablespoons of oil till very hot. Fry celery for ½ minute, push to one side of pan and stir-fry ginger and garlic till light golden brown. Bring back celery and fried beef into pan. Stir in gravy **B** and add to meat mixture. Add spring onions and stir till well combined. Serve hot.

CHINESE BEEF STEAK

INGREDIENTS

1 teaspoon light soya sauce
1 teaspoon dark soya sauce
1 teaspoon sherry or brandy
½ teaspoon oyster sauce
1 teaspoon msg
½ teaspoon pepper
¼ teaspoon bicarbonate of soda
½ teaspoon sesame oil
1 teaspoon ginger juice
2 tablespoons oil
1 egg white, beaten

A

½ tablespoon cornflour
1 tablespoon water

B

225 g (8 oz) bean sprouts; picked, washed and drained
½ teaspoon pounded garlic, fried
A pinch of salt
1 teaspoon sugar

C

225 g (8 oz) fillet or Scotch steak, thinly sliced
4 tablespoons lard
2 sprigs spring onions, cut into 5 cm (2 in) lengths

METHOD

1. Mix **A** in a bowl and marinate beef for 1 hour.

2. Mix **B** in a bowl for the thickening.

3. Heat 2 tablespoons lard in heated wok and stir-fry **C** for 15 seconds. Remove to a serving plate.

4. Place the other 2 tablespoons lard in wok. Stir-fry the marinated beef slices over a high heat for 1 minute. Add spring onions, stir-fry and add thickening. Mix well. Add to fried bean sprouts. Serve immediately.

Beef with Celery

FILLET STEAK

INGREDIENTS

1 teaspoon dark soya sauce ½ teaspoon msg ½ teaspoon sugar ½ teaspoon bicarbonate of soda 1 teaspoon light soya sauce 1 teaspoon sherry *or* brandy 1 teaspoon cornflour 2 tablespoons oil	**A**

1 teaspoon light soya sauce 1 teaspoon oyster sauce ½ teaspoon sugar ½ teaspoon msg ¼ teaspoon salt 1 teaspoon sesame oil 1 teaspoon sherry	**B**

2 tablespoons cornflour 3 tablespoons water	**C**

4 slices ginger 1 teaspoon chopped garlic 115 g (4 oz) snow peas or French beans 1 green pepper, cut into small squares	**D**

225 g (½ lb) beef fillet, sliced into bite-sized pieces
225 ml (8 fl oz) oil
3 tablespoons lard
115 g (4 oz) canned button mushrooms, cut into halves
115 g (4 oz) canned straw mushrooms, cut into halves
2 stalks spring onions, cut into 5 cm (2 in) lengths

METHOD

1. Marinate beef in **A** for ½ hour.
2. Mix **B** and **C** in separate bowls.
3. Heat an iron wok till smoking hot. Heat oil for deep-frying. Add the marinated beef, stir-fry for ½ minute and remove to a plate.
4. Heat 2 tablespoons lard in a clean wok and stir-fry **D** over a high heat. Remove to a plate.
5. Add mushrooms and stir-fry for ½ minute. Add fried mixed vegetables, fried beef, spring onions, **B**, and **C**. Stir in the last tablespoon of lard, and mix well. Serve.

OX TAIL STEW

INGREDIENTS

1 teaspoon salt ½ teaspoon sugar 1 teaspoon msg 1 level teaspoon pepper 1 teaspoon dark soya sauce 1 tablespoon plain flour	**A**

340 g (12 oz) cabbage, cut into pieces 1 carrot, cut into wedges 340 g (12 oz) new potatoes, boiled and skinned 7.5 cm (3 in) piece cinnamon bark 340 g (12 oz) onions, small, whole or halved	**B**

¼ nutmeg 4 cloves 1 tablespoon peppercorns	**C** *to put in a muslin bag*

1 teaspoon msg 1 beef cube ½–1 teaspoon salt 1 teaspoon Bisto gravy powder, optional 2 teaspoons light soya sauce 1 teaspoon sugar 1 teaspoon dark soya sauce 1 teaspoon bicarbonate of soda	**D**

1 kg (2.2 lb) ox tail, chopped. Remove all fat.
1 beef cube
2 tablespoons oil
1 tablespoon butter
55 g (2 oz) thinly sliced shallots or onions
225 g (8 oz) French beans, sliced
115 g (4 oz) tomatoes, quartered
1 tablespoon plain flour mixed with 55 ml (2 fl oz) water, for thickening

METHOD

1. Season ox tail with **A** and leave for ½ hour.
2. Bring 1.4 litres (48 fl oz) water and the beef cube to a fast boil in a saucepan. Add **B** and bring to the boil over high heat for about 10 minutes.
3. Heat oil and butter and fry the sliced onions. Add seasoned ox tail and fry. Add stock, **C**, and **D**, bring to the boil and simmer for 2–2½ hours till meat is tender.
4. Bring vegetables to the boil again with French beans and tomatoes and cook for a further 20 minutes.
5. Add thickening. Serve hot.

Ox Tail Stew

Poultry

Abalone Chicken

Braised Ginger Chicken

Chicken Almond Curry

Chicken Coconut Curry

Chicken Bon Bon

Chicken Curry Devil

Chicken fried with Dried Red Chillies

Chicken in the Basket

Lemon Curried Chicken

Paper-Wrapped Chicken

Roast Turkey with Mince Pork and Rice Filling

Salt-Baked Chicken

Seven-Minute Crispy Chicken

Steamed Stuffed Duck

Stew

Turmeric Chicken

Chicken Curry

ABALONE CHICKEN

INGREDIENTS

6 pieces garlic, lightly bashed
4 stalks spring onion, tied into a knot } **A**
55 g (2 oz) ginger, lightly bashed

115 g (4 oz) abalone liquid
¼ teaspoon salt
½ teaspoon msg
½ teaspoon sugar
1 teaspoon sesame oil
1 teaspoon sherry
Chicken stock (from Method 2) } **B** *mixed in a bowl*

Thickening:
1 tablespoon cornflour
2 tablespoons water } **C**

1 chicken, 1.14 kg (2½ lb)
1 teaspoon salt
Green lettuce and tomato for garnishing
1 can abalone, 455 g (16 oz), cut into slices (reserve liquid)
1 tablespoon lard

METHOD

1. Wash chicken well and rub 1 teaspoon salt all over the skin of chicken. Stuff chicken with **A** and leave for ½ hour.

2. Place chicken on an enamel plate. Pour 3 tablespoons boiling water over chicken. Bring a large saucepan of water to a rapid boil. Place a metal steaming rack in saucepan and steam chicken till cooked (30–45 minutes). Cut into pieces when chicken is cool. Reserve stock for gravy.

3. Place lettuce on a large serving plate, arrange the sliced abalone on top and then the chicken.

4. Boil **B** in a saucepan, stir in **C** and allow to boil. Add the lard, stir and pour over chicken and abalone. Garnish with sliced tomato. Serve immediately.

BRAISED GINGER CHICKEN

INGREDIENTS

8 slices ginger
1 tablespoon sugar } **A**

4 tablespoons dark soya sauce
1 tablespoon sugar
½ teaspoon salt
1 teaspoon msg } **B**

455 g (1 lb) chicken wings
6 chicken livers
6 chicken gizzards
6 chicken drumsticks } **C**

2 tablespoons oil
3 tablespoons lard
½ teaspoon sesame oil

METHOD

1. Preheat wok. When very hot, heat the oil to fry **A**. Add 2 tablespoons lard.

2. Pour in **B** together with 115 ml (4 fl oz) water. Add **C**. Stir and cook for 10 minutes, covered. Remove the livers to a dish. Leave the rest to simmer for ½ hour, covered.

3. Remove the chicken wings to a dish. Pour in another 115 ml water and let the chicken drumsticks and gizzards continue to simmer till tender. Add the remaining tablespoonful of lard and sesame oil.

To serve:
Slice the cooked liver and gizzard. Serve hot or cold.

CHICKEN ALMOND CURRY

INGREDIENTS

8 cloves garlic, sliced thinly ¼ thumb-sized piece turmeric or ¾ teaspoon turmeric powder 2 teaspoons salt 1 teaspoon msg	**A**

8 cashew nuts 8 almonds 3 candlenuts 1 heaped tablespoon cumin seeds or cumin powder ½ cup water	**B**	*blended to a fine paste*

285 g (10 oz) grated coconut, white
115 ml (4 fl oz) water
   Oil for deep frying
285 g (10 oz) shallots, sliced thinly
  4 tablespoons ghee or 2 tablespoons each of oil and butter
 10 dried chillies, soaked and blended to a fine paste
  1 sprig curry leaf

1.6 kg (3½ lb) whole chicken, cut into pieces

METHOD

1. Squeeze grated coconut with 115 ml (4 fl oz) water for milk. Set aside.

2. Heat oil for deep frying. When very hot, fry sliced shallots till light golden brown. Remove to absorbent paper to drain. Divide into two equal parts.

3. Combine **A** with half the coconut milk and rub into chicken pieces to marinate for ¾ hour.

4. Heat ghee in wok. Fry the dried chilli paste and curry leaf till oil turns red.

5. Add chicken and one part crispy shallots and cook over moderate heat. Transfer chicken to a heavy-bottomed aluminium saucepan. Cook for 20 minutes.

6. Remove lid, mix **B** with remaining coconut milk and pour in pan. Stir, reduce heat to low and simmer till chicken is tender.

CHICKEN COCONUT CURRY

INGREDIENTS

6 candlenuts 55 g (2 oz) shallots/onions 6 cloves garlic 5 red chillies ½ thumb-sized ginger 30 dried chillies 6 thin slices galangal ½ teaspoon turmeric powder	**A**	*ground finely*

Seasoning:

2 teaspoons sugar 1 teaspoon salt ½ cube chicken stock	**B**

60 g (2 oz) SANTAN instant coconut cream powder*
1.6 kg chicken, cut into pieces
  4 fragrant lime leaves, sliced thinly
  2 tablespoons lime juice**
  3 tablespoons crispy shallots/onions

METHOD

1. Dissolve SANTAN in 455 ml (16 fl oz) water. Strain.

2. Marinate the chicken with 1 level tablespoon salt and 1 teaspoon sugar.

3. Heat 115 ml (4 fl oz) oil in a hot pan. Fry **A** till oil seeps through and smells fragrant. Add 4 spoonfuls of SANTAN milk while frying.

4. Put in chicken pieces, **B**, fragrant lime leaves and half of the SANTAN milk. Stir and cook over moderate heat for 10 minutes.

5. Pour in remaining SANTAN milk, lime juice and allow to simmer for about 15 minutes. Lastly, add in crispy shallots, stir and remove from heat.

Equivalent to 2 lb white grated coconut.
**The lime juice can be replaced with 2 pieces of dried tamarind.*

CHICKEN BON BON
(SHREDDED CHICKEN AND MIXED
VEGETABLE SALAD)

INGREDIENTS

1 chicken breast, steamed
115 g (4 oz) treated jellyfish (available at wet markets)
2 tablespoons sesame seeds, toasted
1 cucumber
1 cup shredded lettuce

Ingredients for Sauce:
¼ teaspoon fine salt
2½ tablespoons fine sugar
1½ teaspoons vinegar
4 tablespoons mustard powder
1 tablespoon chilli sauce
1½ tablespoons Lea and Perrins Sauce
2 teaspoons sesame oil
115 ml (4 fl oz) evaporated milk
115 g (4 oz) roasted ground peanuts or
chunky peanut butter

*well
blended*

METHOD

1. Rub chicken breast with ½ teaspoon each of
   salt and msg for ½ hour. Then steam for
   ½ hour or till chicken is cooked. Leave to
   cool and shred into long pieces. Set aside.

2. Shred the jellyfish thinly and set aside.

3. Skin cucumber, cut into 3 and shred thinly
   leaving out soft centre.

To serve chicken bon bon:
Put shredded lettuce and cucumber on large
serving plate. Place jellyfish over cucumber,
then put the shredded chicken over and sprinkle the sesame seeds. Pour the sauce over just
before serving.

CHICKEN CURRY DEVIL

INGREDIENTS

1 teaspoon salt	
1 teaspoon msg	**A**
1 teaspoon pepper	

115 g (4 oz) shallots or onions	
4 cloves garlic	**B**
55 g (2 oz) ginger, sliced	*ground*
1 stalk lemon grass, sliced	*to a*
10 fresh red chillies	*fine paste*
8 dried chillies, soaked in warm water	

1½ teaspoons powdered mustard or	
1 tablespoon prepared mustard	
1 tablespoon sugar	
1 teaspoon salt	**C**
1 teaspoon msg	
2 tablespoons sugar	
2 tablespoons vinegar	

1.4 kg (3 lb) chicken, cut into pieces
285 g (10 oz) grated coconut
115 ml (4 fl oz) oil

METHOD

1. Season chicken with **A**.

2. Squeeze coconut in small handfuls through a piece of muslin for No. 1 milk, to obtain approximately 140 ml (5 fl oz). Add 225 ml water to the coconut. Squeeze for No. 2 milk and set aside in another bowl.

3. Grind **B** (or use an electric blender) to a fine paste.

4. Heat oil in wok and fry paste over moderate heat till oil bubbles through and paste is fragrant, adding a few tablespoons of No. 2 milk while frying. Add **C** and the rest of the No. 2 milk, stir till gravy starts to boil, add the chicken and cook over moderate heat for 10 minutes.

5. Add No. 1 milk, stir well, reduce heat to low, cover pan and simmer for 15–20 minutes or till chicken is tender.

CHICKEN FRIED WITH DRIED RED CHILLIES

INGREDIENTS

1 tablespoon honey	
2 teaspoons light soya sauce	**A**
1 teaspoon msg	
1 teaspoon pepper	

1 teaspoon sugar	
½ teaspoon msg	
2 teaspoons oyster sauce	
1 teaspoon dark soya sauce	
1 teaspoon light soya sauce	**B**
1 tablespoon vinegar	
1 teaspoon Lea and Perrins sauce	
1 teaspoon rice wine or sherry	

1 tablespoon cornflour	**C** *blended*
6 tablespoons water	

455 g (1 lb) chicken meat, cut into bite-sized pieces
20–30 dried chillies, remove stems
285 ml (10 fl oz) oil
3 cloves garlic
1 teaspoon ginger, chopped
2 teaspoons spicy soya bean paste★ (page 109)

METHOD

1. Marinate chicken in **A** for ½ hour.

2. Cut dried chillies into big pieces, diagonally across, and remove the seeds. Dip the chillies in cold water and drain immediately in a colander. Set aside.

3. Heat oil in iron wok. When hot, fry chillies till dark brown. Scoop out with perforated ladle and drain. In the same pan, heat oil till smoking hot, and fry chicken till it changes colour. Remove and drain.

4. Remove all oil, except 4 tablespoons, from wok. Fry the garlic and ginger till light brown. Add the spicy soya bean paste, stir, and add chillies, **B** and **C**. Stir till mixture comes to the boil. Add the chicken, toss in pan and remove to a serving plate. Serve immediately.

Note:
It is preferable to use broad, thick dried chillies for this recipe.

CHICKEN IN THE BASKET

Yam Baskets (a pair of perforated ladles for making yam baskets is required):

565 g (20 oz) yam
    4 tablespoons cornflour for dusting
    Oil for deep-frying

METHOD

1. Skin the yam. Do not wash the yam or it will become slimy and difficult to handle. Cut yam into thin strips, about 0.5 cm broad and 18 cm (7 in) long.

2. Place yam strips on a tray and dust with cornflour to keep the strips separated.

3. Put a towel in a bowl. Place a perforated ladle on the towel. Level the yam sticks then spread them, level edge upwards, around the sides of the ladle to form a basket.

4. Fill half a medium-sized saucepan with oil and heat till smoking hot.

5. Press the other ladle lightly over the yam basket and gently dip the sandwiched yam basket into the hot oil to fry for two minutes.

6. Reduce the heat a little to fry till the yam is cooked and turns light brown (about 5–6 minutes). Remove the ladles when the yam basket slips out of the lower ladle. Place on absorbent paper.

7. Make as many baskets as possible, until all the yam strips are used up.

8. Strain the oil to fry the chicken.

Filling:

1 teaspoon bicarbonate of soda	
1 teaspoon msg	
1 teaspoon sugar	
½ teaspoon salt	**A**
2 teaspoons light soya sauce	
2 tablespoons cornflour	
3 tablespoons water	
2 tablespoons oil	

3 Chinese mushrooms	
85 g (3 oz) bamboo shoots	**B**
1 large green pepper	
1 large tomato	

1 teaspoon salt	
1 teaspoon msg	
1 teaspoon sugar	
2 teaspoons light soya sauce	
1 teaspoon sesame oil	**C**
1 teaspoon sherry or brandy	
1 tablespoon oyster sauce	
Dash of pepper	

1 tablespoon cornflour	**D**
4 tablespoons water	

340 g (12 oz) chicken shreds
2 tablespoons lard
4 red chillies, seeded and sliced thinly
2 stalks spring onions, cut into 5 cm (2 in) lengths
115 g (4 oz) lettuce, shredded

METHOD

1. Blend **A** in a bowl and marinate the chicken shreds for 1 hour.

2. Heat the strained hot oil in a clean iron wok till smoking hot. Add the seasoned chicken shreds and deep-fry for 1 minute. Use a perforated ladle to lift chicken shreds on to a plate.

3. Slice **B** thinly into strips.

4. Heat the lard in a clean saucepan. Stir-fry the sliced vegetables and red chillies over high heat.

5. Reduce heat and add the fried chicken shreds. Mix **C** in a bowl, add and stir well.

6. Blend **D** in a bowl and add to sauce in pan. Stir well till sauce thickens.

7. Add the spring onions, stir and remove to a dish.

To serve:
Spread shredded lettuce on a large serving plate. Fill baskets with chicken filling and place on top of the lettuce. Serve hot.

Note:
Oil for frying the yam baskets must be sizzling hot. Test it by putting in a strip of yam. If the yam strip sizzles and floats up immediately, the oil is ready for use. Do not wait for the yam to brown in the oil. Fried yam baskets can be stored in an airtight container for 2–3 weeks.

LEMON CURRIED CHICKEN

INGREDIENTS

12 shallots	
6 candlenuts	
4 stalks lemon grass, thinly sliced	**A**
1 teaspoon shrimp paste	

1 tablespoon sugar	
1–1½ teaspoons salt	
1 teaspoon msg	**B**
1 tablespoon curry powder	

4 tablespoons lemon juice	
1 tablespoon tamarind with 115 ml	**C**
(4 fl oz) water, squeezed and strained	

455 g (16 oz) grated coconut
1.8 kg (4 lb) chicken, cut into pieces
4 tablespoons oil
15–20 pounded dried chillies or 4 tablespoons chilli
    paste
1 stalk lemon grass, bashed lightly
2 lime leaves

METHOD

1. Grind **A** to a fine paste.

2. Squeeze grated coconut for No. 1 milk. Add 170 ml (6 fl oz) water to coconut and squeeze again for No. 2 milk.

3. Mix half of the No. 1 milk with **B** and marinate chicken for ½ hour.

4. Heat aluminium wok. When very hot, heat oil and fry chilli paste over low heat till oil bubbles through. Add the rest of the No. 1 milk, stir-fry for 1 minute, then add Paste **A** (Method 1) and lemon grass. Fry till fragrant.

5. Add the marinated chicken and **C**. Lower heat and stir-fry till chicken is cooked. Add No. 2 milk and bring to the boil.

6. Reduce heat to low. Add the lime leaves and simmer in a covered pan till chicken is tender (½–¾ hour). Add more water if necessary.

PAPER-WRAPPED CHICKEN

INGREDIENTS

1 tablespoon cornflour	
2 tablespoons water	**A**

1 teaspoon salt	
1 teaspoon msg	
1 teaspoon sugar	
2 teaspoons sesame oil	
¼ teaspoon pepper	**B**
1 tablespoon light soya sauce	
1 tablespoon ginger juice	
3 tablespoons lard or oil	
1 tablespoon brandy or sherry	

Cellophane or 'glass' paper
1.4 kg (3 lb) chicken, cut into pieces
Oil for deep-frying

METHOD

1. Cut the cellophane or 'glass' paper into 20 cm (8 in) squares.

2. Blend **A** in a bowl. Add **B**, stir well and pour over the chicken. Marinate chicken for 2 hours.

3. Wrap up a few pieces of chicken in each piece of cellophane paper and staple the edges.

4. Heat oil. Fry paper-wrapped chicken till light brown. Lift chicken onto a wire sieve to drain.

5. Serve hot, leaving wrappers on.

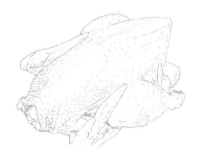

ROAST TURKEY WITH MINCE PORK AND RICE FILLING

INGREDIENTS

1 tablespoon fine salt 1 teaspoon pepper 1 teaspoon honey 1 teaspoon soya sauce	**A**

Filling:
  2 slices bacon, chopped roughly
 55 g (2 oz) butter
 55 g (2 oz) chopped onions
340 g (12 oz) roughly minced pork
  3 cups cooked rice
  1 chicken cube, crushed in 4 tablespoons boiling water

½ cup roughly chopped Chinese parsley ¾ cup sultanas ½ cup blanched almonds, browned and chopped coarsely 120 g (4 oz) spam *or* ham	**B**

  One 3½–4 kg (7½–8½ lb) turkey
  2 tablespoons sherry
  3 tablespoons butter, softened

METHOD

1. Thaw and wash turkey. Pat dry, inside and out, with cloth. Rub inside with 2 tablespoons sherry, 1 teaspoon salt and ½ teaspoon pepper. Brush the turkey with butter and rub all over with **A**. Set aside for ½ hour.

To make filling:
2. Fry bacon in a dry frying pan till oil runs out and bacon turns crisp. Remove to a plate. Heat butter and fry onions in the same pan till onions become soft. Increase heat to high, add minced pork to stir-fry till pork changes colour. Put in rice and stir for a moment. Stir in chicken cube stock. Add **B** and mix till well combined.

To prepare and roast turkey:
3. Fill turkey, but not too tightly as filling will expand on cooking. Secure cavity to prevent filling from spilling. Brush again with butter. Cross end of drumstick and secure with string.

4. Place turkey on a rack over a baking tray lined with foil to catch drippings. Bake in a preheated oven (220°C or 425°F) for about 2½–3 hours. Reduce heat after turkey turns light brown and continue baking till golden brown.

5. Baste turkey with drippings regularly. Use foil to cover parts that brown too quickly before turkey is cooked.

6. Allow turkey to cool for 15–20 minutes before carving.

SALT-BAKED CHICKEN

INGREDIENTS

½ teaspoon fine salt 1 teaspoon msg ¼ teaspoon five-spice powder	**A**

1 teaspoon salt 1 teaspoon sherry 1 teaspoon oil	**B**

  1 young tender chicken (905 g or 2 lb)
3.6 kg (8 lb) coarse salt

METHOD

1. Clean and wash chicken, both outside and inside. Cut off the neck and legs. Wipe dry.

2. Rub **A** on the inside of chicken. Rub **B** all over surface of chicken and set aside for 1 hour.

To cook chicken:
1. Wrap up chicken with 2 large white paper napkins.

2. Line a shallow baking tin with tin foil. Fill with salt and heat in oven till salt becomes very hot. Alternatively, fry salt in an old wok till very hot and immediately pour half into large Chinese clay pot. Put the chicken in the middle of the pot and pour in the rest of the salt over the chicken.

3. Place clay pot over low heat on stove and cook for 1 hour or till chicken is well done. Serve hot.

Roast Turkey

SEVEN-MINUTE CRISPY CHICKEN

INGREDIENTS

2 tablespoons light soya sauce
4 tablespoons water
1 tablespoon sugar
1 tablespoon ginger juice   **A**
1 teaspoon sherry
1 teaspoon msg
¾ teaspoon salt
½ teaspoon cinnamon powder

115 g (4 oz) self-raising flour
¼ teaspoon salt   **B**
¼ teaspoon msg
¼ teaspoon pepper

0.8 kg (1½–1¾ lb) spring chicken, whole
   Oil for deep-frying
1 cucumber, sliced

METHOD

1. Cut chicken open from the breast downwards.
2. Turn over and crack backbone and thigh bones with blunt edge of a chopper.
3. Mix **A** in a bowl and marinate the chicken for 1 hour.
4. Sift **B** together to coat the chicken.
5. Heat oil in wok and deep-fry chicken for 1 minute on each side over high heat. Lower the heat. Fry for another 5 minutes. Turn chicken over once to brown. Lift chicken to drain.
6. Cool for a while before cutting it into pieces. Arrange on a serving dish and garnish with cucumber slices. Serve hot.

STEAMED STUFFED DUCK

INGREDIENTS

2 slices ginger   **A**
2 cloves garlic, bashed

½ teaspoon salt
1 teaspoon msg
2 teaspoons light soya sauce
1 teaspoon brandy   **B**
4 tablespoons pearl barley, soaked in water
   and drained
55 g (2 oz) lotus seeds, boiled and drained
55 g (2 oz) gingko nuts, shelled and skinned

1.8 kg (4 lb) duck, whole
   Salt water
2 tablespoons ginger juice
2 tablespoons lard or oil
4 Chinese mushrooms, soaked in hot water and sliced thinly
225 g (½ lb) pork, chopped coarsely
   Liver and gizzard, diced

METHOD

1. Wash duck thoroughly with salt water. Wipe dry. Rub ginger juice over the whole duck, including the inside.
2. Heat lard or oil in heated wok and stir-fry **A** till brown. Add mushrooms and stir-fry for 1 minute. Add the chopped pork, stir-fry for 2 minutes then add the diced liver and gizzard. Cook for 5 minutes.
3. Remove fried mixture to a saucepan. Add **B**. Pour in 680 ml (24 fl oz) boiling water and let simmer for ½ hour. Remove the meat mixture and keep gravy aside.
4. Stuff duck with meat mixture. Place duck in large bowl and pour gravy over. Steam over rapidly boiling water for 3 hours or till duck is tender. Serve hot.

Note:
Add boiling water to the steamer if necessary. Keep the water boiling all the time.

STEW

INGREDIENTS

1 tablespoon light soya sauce 1 teaspoon msg 1 teaspoon sugar 1 teaspoon salt 1 teaspoon pepper	**A**

10 new potatoes, skinned 1 teaspoon peppercorns 1 carrot, cut into wedges 2 onions, cut into quarters 1 chicken cube 455 ml (16 fl oz) water	**B**

10 shallots, pounded coarsely 1 thumb-sized piece cinnamon bark	**C**

1 teaspoon dark soya sauce 1 teaspoon msg ¾ teaspoon salt 2 tablespoons flour 4 tablespoons water	**D**

1.2 kg (2½ lb) chicken, cut into pieces
2 tablespoons oil
3 tablespoons butter or margarine
8 tomatoes, cut into halves

METHOD

1. Marinate the chicken in **A** for ½ hour.
2. Boil **B** in a saucepan for 10 minutes.
3. Heat the oil in a frying pan and brown **C**. Remove to a plate.
4. In the same pan, add the butter and fry the marinated chicken till brown on all sides.
5. Mix **D** in a bowl and add to pan together with **B** (Method 2) and **C** (Method 3).
6. Stir and let simmer till chicken is tender, (20 minutes). Add the tomatoes and cook for 5 minutes. Remove from heat. Serve hot or cold.

TURMERIC CHICKEN

INGREDIENTS

1 tablespoon coriander powder 2½ tablespoons cumin powder 1 teaspoon pepper powder ½ teaspoon cinnamon powder 1 tablespoon turmeric powder 1 tablespoon curry powder	**A** *mixed in a bowl*

170 g (6 oz) onions 2 cloves garlic ½ thumb-sized piece ginger	**B** *ground to a fine paste*

1.6 kg (3½ lb) chicken, cut into big pieces
6 tablespoons natural yogurt
170 ml (6 fl oz) evaporated milk
2 stalks coriander, with roots intact

Seasoning:
2 tablespoons lemon juice
1½ tablespoons sugar
1½ teaspoons salt
1 teaspoon msg

200 g (7 oz) ghee or 140 g (5 oz) butter and 55 ml (2 fl oz) oil

METHOD

1. Marinate chicken pieces for ¾ hour with yogurt, 1½ teaspoons salt, 1 teaspoon each of sugar, msg and pepper.
2. Mix evaporated milk, 225 ml (8 fl oz) water, **A** and seasoning in large bowl. Add in chicken and mix well. Set aside.
3. Heat a heavy bottomed saucepan or aluminium wok. Heat ghee and fry **B** over medium heat till oil comes through and is fragrant. Add in chicken mixture, stir and cook over moderate heat for 15 minutes. Stir occasionally to prevent burning. Reduce heat to low, add coriander leaves and stalk. Cover pan to simmer for another 15–20 minutes or till chicken is tender and gravy is rather thick.
4. Add another 225 ml (8 fl oz) water. Stir and continue cooking for 2 minutes. Remove from heat.

Note:
If a thick gravy is preferred, omit Method (4).

Seafood

Braised Grouper with Black Soya Bean Sauce

Baked Crabs

Crabs in Spicy Soya Bean Paste

Crabs in Tomato Chilli Sauce

Dry Fish Curry

Fish Head Curry

Ikan Masak Kuah Lada

Rendang Ikan

Steamed Pomfret

Chilli Prawns

Glassy Prawns

Prawns in Soya Sauce

Sweet Sour Prawns

Tempura Prawns

Crayfish Mornay

Chilli Cuttlefish

Stuffed Cuttlefish Soup

Spicy Cockles

Crabs in Tomato Chilli Sauce

BRAISED GROUPER WITH BLACK SOYA BEAN SAUCE

INGREDIENTS

2 teaspoons light soya sauce	
½–1 teaspoon msg	
2 teaspoons sugar	**A** *mixed in a bowl*
1–2 teaspoons vinegar	
½ teaspoon sesame oil	
½ teaspoon cornflour	

1 grouper, approximately 680 g (1½ lb)
1 teaspoon salt
½ teaspoon pepper
    Oil for frying fish
3 tablespoons lard
6 slices ginger
1 teaspoon pounded garlic
3–4 tablespoons black soya beans, pounded to a paste
285 ml (10 fl oz) chicken stock or 285 ml (10 fl oz) water with ½ chicken cube

1 red chilli	*seeded and cut into thin strips*
1 green chilli	

3 stalks spring onions, cut into 4 cm (1½ in) lengths

METHOD

1. Scale and clean fish. Cut slits on both sides of fish. Rub in salt and pepper including inside of fish. Leave for ½ hour.

2. Heat iron wok. Put in enough oil to pan-fry fish and heat till very hot. Fry fish to a crisp golden brown on both sides. Remove fish to a serving plate.

3. Drain oil from pan, heat 2 tablespoons of the lard and fry the ginger and garlic till light brown. Add soya bean paste, **A** and chicken stock and stir-fry for short while. Lastly, add the red and green chillies and spring onions. Put fish in and cook for 1 minute adding extra tablespoon lard. Remove to a serving plate. Serve hot.

BAKED CRABS

INGREDIENTS

1 teaspoon salt	
1 teaspoon msg	
½ teaspoon pepper	
2 tablespoons lard	**A**
1 teaspoon dark soya sauce	
1 teaspoon light soya sauce	
1 egg, beaten	

225 g (½ lb) minced pork, with some fat	
225 g (½ lb) prawns, shelled, deveined and chopped finely	**B**
2 tablespoons breadcrumbs, soaked in 2 tablespoons water	

8 medium-sized fresh crabs, whole
    Flour for dusting
1 egg, breaten
    Breadcrumbs

METHOD

1. Steam the crabs, whole, over rapidly boiling water for 20 minutes. Do not remove lid while steaming. Cool. Remove meat and set aside the shells for stuffing.

2. Mix **A** in a bowl.

3. Add **B** and mix thoroughly. Add the crab meat and mix lightly.

4. Dust crab shells with flour. Fill the shells with the crab meat mixture and grill or bake in a pre-heated oven at 190°C (375°F) or Regulo 7 till cooked, (about ½–¾ hour).

5. Remove baked crabs from oven. Brush with beaten egg and sprinkle on breadcrumbs. Return to oven for another 5–7 minutes. Serve hot or cold.

CRABS IN SPICY SOYA BEAN PASTE

INGREDIENTS

8 shallots
4 cloves garlic
2 red chillies, seeded
4 slices ginger

A *ground to a paste*

3 large crabs weighing approximately 1.8 kg (4 lb)
4 tablespoons lard or oil
2 tablespoons spicy salted soya bean paste (*see recipe below*)

1 cup water, 225 ml (8 fl oz)
1 tablespoon sugar
1 teaspoon vinegar
1 teaspoon msg
¼ teaspoon salt
2 tablespoons light soya sauce

gravy sauce

1 large egg, lightly beaten
3 stalks spring onions, cut into 3 cm (1½ in) lengths
2 tablespoons lard

METHOD

1. Clean crabs and cut into 4 pieces. Cut off claws and crack them lightly.

2. Heat a pan, add lard and fry **A** till fragrant, stirring frequently. Add salted bean paste; fry for ½ minute. Pour in gravy sauce and bring it to boil. Put in crabs, stir well and cook for 10–15 minutes or till crabs are well done.

3. Add more water if gravy is too dry, pour in the beaten egg, add spring onions and lard, stir in pan for a moment and remove crabs to a serving dish.

SPICY SOYA BEAN PASTE

115 g (4 oz) preserved soya beans (brown)
2 tablespoons plum paste
4 tablespoons hot chilli sauce
2 teaspoons sesame oil

Combine all ingredients in a bowl and blend well.

CRABS IN TOMATO CHILLI SAUCE

INGREDIENTS

1 tablespoon chilli sauce
2 tablespoons light soya sauce
¼ teaspoon salt
1 tablespoon sugar
½ teaspoon msg
2 tablespoons vinegar
8 tablespoons tomato ketchup
1 teaspoon sesame oil
340 ml (12 fl oz) water

A

4 cloves garlic
10 shallots
½ thumb-sized piece ginger

B

2 tablespoons cornflour
4 tablespoons water

C

6 tablespoons lard

1.5 kg (3¼ lb) crabs, cleaned and cut into pieces
1 egg, beaten

METHOD

1. Mix **A** in a bowl for the sauce.

2. Pound **B** to a fine paste.

3. Blend **C** in a separate bowl for the thickening.

4. Heat 6 tablespoons lard in wok and fry paste till fragrant. Add crabs and one-third of the sauce. Stir-fry for 2 minutes over a high heat.

5. Add the rest of the sauce; stir and cover wok for 10 minutes. (Do not remove the lid.)

6. Pour in thickening and stir well. Add beaten egg, mix thoroughly with the chillied crabs and remove to a serving plate. Serve at once.

DRY FISH CURRY

INGREDIENTS

1½ teaspoons turmeric powder	
1½ teaspoons dried chilli powder	
1 tablespoon cumin powder	**A**
1 tablespoon cinnamon powder	
1 teaspoon aniseed powder	
1 teaspoon black pepper powder	

455 g (1 lb) coconut
680 g (24 oz) Spanish mackerel

Marinade:
   2 tablespoons fish sauce
   1 teaspoon pepper
   1 tablespoon lime juice
   1 tablespoon sugar

115 ml (4 fl oz) oil for frying fish
   3 tablespoons oil for frying paste
  55 g (2 oz) onions, sliced thinly
  ½ thumb-sized piece ginger, shredded thinly
   1 teaspoon rempah tumis (*see recipe*)
   2 sprigs curry leaves
   2 cloves garlic, chopped finely
  55 g (2 oz) shallots, pounded coarsely
   2 ripe tomatoes, peeled and sliced thickly

Seasoning:
1 teaspoon salt
1 teaspoon sugar
1 teaspoon msg

METHOD

1. Squeeze coconut with 225 ml (8 fl oz) water to extract milk. Set aside.
2. Wash and cut fish into pieces. Soak in marinade for 20 minutes. Drain fish and fry till lightly browned on both sides. Remove and set aside.
3. Heat 3 tablespoons oil in an aluminium wok. Fry sliced onions till soft; add ginger, rempah tumis and curry leaves. Fry till ginger turns light brown. Stir in garlic, fry for 1 minute; add shallots and stir-fry till light brown.
4. Add **A** with ½ cup coconut milk. Stir for ½ minute and add 115 ml (4 fl oz) water and tomatoes. Simmer for 5 minutes, stirring constantly to prevent burning.
5. Pour in remaining milk and seasoning. Cook over low heat till it reaches a boil. Put in fish and continue cooking till gravy is thick. Remove from heat. Serve hot or cold.

Note:
Cut Spanish mackerel into pieces 2.5 cm (1 in) thick. Then cut each piece into four. Ingredients **A** *may be substituted with 4 tablespoons curry powder and 1 teaspoon turmeric powder.*

REMPAH TUMIS

INGREDIENTS

55 g (2 oz) cumin seeds
55 g (2 oz) cinnamon bark
55 g (2 oz) fenugreek
55 g (2 oz) split black beans
30 g (1 oz) poppy seeds

METHOD

1. Wash cumin seeds and cinnamon bark. Drain. Dry in sun or under a warm grill for 35–45 minutes till ingredients are heated through and smell fragrant.
2. Mix everything together. Keep in a bottle and store in refrigerator.

Curry leaves give this dish a delightful aroma. Use 1–2 sprigs.

FISH HEAD CURRY

INGREDIENTS

1–2 teaspoons salt
2–3 teaspoons sugar
  1 teaspoon msg
  3 tomatoes, quartered   **A**
55 g (2 oz) tamarind with 225 ml (8 fl oz) water, squeezed and strained
  2 sprigs curry leaves

  6 red chillies
  8 green chillies
  5 tablespoons oil
  1 tablespoon mixed curry seeds for fish curry★
½ thumb-sized piece ginger, thinly shredded
  2 cloves garlic, sliced thinly
  2 onions, sliced thinly
  4 tablespoons curry powder, mixed into a paste with 225 ml (8 fl oz) water
225 g (8 oz) grated coconut, squeezed with 225 ml (8 fl oz) water
225 g (8 oz) tender lady's fingers
625 g (1 lb 6 oz) fish head

METHOD

1. Slit the chillies half-way, lengthwise.

2. Heat oil in wok and fry curry seeds and ginger till light brown. Add garlic and stir-fry for ½ minute. Add sliced onion and fry till soft and transparent. Add curry paste and 115 ml of the coconut milk. Stir-fry till oil comes through.

3. Add **A** and continue to cook over a low heat. Add remaining coconut milk. Let simmer for 5 minutes.

4. Add lady's fingers, fish head and sliced chillies, cover pan and let simmer till cooked.

★*See "Helpful Hints".*

Note:
You can add 3–4 dried tamarind slices for a sharp, sourish taste.

IKAN MASAK KUAH LADA
(FISH IN MILD SPICY PASTE)

INGREDIENTS

½ thumb-sized piece turmeric
10 slices galangal
  2 stalks lemon grass, sliced
  4 candlenuts
  1 tablespoon shrimp paste   **A**
  1 red chilli
12 shallots
  1 clove garlic
  2 teaspoons pepper

½ teaspoon salt
½ teaspoon msg   **B**
455 ml (16 fl oz) water

  3 green egg plants
  Salt water
625 g (1 lb 6 oz) Spanish mackerel or ray fish
  Sugar and salt for seasoning
  5 tablespoons oil
  1 walnut-sized tamarind with 225 ml (8 fl oz) water, squeezed and strained

METHOD

1. Grind **A** to a fine paste.

2. Cut the egg plants into 6 cm (2½ in) lengths. Halve each piece lengthwise and score the cut surface. Soak in salt water until needed.

3. Wash and cut the fish. Season with 1 teaspoon salt and 1 teaspoon sugar. Set aside.

4. Heat an aluminium wok. Heat oil and stir-fry paste (Method 1) over a moderate heat till fragrant. Add the tamarind juice, 2 tablespoonfuls at a time.

5. Add **B** and boil for 5 minutes. Add the egg plants. Cover wok and cook for 5 minutes. Add the fish and cook till fish is done.

RENDANG IKAN
(FISH IN RICH COCONUT SAUCE)

INGREDIENTS

455 g (1 lb) Spotted Spanish Mackerel (Tenggiri Papan), cut into pieces
455 g (1 lb) grated coconut, white
  2 teaspoons curry powder

115 g (4 oz) shallots
  1 stalk lemon grass
  ½ thumb-sized piece galangal
  6 red chillies, seeded
  4 slices ginger
  1 teaspoon shrimp paste
  1 clove garlic
  ½ thumb-sized piece fresh turmeric or
    ½ teaspoon turmeric powder
  4 daun limau purot

  } *ground to a fine paste*

  1 walnut-sized piece tamarind mixed with 115 ml (4 fl oz) water, strained
  1 slice dry tamarind

METHOD

1. Marinate fish pieces with 1 teaspoon sugar, ¾ teaspoon salt and 1 tablespoon tamarind with 2 tablespoons water, for 20 minutes.

2. Squeeze coconut for No. 1 milk, set aside. Add 225 ml water to coconut and squeeze for No. 2 milk. Set aside.

3. Heat wok. Add 4 tablespoons oil and when hot, fry curry powder and paste over moderate heat till oil bubbles through, adding 3 tablespoons No. 1 milk a spoonful at a time. Fry till paste is oily and fragrant.

4. Pour in No. 2 milk and tamarind juice and bring to a boil. Add slice of tamarind, fish, 2 teaspoons sugar and 1 teaspoon each of salt and msg to cook over moderate heat for 7–8 minutes. Reduce heat to low. Pour in the remaining No. 1 milk, stir well and simmer for 5 minutes uncovered. Remove from heat. Serve hot or cold.

STEAMED POMFRET

INGREDIENTS

  2 teaspoons light soya sauce
  1 teaspoon msg
  ½ teaspoon sugar
  ½ teaspoon sesame oil
  ¼ teaspoon fine salt
225 ml (8 fl oz) chicken stock

  } **A**

  1 tablespoon *kiam chye*, finely shredded
  1 stalk Chinese parsley, cut
  2 red chillies, cut into strips
  2 stalks spring onions, cut into 5 cm (2 in) lengths

  } **B**

  2 dried mushrooms, soaked in hot water
  1 pomfret, 455–680 g (1–1½ lb)
    Salt
 10 thin slices ginger
  2 tablespoons lard
  1 tablespoon pork fat, finely shredded

METHOD

1. Mix **A** in a bowl for the sauce.

2. Slice mushrooms into strips.

3. Clean fish and make two shallow slits on each side. Season with salt.

4. Arrange half of the ginger slices and spread 1 tablespoonful of the lard on a plate. Place fish on top.

5. Spread the rest of the ginger, pork fat and mushroom strips over the fish.

6. Steam for 12–15 minutes over a very high heat or till cooked.

7. Boil the sauce in another pan. Stir in the other tablespoonful of lard.

8. Place the steamed fish on a hot serving dish and pour the cooked sauce over the fish. Garnish with **B** and serve while very hot.

Steamed Pomfret

CHILLI PRAWNS

INGREDIENTS

15 red chillies
1 teaspoon shrimp paste **A**
¼ teaspoon salt

1 teaspoon sugar **B**
1 tablespoon lime juice

6 tablespoons oil
625 g (22 oz) king prawns, trimmed
½ teaspoon salt
1 big onion sliced

METHOD

1. Pound **A** till fine.
2. Heat oil in wok. Fry prawns till cooked. Add salt and sliced onions.
3. Push to one side of the wok and fry the chilli paste (Method 1). Stir in the prawns and onions, add **B**, and fry for 1 minute. Remove to a serving plate.

GLASSY PRAWNS

INGREDIENTS

680 g (1½ lb) big prawns

1 tablespoon *pheng say* powder (available at Chinese medicine shops) **A**
1 tablespoon bicarbonate of soda
225 g (8 oz) castor sugar

170 ml (6 fl oz) water
1 tablespoon cornflour
½ teaspoon sesame oil *sauce*
2 teaspoons light soya sauce *mixed in*
1 teaspoon msg *a bowl*
½ teaspoon sugar
Pinch of salt
1 teaspoon oyster sauce

225 ml (8 fl oz) oil to deep fry prawns
2 tablespoons lard
1 teaspoon coarsely chopped ginger
2 cloves garlic, coarsely chopped
3 stalks spring onion, cut into 5 cm (2 in) lengths

PRAWNS IN SOYA SAUCE

INGREDIENTS

4 tablespoons light soya sauce
1 tablespoon sugar **A**
1 teaspoon cornflour
2 tablespoons water

455 g (1 lb) prawns, fairly large
Salt water
8 tablespoons lard or oil
2 thumb-sized pieces ginger, shredded finely
¼ teaspoon salt
2 stalks spring onions, cut into short lengths

METHOD

1. Mix **A** in a bowl for the sauce.
2. Trim prawns and wash in salt water. Drain.
3. Heat the lard in an iron wok. When very hot, fry ginger till it turns brown. Add prawns, salt and stir-fry for ½ minute. Cover and cook for 5–7 minutes.
4. Remove lid, add **A**, stir well with the prawns and add the spring onions. Serve.

METHOD

1. Shell prawns, slit lengthwise from the head to the tail without cutting through the prawns. Remove dark veins.
2. Wash prawns and drain. Season with **A** and set aside for 4 hours or leave overnight in the refrigerator. Add water to cover 8 cm (3 in) above the prawns in a bowl.
3. Place bowl of prawns under a slow running tap for ½ hour, stirring at 5 minute intervals. Leave in colander to drain.
4. Pour oil in heated wok. When very hot, put in prawns. Cover pan with lid and cook over high heat for 2 minutes or till prawns turn transparent. Remove prawns to a bowl.
5. Remove oil from the wok, add lard, and stir fry ginger and garlic till light brown. Return prawns to pan, stir sauce and pour over prawns. Toss in pan till gravy boils and thickens. Remove to a serving plate. Garnish with spring onions and serve.

SWEET SOUR PRAWNS

INGREDIENTS

6 tablespoons tomato sauce
2 tablespoons sweet chilli sauce
1 teaspoon light soya sauce
¼ teaspoon pepper
½ teaspoon msg
1 teaspoon sugar
1 teaspoon vinegar
1 tablespoon cornflour mixed with
   3 tablespoons water

A *mixed in a bowl*

1 tablespoon lard

605 g (21 oz) medium-sized prawns
4 tablespoons castor sugar
4 tablespoons lard or oil
2 cloves garlic, finely chopped
1 tablespoon chopped ginger
6 tablespoons spring onion, chopped
6 tablespoons Chinese celery, cut into 0.5 cm (¼ in) pieces

METHOD

1. Shell prawns, slit lengthwise and devein. Wash and drain in a colander.

2. Place prawns in a bowl, season with 4 tablespoons castor sugar and leave for 1 hour. Wash prawns under a running tap for a minute to remove all the sugar and put in colander to drain.

3. Heat lard in wok till very hot. Fry the garlic and ginger till light brown. Add prawns and stir fry over high heat for 2 minutes or till prawns are cooked. Add chopped spring onions and celery and stir-fry for 1 minute.

4. Stir **A** and pour over prawns. Add the extra tablespoon of lard, mix well, and remove to a serving plate. Serve hot.

TEMPURA PRAWNS
(FRIED PRAWNS, JAPANESE-STYLE)

INGREDIENTS

¼ teaspoon salt
½ teaspoon brandy
½ teaspoon msg

A

85 g (3 oz) cauliflower
55 g (2 oz) green peppers

B

85 g (3 oz) self-raising flour

½ teaspoon salt
½ teaspoon sugar
½ teaspoon msg
½ teaspoon pepper
1 tablespoon oil
130 ml (4½ fl oz) water

C

225 g (½ lb) small prawns, shelled and deveined
55 g (2 oz) pork chop meat, sliced thinly
Oil for deep-frying

METHOD

1. Marinate prawns and pork in **A** for 10 minutes.

2. Slice **B** thinly.

3. Place flour in a bowl. Stir **C** till well mixed and pour gradually into the flour. Mix well to form a smooth batter. Leave to stand for 20 minutes.

4. Add the marinated prawns, pork and **B** to batter. Mix well.

5. Heat oil. When very hot, fry battered ingredients till golden brown. Drain on a wire sieve and leave to cool on absorbent paper. Serve hot with sauce.

SAUCE:
4 tablespoons tomato ketchup
1 tablespoon sweet chilli sauce
1 teaspoon 'A1' brand sauce
1 teaspoon vinegar
1 teaspoon msg
1 teaspoon lime juice
4 tablespoons boiled water, cooled

1. Mix all the ingredients and serve in a separate bowl.

CRAYFISH MORNAY

INGREDIENTS

340 g (12 oz) cooked crayfish meat
55 g (2 oz) butter with 1 tablespoon oil
85 g (3 oz) onions, sliced
4 tablespoons celery, sliced thinly
2 heaped tablespoons flour
285 ml (10 fl oz) milk

Seasoning:
½ teaspoon sugar
¼ teaspoon salt
½ teaspoon pepper

2 egg whites, lightly beaten
115 g mozzarella cheese, coarsely grated

Topping:
½ cup dry breadcrumbs
140 g (5 oz) chopped salami
½ cup mozzarella cheese, coarsely grated

METHOD

1. Chop crayfish into big serving chunks.
2. Heat the butter and oil to fry onions and celery till soft and transparent. Add in the flour and stir for a moment.
3. Pour in the milk and stir well in pan. Reduce heat to low and add crayfish, seasoning and egg whites. Cook for a minute and then add the cheese. Stir and remove from heat.
4. Grease a deep oven-proof dish; dust with flour and pour in crayfish mixture. Spread on ½ of breadcrumbs, put in salami and remaining cheese and top with remaining breadcrumbs.
5. Bake in a moderate oven (121°C) for ½ hour. Serve hot.

CHILLI CUTTLEFISH

INGREDIENTS

15 red chillies
½ teaspoon shrimp paste ⎱ **A**

½ teaspoon salt
1 teaspoon sugar
½ teaspoon msg ⎱ **B**
1 teaspoon lime juice

455 g (1 lb) cuttlefish
6 tablespoons lard or oil
2 big onions, sliced thinly

METHOD

1. Pound **A** to a fine paste.
2. Remove ink bag and bone from cuttlefish. Wash, drain and cut cuttlefish into 2.5 cm (1 in) rings.
3. Heat iron wok. When very hot, heat 3 tablespoons lard. Fry cuttlefish over high heat for 5 minutes. Remove to a dish.
4. Heat the rest of the lard and fry the sliced onions over a high heat for 1 minute. Reduce heat, add the paste and **B** and stir-fry for another minute. Add cuttlefish and stir well with the paste. Serve hot or cold.

STUFFED CUTTLEFISH SOUP

INGREDIENTS

310 g (11 oz) small cuttlefish

310 g (11 oz) minced pork
225 g (½ lb) prawns; shelled, deveined and
 chopped
¼ teaspoon salt
½ teaspoon msg
¼ teaspoon cornflour

A

1 teaspoon salt
1 teaspoon msg
1 chicken cube

B

15 g (½ oz) vermicelli, soaked in hot water

2 sprigs Chinese celery
2 cloves chopped garlic, fried in oil
 Dash of pepper

C

METHOD

1. Remove head, ink bag and cartilage from each cuttlefish. Set aside the heads. Wash and clean the inside of the cuttlefish. Drain cuttlefish in a colander.

2. Mix **A** thoroughly to stuff three-quarters of each cuttlefish. Re-attach head. Shape little meat balls with the remaining meat.

3. Boil 680 ml (1½ pints) water in a saucepan. Add the stuffed cuttlefish and meat balls. Boil for 3 minutes. Season with **B**. Cut up the vermicelli and add to the soup. Garnish with **C** and serve in a large bowl.

Note:
When cleaning the cuttlefish, remove the brown outer skin from the body. In this way, the soup remains clear. Before stuffing meat into the cuttlefish, make a slit at the tail end of the cuttlefish. This will prevent the heat from pushing the meat out.

SPICY COCKLES

INGREDIENTS

10 shallots
6 dried chillies or 1 tablespoon chilli paste
1 teaspoon shrimp paste
1 candlenut
1 stalk lemon grass, sliced

A

115 ml (4 fl oz) water
1 teaspoon tamarind with 115 ml (4 fl oz)
 water, squeezed and strained
1 teaspoon sugar
1 teaspoon salt
½ teaspoon msg

B

310 g (11 oz) shelled cockles
5 tablespoons oil
1 stalk lemon grass, bruised
115 g (4 oz) grated coconut, squeezed with 115 ml (4 fl oz) water for milk

METHOD

1. Pound **A** to a fine paste.
2. Scald the cockles and drain in a colander.
3. Heat oil in very hot pan. Fry the paste and bruised lemon grass till fragrant.
4. Add **B**. Allow mixture to boil.
5. Add the cockles and coconut milk.
6. Cook for 1 minute and remove to a dish.

Starters and Salads

Chinese Rojak

Indian Rojak

Cold Dish Salad

Gado Gado

Nonya Salad

Shredded Duck and Fruit Salad

Yue Sung

Chinese Rojak

CHINESE ROJAK

INGREDIENTS

7–8 tablespoons sugar	
1–1¼ teaspoons salt	
2–4 tablespoons dried chilli paste	**A**
2–2½ tablespoons black prawn paste (hay ko)	

170 g (6 oz) sliced cucumber	
115 g (4 oz) beansprouts, blanched and drained	
170 g (6 oz) sliced Chinese turnip	**B**
170 g (6 oz) sliced pineapple	
115 g (4 oz) water convolvulus, blanched, drained and cut into 5 cm (2 in) lengths	

1 tablespoon juice of local lime (*limau kesturi*)
1 walnut-sized knob of tamarind, soaked in 85 ml (3 fl oz) water and strained
225 g (8 oz) ground roasted peanuts
2 crispy Chinese crullers, sliced thickly
4 squares fried spongy bean curd, cut into pieces

METHOD

1. Put **A** into a large bowl and blend to a paste with the back of a wooden spoon. Add the lime juice and 4-5 tablespoons of the tamarind juice and stir.

2. Add peanuts with rest of the tamarind juice and stir well. Add **B** and stir with a wooden spoon. Just before serving, add the crispy Chinese crullers and fried spongy bean curd. Mix well.

Note:
Cuttlefish and jellyfish soaked in alkaline water can be purchased from local markets and included in the salad. Rinse, blanch, cut into thick strips and add with the other salad ingredients (Method 2).

INDIAN ROJAK

INGREDIENTS

225 g (8 oz) potatoes, boiled in jackets, peeled and quartered
8 eggs, hard boiled and quartered
5 big firm bean curd cakes, fried and cut into pieces
Coconut fingers★, sliced thickly
Wardays★★
Prawn fritters★★★
Spicy cuttlefish★★★★
2 cucumbers, skinned and sliced
2 lettuce leaves, shredded

Sauce:

30–40 dried chillies	
2 tablespoons chopped onions	
1 clove garlic, chopped finely	**A**
1 teaspoon shrimp paste	

4 tablespoons oil
400 g (14 oz) boiled sweet potatoes, mashed

Seasoning:

225–285 g (8–10 oz) sugar	
1½–2 teaspoons salt	
2 tablespoons vinegar	**B**
55 g (2 oz) tamarind soaked in 115 ml (4 fl oz) water and strained	

30 g (1 oz) toasted sesame seeds, finely ground
30 g (1 oz) toasted sesame seeds

To make the sauce:

1. Grind or blend **A** to a fine paste.

2. Heat the oil in a pan and fry the paste over moderate heat till it is fragrant and oil bubbles through. Set aside.

3. Put mashed sweet potatoes in a heavy aluminium saucepan. Add 560 ml (1¼ pints) water in small amounts and stir till well-blended. Add **B** (seasoning), fried paste, and the ground sesame seeds. Boil gently for ½ hour to thicken, stirring occasionally to prevent sauce sticking to bottom of pan.

4. Remove from heat, add the rest of the sesame seeds, stir and cool.

*Coconut fingers

115 g (4 oz) plain flour
1 tablespoon dried prawns, pounded
½ teaspoon salt   **A**
1 teaspoon sugar
½ teaspoon msg
½ teaspoon pepper

30 g (1 oz) chickpea flour
115 g (4 oz) coarsely grated coconut, white
115 ml (4 fl oz) water

1. Put **A** in a bowl and stir till well mixed. Add chickpea flour and coconut and mix. Add water and knead lightly to make a soft dough.
2. Shape mixture into small 6.5 cm (2½ in) long rolls, tapering at both ends. Deep fry in hot oil for 5 minutes till golden brown and well cooked inside. Drain in a metal colander. Cool and set aside.

**Warday

2 eggs
1 teaspoon sugar
¼ teaspoon salt
¼ teaspoon pepper   **A**
¼ teaspoon msg
85 ml (3 fl oz) water

¼ teaspoon bicarbonate soda
85 g (3 oz) chickpea flour
100 g (3½ oz) plain flour   **B**
3 tablespoons chopped onions

1. Put **A** in a bowl, beat lightly with a fork till well mixed.
2. Put **B** in a mixing bowl. Pour in the egg mixture and stir till batter is smooth and free of lumps.
3. Divide batter into two, setting aside one half to fry the prawn fritters.
4. Heat oil in an aluminium wok for deep frying. Spoon tablespoons of the remaining batter into the hot oil, allowing space for *warday* to expand. Fry over moderate heat till golden brown.
5. Drain in a colander and set aside.

***Prawn fritters

¼ teaspoon bicarbonate of soda
¼ teaspoon pepper   **A**
Pinch of salt
2 tablespoons self-raising flour

2 tablespoons water
½ *warday* batter   **B**

285 g (10 oz) small prawns, shelled and deveined

1. Put **A** in a bowl and mix well.
2. Add **B** and stir till batter is smooth. Coat prawns.
3. Fry fritters over moderately high heat till golden brown and set aside.

****Spicy cuttlefish

1 tablespoon chilli powder
1 candlenut   **A** *ground to a*
4 shallots   *fine paste*
1 teaspoon shrimp paste

115 g (4 oz) grated coconut
1 large cuttlefish (soaked in alkaline water)
6 tablespoons oil

1 teaspoon sugar
½ teaspoon msg
½ teaspoon pepper   **B**
½ teaspoon cumin powder

1. Squeeze coconut for No. 1 milk.
2. Cut cuttlefish into small pieces. Pat with kitchen towel to dry.
3. Heat oil in wok. When very hot, fry the cuttlefish a few at a time, for 1 minute. Remove to a bowl.
4. In the same wok, heat oil and fry **A** till oil bubbles through and smells fragrant. Add coconut milk and **B**, stir and continue cooking over moderate heat till dry.
5. Put in the fried cuttlefish, stir and cook over gentle heat.

To serve:
Put small amounts of each of the ingredients on individual plates, garnish with sliced cucumber and lettuce. Serve with sauce in separate small bowls.

COLD DISH SALAD

INGREDIENTS

1 tablespoon sugar
¼ teaspoon salt
4 tablespoons salad cream
1 tablespoon sweet chilli sauce   **A**
½ teaspoon pepper
1 teaspoon sesame oil
3 tablespoons chunky peanut butter

1 chicken breast, about 170–230 g (6–8 oz)
½ teaspoon salt
½ teaspoon msg
½ teaspoon sherry
1 tablespoon vinegar
1 tablespoon dry mustard
115 g (4 oz) lettuce, finely shredded
225 g (8 oz) shredded jellyfish, treated and seasoned*
2 stalks Chinese celery
2 tablespoons roasted sesame seeds

METHOD

1. Rub chicken with the salt, msg and sherry. Place on a small enamel plate in a steamer and steam for ½ hour. Leave to cool. Cut chicken in half lengthwise and then into thick shreds. Set aside.

2. Mix vinegar and mustard in a big bowl and add **A**. Mix well till sauce is smooth. Set aside.

3. Place the shredded lettuce on a large serving plate. Arrange jellyfish on the lettuce and spread the shredded chicken over it. Pour the sauce over and garnish with celery and sesame seeds. Chill for 1–2 hours. Serve as a cold starter to a Chinese meal.

To make alkaline water:

625 g (22 oz) white crystal balls, obtainable from local markets, finely pounded
680 ml (24 fl oz) boiling water

1. Place pounded alkaline crystal balls in a porcelain jar. Add boiling water and stir with a wooden spoon till crystal balls dissolve. Leave to stand overnight.

2. Strain alkaline water through fine muslin. Store the alkaline water in a bottle for future use. (Prepared alkaline water can be kept for almost a year.)

★To prepare jellyfish:

6 tablespoons alkaline water
1.7 litres (4 pints) cold water
605 g (20 oz) salted jellyfish

Seasoning:

3 teaspoons light soya sauce
1 teaspoon sugar
1½ teaspoons msg   *seasoning for 225 g jellyfish*
2 teaspoons peanut or corn oil
1 teaspoon sesame oil

1. Mix the alkaline water with the cold water in an enamel container and soak the jellyfish for 48 hours or till jellyfish swells and softens.

2. Wash in cold water and cut each into 2 or 4 pieces.

3. Bring a saucepan of water to a rapid boil. Blanch 2 or 3 pieces of jellyfish at a time in the boiling water. Scoop out immediately and soak in a basin of cold water. Bring water to a fast boil each time you add jellyfish. Drain jellyfish. Pat dry and shred thinly. Mix well with seasoning. Keep the rest in a container of water and store in the refrigerator for future use. (Prepared jellyfish can be stored in the refrigerator for at least 2–3 weeks if the water is changed every fourth day. Blanch in hot water and roll in dry tea towel before use.)

GADO-GADO

(INDONESIAN SALAD WITH PEANUT SAUCE)

INGREDIENTS

625 g (22 oz) bean sprouts
625 g (22 oz) cabbage, diced
625 g (22 oz) long beans, cut into 3.5 cm (1½ in) lengths
2.7 litres (6 pints) water
1 teaspoon salt
1 tablespoon sugar
4 stalks lettuce, cut into 2.5 cm (1 in) pieces
225 g (8 oz) potatoes, boiled, peeled and cut into pieces
6 soya bean cakes, fried and cut into pieces
3 packets fermented soya bean cake, fried and cut into pieces
10 hard-boiled eggs, sliced
Cucumber wedges

METHOD

1. Boil separately: bean sprouts (½ minute), cabbage (5 minutes) and long beans (5 minutes) in the water with 1 teaspoon salt and 1 tablespoon sugar.

2. Lift and drain. Soak bean sprouts immediately in a basin of cold water.

SAUCE:

680 g (24 oz) roasted groundnuts, pounded 1 litre (2 pints) water 10 tablespoons sugar 1½ tablespoons salt	**A**
15 shallots 6 cloves garlic 1 tablespoon shrimp paste 20–30 dried chillies	**B**

225 ml (8 fl oz) oil
6–8 tablespoons vinegar
½ cup crispy shallots

METHOD

1. Boil **A** for 10 minutes.

2. Grind **B** to a paste.

3. Heat oil in wok and fry paste till fragrant and oil comes through.

4. Add fried paste to the boiled groundnut sauce (Method 1). Stir, reduce the heat and let simmer for 10–15 minutes. Add vinegar to taste. Remove from heat. Set aside sauce to cool. Mix in half cup of the crispy shallots.

To serve:
Arrange the lettuce on a large serving plate. Place bean sprouts, cabbage, long beans, potatoes, soya bean cakes, and fermented soya bean cake on it. Garnish with sliced eggs and cucumber wedges. Serve with groundnut sauce separately.

NONYA SALAD

INGREDIENTS

1 lime leaf ¼ teaspoon salt	**A**
2 or 3 red chillies 2 tablespoons toasted shrimp paste	**B**
2–3 tablespoons vinegar ½–1 tablespoon sugar 1 teaspoon lime juice	**C**

2 cucumbers
½ pineapple
4 tablespoons dried prawns, pounded

METHOD

1. Cut off the ends of each cucumber. Wash and dice cucumbers into 1 cm cubes (with skin).

2. Remove pineapple skin and dice pineapple into 1 cm cubes.

3. Pound **A** till fine. Add **B** and pound together till fine. Remove to a dish.

4. Add **C** to the shrimp paste mixture and stir till well mixed.

To mix the salad:
1. Place the cucumber and pineapple cubes in a large bowl. Add dried prawns and mix thoroughly by hand.

2. Add shrimp paste mixture, stir thoroughly, and serve.

SHREDDED DUCK AND FRUIT SALAD

INGREDIENTS

1 cup shredded green lettuce
1 cup shredded treated jellyfish
1 cup shredded cucumber
1 cup shredded honey-dew melon
1 cup shredded roast duck

Garnish:
¼ cup chopped walnuts
¼ cup ground roasted peanuts
3 tablespoons toasted sesame seeds

1. Place shredded ingredients in a large serving plate with green lettuce on the bottom and roast duck on top. Chill in refrigerator.
2. Before serving, sprinkle salad with walnuts, peanuts and sesame seeds. Pour sauce (see recipe below) over and serve.

Sauce:
4 tablespoons sour plum sauce (sung boey chew)
4 tablespoons apricot jam
1 tablespoon sweet chilli sauce
1 teaspoon vinegar
1 tablespoon peanut oil
1 teaspoon ginger wine (optional)
1 teaspoon sugar
½ teaspoon sesame oil

METHOD

1. Mix all ingredients in a small saucepan. Cook over low heat till heated through and well blended.
2. Strain mixture, cook and serve with cold salad.

YUE SUNG
(CANTONESE RAW FISH SALAD)

INGREDIENTS

455 g (1 lb) Chinese radish
115 g (4 oz) sweet potato
115 g (4 oz) carrot
55 g (2 oz) sweet crisp flakes (available in Chinatown confectionaries)
55–85 g (2–3 oz) roasted peanuts, coarsely ground
4 tablespoons sesame seeds, toasted
1 small segment pomelo
2 sprigs Chinese celery (short, dark green variety), cut leaves and tender stalks into short pieces
115 g (4 oz) preserved jellyfish, sliced thinly

30 g (1 oz) fresh young ginger
30 g (1 oz) preserved sweet ginger
30 g (1 oz) preserved sweet red ginger
2 fresh chillies, seeded
3 preserved, sweet and sour leeks
2 lime leaves
1 small piece preserved candied orange
55 g (2 oz) preserved candied winter melon   *finely shredded*

4–5 tablespoons corn oil
2 tablespoons lime juice
4 teaspoons castor sugar
¼ teaspoon five-spice powder
½ teaspoon fine salt
¼ teaspoon pepper
3–4 tablespoons vinegar, set aside 1 tablespoon for fish   *seasoning*

225 g (8 oz) thinly sliced wolf herring

METHOD

1. Skin radish, sweet potatoes and carrots. Soak in cold water for an hour and drain. Leave in a colander to air.
2. Grate sweet potatoes, immerse in water briefly, stir and strain immediately to drain well.
3. Grate carrot and radish and set aside. Do not immerse in water.

To serve:
Arrange all ingredients except fish, crispy flakes and seasoning on a large round tray. Place fish and flakes last with tablespoon of vinegar. Mix well with seasoning.

Yue Sung

Vegetarian Greens

Bean Sprouts fried with Crispy Salted Fish
Cauliflower and Long Beans in Creamy Sauce
Chinese Mustard with Abalone
Chop Suey
Egg Plant with Pork and Prawns
Egg Plant in Spicy Sauce
Loh Hon Chye
Long Beans with Minced Meat
Mustard with Crab Meat Sauce
Rebong Masak Lemak
Vegetarian Spring Rolls
Vegetarian Beehoon
Vegetarian Curry

Vegetarian Spring Rolls

BEAN SPROUTS FRIED WITH CRISPY SALTED FISH

INGREDIENTS

  30 g (1 oz) Penang salted fish
  Oil
  3 tablespoons lard
  ½ teaspoon pounded garlic
285 g (10 oz) bean sprouts, picked, washed and drained
  2 stalks spring onions, cut into 4 cm (1½ in) lengths

Seasoning:
½ teaspoon salt
1 teaspoon sugar
½ teaspoon msg
¼ teaspoon pepper

METHOD

1. Cut salted fish into thin strips, immerse in water and drain immediately. Heat oil in a small saucepan and fry salted fish over moderate heat till lightly browned and crispy. Drain on absorbent paper and leave to cool slightly. Keep in a bottle to keep it crisp.

2. Heat an iron wok. When very hot, heat 2 tablespoons lard and fry garlic till light brown, add bean sprouts, spring onions and seasoning. Sprinkle a little water and stir-fry for short while over high heat. Remove from heat and pour in the rest of the lard, stir and remove to a serving plate. Break crispy salt fish into fine pieces and place over bean sprouts before serving.

CAULIFLOWER AND LONG BEANS IN CREAMY SAUCE

INGREDIENTS

115 g (4 oz) peas
455 g (1 lb) cauliflower, cut into florets
455 g (1 lb) long beans, cut into 7 cm (3 in) lengths
  1 carrot, sliced
  2 tablespoons each of butter and oil
  1 onion, thinly sliced
  1 clove garlic, finely chopped
  2 tablespoons plain flour

Seasoning:
  1 chicken cube, crushed
½ teaspoon turmeric powder
  1 teaspoon sugar
¼ teaspoon salt
  Dash of pepper
  2 teaspoons light soya sauce

225 ml (8 fl oz) evaporated milk diluted in 225 ml (8 fl oz) water

METHOD

1. Blanch vegetables separately. Drain and set aside.

2. Heat butter and oil in wok. Fry onion and garlic till light brown. Add in flour and stir-fry for short while. Put in scalded vegetables and stir-fry over high heat for 1 minute.

3. Add seasoning with ½ of diluted milk into pan. Stir well, reduce heat to moderate and cook for 5–7 minutes. Pour in remaining milk and cook for another 5 minutes or till vegetables are tender.

CHINESE MUSTARD WITH ABALONE

INGREDIENTS

1 tablespoon oyster sauce
½ teaspoon sugar
½ teaspoon msg
Dash of pepper
½ teaspoon sesame oil
Abalone sauce from the can
1 teaspoon light soya sauce
A

1 tablespoon cornflour
4 tablespoons water
B

1 can 455 g (16 oz) abalone

285 g (10 oz) *poh chye* or Chinese mustard
1 teaspoon salt
1 tablespoon sugar
1 tablespoon oil
3 tablespoons lard
4 slices ginger
1 clove garlic, minced
2 slices cooked ham, cut into strips
1 tablespoon crispy shallots

METHOD

1. Slice abalone thinly and retain liquid.

2. Mix **A** in a bowl and set aside.

3. Wash Chinese mustard, drain and cut into 15 cm (6 in) lengths. Bring 1 litre (32 fl oz) water to a rapid boil with the salt, sugar and oil. Add Chinese mustard and boil over high heat for ¼ minute. Remove and immerse in a large bowl of cold water for 1 minute. Drain in colander and set aside.

4. In a hot iron wok, put in 2 tablespoons lard and fry the sliced ginger and minced garlic till lightly browned. Add **A** and bring to the boil gently. Add **B** and stir well. When gravy comes to a boil, place the Chinese mustard and sliced abalone separately in the pan. Cook till gravy starts to boil again. Boil for further 5 seconds, then add the remaining tablespoon of lard.

5. Remove the mustard to a serving plate and then arrange the abalone on top. Garnish with shredded ham and crispy shallots.

CHOP SUEY
(MIXED VEGETABLES)

INGREDIENTS

1 teaspoon light soya sauce
½ teaspoon msg
1 teaspoon ginger juice
Dash of pepper
A

85 g (3 oz) canned bamboo shoots
115 g (4 oz) French beans
B

1 teaspoon msg
½ teaspoon salt
½ teaspoon sugar
2 tablespoons light soya sauce
1 tablespoon oyster sauce
½ tablespoon dark soya sauce
½ tablespoon sesame oil
½ tablespoon sherry or wine
C

1 tablespoon cornflour
170 ml (6 fl oz) water
D

115 g (4 oz) pork fillet, sliced
115 g (4 oz) pork liver, sliced
6 red chillies, seeded
455 g (1 lb) prawns, shelled and deveined
1 onion, peeled and quartered
4 Chinese mushrooms, soaked in hot water and sliced
1 can button mushrooms

METHOD

1. Marinate pork and liver in **A** for 10 minutes.

2. Cut chillies into thick long strips.

3. Slice **B** thinly.

4. Heat a pan till very hot. Use 2 tablespoons lard, fry prawns for ½ minute. Remove. In the same pan, fry the following separately over a very high heat: onion, chillies, French beans and bamboo shoots. Remove to a dish.

5. Mix **C** in a bowl. Heat 2 tablespoons lard in a clean pan and fry the mushrooms, pork and liver for 2 minutes.

6. Add the fried ingredients and toss mixture in pan. Add **C**, stir for 1 minute. Blend **D** and add to pan. Stir-fry so that all ingredients are mixed thoroughly.

EGG PLANT WITH PORK AND PRAWNS

INGREDIENTS

3 teaspoons chopped garlic
1 teaspoon chopped ginger
1 tablespoon preserved salted soya beans, pounded   **A**
1 teaspoon chilli sauce

455 g (1 lb) egg plant (purple or green)
1 cup oil for frying
3 tablespoons lard or oil
4 dried Chinese mushrooms, sliced thinly
225 g (8 oz) minced pork
115 g (4 oz) shelled prawns, chopped coarsely

Seasoning:
½ teaspoon salt
½ teaspoon msg
2 teaspoons sugar
1 tablespoon Thai fish sauce
1 teaspoon sesame oil   **B**
2 teaspoons tapioca flour dissolved in
2 tablespoons water
¼ teaspoon pepper

METHOD

1. Remove stems and skin from egg plants. Cut into thick slices and soak in salt water. Drain before frying.

2. Heat 1 cup oil in an iron wok till very hot. Fry egg plant till lightly browned. Remove to a metal colander to drain oil.

3. Heat 3 tablespoons lard or oil in a heated wok. Fry **A** over moderate heat, till garlic and ginger brown. Add mushrooms and stir for 1 minute. Put in pork and prawns and stir fry for another minute before pouring in **B** (seasoning). Cook for 1 minute and add egg plant. Mix well and allow to simmer for 5 minutes. Serve.

EGG PLANT IN SPICY SAUCE

INGREDIENTS

6 fresh red chillies, seeded
20 dried chillies, seeded   **A**
1 teaspoon shrimp paste

½ teaspoon salt
1 level teaspoon sugar   **B**
½ teaspoon msg

6 green egg plants
4 tablespoons oil

METHOD

1. Remove stalks and cut egg plant into halves lengthwise. Soak in a bowl of slightly salted water.

2. Grind or blend **A** to a fine paste.

3. Heat the oil in a non-stick pan and fry the sliced egg plant lightly until cooked. Remove to a plate. Fry paste and **B** with remaining oil. Fry over low heat till oil bubbles through then add 2 tablespoons water. Stir for short while and pour over fried egg plant. Serve hot or cold.

Note:
Sprinkle water in pan, then cover while frying egg plant. This helps it cook right through quickly.

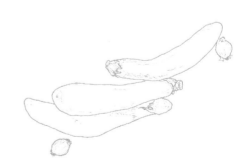

LOH HON CHYE
(MIXED VEGETABLES)

2 teaspoons sugar
1 tablespoon oil   } **A**
½ teaspoon salt
½ teaspoon bicarbonate of soda

2 teaspoons light soya sauce
1 teaspoon msg
½ teaspoon sesame oil   } **B**
1 teaspoon sugar
2 tablespoons oyster sauce

455 g (16 oz) green mustard, stalks only
115 g (4 oz) lard or oil
6 slices ginger
½ teaspoon pounded garlic
6–8 dried Chinese mushrooms, softened and quartered
115 g (4 oz) snow peas
½ can young corn, cut into halves
115 g (4 oz) sliced bamboo shoots
½ can button mushrooms, cut into halves
1 handful gingko nuts, boiled for ½ hour till softened
½ can mock abalone (obtainable from soya bean stalls at wet markets)
455 ml (16 fl oz) chicken stock or 455 ml boiling water with 1 chicken cube

1½ tablespoons tapioca flour or cornflour
4 tablespoons water   } **C**

METHOD

To boil green mustard:

1. Cut mustard stalks into big pieces, wash and drain. Boil 850 ml (30 fl oz) water in a saucepan. Put in stalks and **A**. Allow water to boil again over very high heat and cook for 3 minutes only.

2. Drain and immerse stalks in a large bowl of cold water for 2 minutes, drain in colander and keep in the refrigerator till ready for use.

To prepare *Loh Hon Chye:*

1. Heat 2 tablespoons lard in pre-heated wok and fry ginger and garlic till lightly browned. Stir-fry Chinese mushrooms and snow peas and remove.

2. Add another 2 tablespoons of lard and stir-fry the corn, bamboo shoots, button mushrooms, gingko nuts and mock abalone for ½ minute. Add in **B**, chicken stock and the rest of the ingredients and bring to the boil.

3. Lastly add the mustard stalks, cover pan and allow to boil. Remove lid, pour in **C** and stir well. Serve hot.

LONG BEANS WITH MINCED MEAT
(SICHUAN STYLE)

INGREDIENTS

2 teaspoons fine sugar
½ teaspoon msg
¼ teaspoon pepper
1 teaspoon oyster sauce   } **A** *mixed in a bowl*
½ teaspoon sesame oil
1 teaspoon sago flour
115 ml (4 fl oz) water

170 ml (6 fl oz) oil
225 g (8 oz) long beans, cut into 6 cm lengths

2 tablespoons lard or oil
3 cloves garlic, chopped coarsely
1½ tablespoons spicy soya bean paste★
115 g (4 oz) minced pork
55 g (2 oz) chopped prawn meat

METHOD

1. Heat iron wok. When very hot, add oil, and fry long beans till tender. Sprinkle a little water to avoid burning. Remove and drain.

2. Heat oil and fry garlic till very lightly browned. Add spicy soya bean paste, pork and prawns, and stir-fry till pork changes colour. Add **A**, then fried long beans. Continue cooking over low heat for 1–2 minutes. Remove and serve immediately.

★*See page 109.*

MUSTARD WITH CRAB MEAT SAUCE

INGREDIENTS

455 g (1 lb) crab (blue flowery or *kepiting batu*)
  3 tablespoons dried prawns, pounded finely
  6 tablespoons lard or oil
455 g (1 lb) green mustard stalks, cut into big pieces
  1 can straw mushrooms, cut into halves
  4 slices ginger
  3 shallots, thinly sliced
  2 level tablespoons plain flour (*for thickening*)
115 ml (4 fl oz) evaporated milk and 340 ml (12 fl oz) chicken stock

1 tablespoon light soya sauce	
1 teaspoon msg	
1 teaspoon sugar	
Dash of pepper	**A**
1 tablespoon oyster sauce	
½ teaspoon sesame oil	

METHOD

1. Steam crabs over high heat for 20 minutes. Immerse in cold water for 1 minute. Clean and remove meat. Keep in refrigerator before use.

2. Fry dried prawns in oil till golden brown, drain and spread on a piece of absorbent paper. Keep prawns in a bottle till ready to use.

3. Pour 3 tablespoons lard in heated wok and stir-fry green mustard for short while. Remove to a bowl. In the same pan, add 1 tablespoon lard, stir-fry the straw mushrooms over high heat and remove.

4. Add the rest of the lard, fry ginger and shallots till lightly browned. Stir-fry the flour for short while till bubbly; reduce heat and pour in the milk mixture and **A**. Stir till well blended and bring to the boil. Put in green mustard and straw mushrooms, stir lightly and wait till gravy boils. Place crab meat over green mustard, cover pan with lid and simmer for 1 minute. Sprinkle the dried prawns over dish with a dash of pepper, and serve.

REBONG MASAK LEMAK
(BAMBOO SHOOTS IN SPICY COCONUT GRAVY)

INGREDIENTS

1 teaspoon peppercorns	
2 teaspoons roasted coriander seeds	
14 slices galangal	
½ thumb-sized piece turmeric	
5 candlenuts	**A**
14 shallots	
1 clove garlic	
2 red chillies	
2 tablespoons shrimp paste	

¾ tablespoon salt	
1 teaspoon sugar	**B**
½ teaspoon msg	

455 g (16 oz) boiled tender bamboo shoots, sliced thinly	
905 g (2 lb) chicken, cut into pieces	**C**
340 g (12 oz) pork ribs, cut into pieces	

455 g (16 oz) grated coconut

115 ml (4 fl oz) oil
  2 stalks lemon grass

METHOD

1. Pound **A** together in the given order to a very fine paste.

2. Use a piece of muslin to squeeze coconut for No. 1 milk. Set aside.

3. Add 900 ml (32 fl oz) water to the grated coconut and squeeze again for No. 2 milk. Set aside.

4. In a very hot aluminium wok, heat oil. Stir-fry paste and bruised lemon grass over moderate heat, till oil bubbles through and paste is fragrant.

5. Add **B** and half of the No. 2 milk. When mixture boils, add **C**. Cook for 10 minutes, stirring occasionally.

6. Add remaining No. 2 milk, stir and cover. Cook over low heat for 20 minutes or till chicken is tender.

7. Finally, add No. 1 milk. Stir for 1 minute, remove from the heat.

VEGETARIAN SPRING ROLLS

INGREDIENTS

Seasoning:

1 teaspoon salt
1 teaspoon sugar   **A**
1 teaspoon black soya sauce

5 dried Chinese mushrooms
1 kg yambean (bangkuang)
1 carrot, approximately 115 g (4 oz)
10 sweet soya bean strips
6 tablespoons peanut oil
1 teaspoon shredded ginger
1 tablespoon preserved salted soya bean, pounded
  Oil for deep frying
1 tablespoon tapioca flour blended in 3 tablespoons
  water for thickening
1 small packet spring roll wrappers (50 pieces)

METHOD

1. Soak mushrooms in 225 ml (8 fl oz) hot water. Remove stalks and cut caps into thin slices. Reserve water for cooking.

2. Grate yambean using a coarse scraper. Rinse under cold water in a colander. Drain well. Using same scraper, grate carrot. Do not wash. Use scissors to cut the sweet soya bean strips into thin strips.

3. Heat 6 tablespoons peanut oil. Fry sweet bean strips till they blister and are slightly browned. Remove to a dish.

4. Reheat oil in pan. Saute 1 teaspoon ginger till light brown, adding preserved soya bean sauce to fry for short while. Add **A** (seasoning) and ½ of the water reserved. Stir till mixture boils, then put in the grated yambean and sweet soya bean curd strips. Cook for 10 minutes then add remaining water.

5. Put in carrots. Stir mixture and continue cooking till moist. Pour in thickening and stir well. Remove to a large plate to cool completely before making spring rolls.

To prepare spring rolls:

INGREDIENTS

2 tablespoons tapioca flour
2 tablespoons plain flour

METHOD

1. Mix 2 tablespoons each of tapioca flour and plain flour with 6 tablespoons water in a cup.

2. Scoop 2 tablespoons of filling on the lower half of the wrapper. Fold over to cover filling, fold sides, and roll wrapper to make spring roll. Seal with flour mixture. Repeat with remaining ingredients.

3. Heat oil for deep frying in an aluminium wok. Put in spring rolls a few at a time and fry till light brown. Remove to a steel colander to drain before putting on absorbent paper for a while. Serve hot with sweet chilli sauce.

VEGETARIAN BEEHOON

INGREDIENTS

225 g (8 oz) cabbage, thinly shredded
170 g (6 oz) french beans, cut diagonally   **A**
200 g (7 oz) carrots, grated

340 ml (12 fl oz) water
  1 level tablespoon salt
  2 tablespoons msg
  3 tablespoons sugar
  2 teaspoons dark soya sauce   **B**
  2 tablespoons light soya sauce
  1 teaspoon pepper
  2 teaspoons sesame oil

285 g (10 oz) rice vermicelli
170 ml (6 fl oz) peanut or corn oil
  Pinch of salt and sugar
  1 teaspoon each pounded garlic and ginger
  8 pieces sweet soya bean strips (tow kee), cut into thin slices
  6 dried Chinese mushrooms, soaked and thinly sliced
285 g (10 oz) prepared gluten (mock duck or mock abalone), thinly sliced
  4 tablespoons crispy shallots
  4 strips sweet soya bean strips, shredded, fried to a crisp
  4 tablespoons roasted sesame seeds

METHOD

1. Soak rice vermicelli in boiling water for 3 minutes. Drain and set aside for ½ hour.

2. In a heated iron wok, heat 2 tablespoons oil. Fry **A** separately for 1 minute each. Sprinkle water, a pinch of sugar and salt and a little oil for each vegetable. Set aside.

3. In the same wok, heat 4 tablespoons oil and fry garlic and ginger till light brown. Add sweet soya bean strips and Chinese mushrooms. Fry for 1 minute.

4. Add the sliced gluten and **B**. Allow to boil for 3 minutes.

5. Put in drained vermicelli and use fork to stir till gravy is absorbed. Add vegetables and stir well to mix evenly.

6. Garnish with crispy shallots and fried soya bean strips. Sprinkle with sesame seeds, pepper and sesame oil.

VEGETARIAN CURRY

INGREDIENTS

455 g (1 lb) cabbage, cut into bite-sized pieces
170 g (6 oz) long beans, cut into short lengths
  1 carrot, cut into bite-sized pieces
170 g (6 oz) cauliflower, cut into florets
170 g (6 oz) potatoes, cut into bite-sized pieces   **A**
115 g (4 oz) soya bean strips (foo chok)
  6 spongy fried soya bean cubes
  1 tin mock abalone, pour boiling water over and drain

455 g (1 lb) grated coconut
  6 tablespoons oil
115 g (4 oz) onions, sliced thinly
  2 cloves garlic, sliced thinly
  ½ thumb-sized piece ginger, sliced thinly
  1 tablespoon shrimp paste mixed in 4 tablespoons water
  4 tablespoons curry powder

Seasoning:
1 teaspoon salt
1 tablespoon sugar
1 teaspoon msg

METHOD

1. Squeeze coconut for No. 1 milk. Set aside. Add 570 ml (20 fl oz) water and squeeze for No. 2 milk. Set aside.

2. Heat oil in pan. Fry onions, garlic and ginger till lightly browned. Add shrimp paste and stir for a while.

3. Put in curry powder and ½ of No. 2 milk. Stir-fry till oil bubbles through. Add remaining No. 2 milk and bring to a boil. Put in all of **A** with seasoning and cook over moderate heat till vegetables are tender. Reduce heat to low, add No. 1 milk, stirring as you pour and cook for ½ minute. Remove from heat and serve.

Vegetarian Curry

Special Combinations
featuring dishes that are traditionally served together

Kuey Chap
Braised Belly Pork, Soya Bean Cakes and Eggs in Soya Sauce

Nasi Lemak
Crispy Anchovies with Sambal
Otak-Otak Rhio
Sambal Udang
Spicy Sambal Kangkong

Nasi Padang *(served with white rice)*
Beef Rendang
Cucumber Pickle
Sambal Telor
Spicy Fried Chicken

Nasi Lontong
Beef Serondeng
Sambal Goreng
Sayor Loday

Nasi Minyak
Achar
Dhal Char
Satay Ayam Panggang

Taiwan Porridge
Tow Yew Bak
Fried Anchovies and Groundnuts
Fried Salted Mustard
Steamed Minced Pork
Long Bean Omelette
Sweet and Spicy Fish
Threadfin fried with Soya Sauce and Pepper

Braised Belly Pork, Soya Bean Cakes and Eggs in Soya Sauce with Kuey Chap

BRAISED BELLY PORK, SOYA BEAN CAKES AND EGGS IN SOYA SAUCE

INGREDIENTS

4 large soya bean cakes, cut into small squares
2 tablespoons oil
2 tablespoons sugar
6 cloves garlic, lightly bashed

2 tablespoons light soya sauce
4 tablespoons dark soya sauce   **A**
225 ml (8 fl oz) boiling water
½ teaspoon salt

605 g (21 oz) belly pork, cut into pieces
10 hard-boiled eggs

METHOD

1. Immerse soya bean cakes in salted water for 5 minutes, drain and fry in a non-stick pan till lightly browned on all sides. Remove to a dish.

2. Heat a heavy-bottomed aluminium saucepan. Put in oil and sugar and leave till sugar turns a light golden brown. Add garlic, cook for a moment, add **A** and bring to the boil. Put in pork and cook briskly for about 20 minutes or till pork is well done.

3. Add eggs and leave to simmer for another ½ hour or till pork is tender. Add the fried soya bean cakes 10 minutes before the pork becomes tender and leave to simmer for 5 minutes. Serve hot.

Note:
Add small amounts of boiling water if gravy thickens before meat is tender.

Kuey Chap, a fatter smoother version of Kwayteow, can be bought from fresh noodle stalls at wet markets.

NASI LEMAK
(COCONUT MILK RICE)

INGREDIENTS

680 g (24 oz) No 1 Thai rice
625 g (22 oz) grated coconut, white
455 ml (16 fl oz) water
1½ teaspoons salt
6 screw pine leaves, tied into a knot

METHOD

1. Wash the rice and soak it in water for 2 hours. Drain before use.

2. Use a piece of muslin to squeeze 225 ml (8 fl oz) No. 1 milk from the grated coconut.

3. Add 455 ml water and squeeze for No. 2 milk. Measure, then add water to obtain 740 ml (26 fl oz) No. 2 milk.

4. Place rice in the rice cooker, stir in the No. 2 milk and the salt. Boil till rice is dry. Place the screw pine leaves on top and leave rice in the cooker for a further ½ hour.

5. Rake the rice with a fork, add the No. 1 milk and stir lightly to mix.

6. Leave the rice in the cooker to absorb the milk for another 20 minutes. Serve hot or cold.

Note:
Stir rice once or twice whilst boiling. Do not stir any more when the rice is dry. Stir again only when adding the No. 1 milk.

(10 servings)

Nasi Lemak

CRISPY ANCHOVIES WITH SAMBAL

INGREDIENTS

Sambal:
115 g (4 oz) dried chillies
1 clove garlic   **A**
115 g (4 oz) shallots *or* onions
55 g (2 oz) shrimp paste

170 g (6 oz) grated coconut
170 ml (6 fl oz) oil

4 level tablespoons sugar
¼ teaspoon salt
1 teaspoon msg   **B**
1 tablespoon tamarind, squeezed and
    strained with 4 tablespoons water

METHOD

1. Wash and soak dried chillies to soften. Grind or use electric blender to blend **A** to a fine paste.
2. Add 225 ml (8 fl oz) water to grated coconut and squeeze through muslin for milk.
3. Heat oil in aluminium wok and fry the chilli paste and one-third of the milk over moderate heat till oil bubbles through and smells fragrant.
4. Add **B**, stir and pour in the rest of the coconut milk. Lower heat and simmer for 2 minutes.

Anchovies:
1. Remove heads of 455 g (1 lb) medium sized anchovies. Wash and drain the anchovies.
2. Heat oil for deep frying till very hot. Put in the anchovies and fry over moderate heat to a light brown and to a crisp. Lower heat at the end of cooking time to prevent it from turning too dark. Remove anchovies to cool slightly on a paper towel and keep in container.
3. Mix in sambal when ready to serve.

OTAK-OTAK RHIO

INGREDIENTS

570 g (20 oz) grated coconut, white

85 g (3 oz) galangal, sliced
6 candlenuts
1 teaspoon shrimp paste   **A**
340 g (12 oz) shallots
30–40 g (1–1½ oz) dried chillies, cut into
    small pieces, soaked in warm water and
    drained

1.2 kg (2½ lb) spanish mackerel
Pinch of salt
6 tablespoons oil

4 teaspoons sugar
2 level teaspoons msg   *seasoning*
½ teaspoon pepper
2 level teaspoons salt

4 eggs
6 lime leaves, sliced finely
1 turmeric leaf, sliced finely
24 banana leaves (*daun pisang batu*), or heavy duty tin foil

METHOD

1. Squeeze grated coconut, without adding water, through a piece of muslin for No. 1 milk. Set aside.
2. Grind or use electric blender to blend **A** to a fine paste. Set aside.
3. Slit the fish right through lengthwise, and remove bones. Slice the meat from half the fish and set aside.
4. Pound or mince the other half of the fish until smooth, add a pinch of salt and 6 tablespoons of the coconut milk. Mix till well blended.
5. Heat an iron or aluminium wok and when hot, add 4 tablespoons oil and fry the paste over moderate heat till oil bubbles through and the paste is fragrant. Add seasoning and 12 tablespoons coconut milk, cooking over low heat till paste is almost dry. Stir frequently to prevent burning. Remove to a large plate to cool.

6. Into a large mixing bowl, put the minced fish, fried paste, eggs, sliced lime leaves, turmeric leaf and mix well. Lastly add the sliced fish and remaining oil. Stir lightly with a wooden spoon till well mixed. Cut 24 banana leaves into pieces, 21 cm × 22 cm (8 in × 8½ in).

7. Wash banana leaves and put into a saucepan of boiling water. Simmer for ½ minute to soften. Drain. Put 2–3 tablespoons of the fish mixture in the centre of each leaf, fold short ends of rectangle to cover mixture, then overlap left and right ends to form a neat square or oblong packet. Staple both ends of the leaf to seal before cooking.

To grill otak-otak:
Pre-heat grill and place the packets of otak-otak on a wire rack and grill for 5–7 minutes on each side. Leave to cool before serving.

To dry-fry otak-otak in an iron wok:
Heat an iron wok till hot. Place otak-otak side by side in the wok and cook over moderate heat for 5–6 minutes on each side. Serve cold.

Note:
Heavy duty tin foil is a good substitute for banana leaves.

SAMBAL UDANG
(PRAWNS IN HOT SPICY PASTE)

INGREDIENTS

605 g (21 oz) medium sized prawns, shelled and deveined
    Pinch of salt
½ teaspoon sugar
115 g (4 oz) frozen spicy paste, thawed (Page 186)
½ teaspoon salt
1 teaspoon sugar
½ teaspoon msg
1 teaspoon tamarind, mixed with 85 ml (3 fl oz) water and strained
115 g (4 oz) grated coconut squeezed to obtain 3 tablespoons No. 1 milk

METHOD

1. Season prawns with pinch of salt and ½ teaspoon sugar and set aside.

2. Heat an aluminium wok. Put in frozen spicy paste, and cook over low heat till oil bubbles through (½ minute).

3. Add the rest of the ingredients except the prawns and cook till mixture comes to the boil.

4. Add prawns and stir in pan till prawns are cooked, about 3-4 minutes. Serve hot or cold.

SPICY SAMBAL KANGKONG

INGREDIENTS

455 g (1 lb) water convolvulus (kangkong)
4 tablespoons lard or oil

3 fresh red chillies | *pounded to a fine paste*
1 tablespoon shrimp paste |

2 teaspoons sugar
    Pinch of salt
2 teaspoons pounded dried prawns

METHOD

1. Cut the water convolvulus into 7.5 cm (3 in) lengths, omitting the tough stalks and roots. Wash thoroughly and drain in a colander.

2. Heat an iron wok, put in 3 tablespoons oil to fry the chilli paste for half a minute. Add the water convolvulus, sugar, salt and dried prawns. Stir fry over high heat for 1 minute. Toss the water convolvulus in the wok to ensure that it is well cooked.

3. Add the remaining tablespoon of lard or oil, stir well and remove to a serving plate. Serve immediately.

BEEF RENDANG

INGREDIENTS

570 g (20 oz) coconut, white
605 g (21 oz) beef brisket or topside

1 teaspoon salt
½ teaspoon msg   **A**
2 teaspoons sugar
1½ teaspoons tamarind, remove seeds

1 turmeric leaf
2 lime leaves   **B**
1 stalk lemon grass, bashed
1 thick slice galangal

10 shallots
6 fresh red chillies
14 dried chillies
30 g (1 oz) ginger   **C** *ground to*
1 stalk lemon grass   *a fine paste*
2 thin slices galangal
2 cloves garlic
2 tablespoons fried coconut

1–1½ tablespoons palm sugar
1 level teaspoon salt
½ teaspoon pepper   **D**
½ teaspoon msg
2 teaspoons dark soya sauce

2 tablespoons oil
170–225 ml (6–8 fl oz) boiling water

METHOD

1. Dry-fry 115 g of the coconut till dark brown. Cool.
2. Season beef with **A** and dry coconut and leave for 2 hours.
3. Squeeze remaining coconut for No. 1 milk. Set aside. Add 225 ml water and squeeze for No. 2 milk. Set aside.
4. Combine **B**, **C** and **D** in a saucepan. Add No. 2 milk and bring to the boil. Add meat and boil, uncovered, over moderately high heat for 1 hour, stirring occasionally to prevent burning.
5. Add No. 1 milk and stir well. Reduce heat, cover pan and cook for ¾–1 hour till gravy mixture turns oily and fragrant.

CUCUMBER PICKLE

INGREDIENTS

To boil vegetables:
225 ml (8 fl oz) vinegar
225 ml (8 fl oz) water   **A**
2 tablespoons sugar

55 g (2 oz) shallots, sliced thinly
30 g (1 oz) garlic, sliced thinly   **B**
1 thumb-sized piece ginger, sliced thinly

1.8 kg (4 lb) cucumber
2 tablespoons salt
305 g (11 oz) shallots (choose tiny ones)

1 thumb-sized piece turmeric   **C** *ground to*
1 tablespoon shrimp paste   *a fine paste*

115 ml (4 fl oz) oil for frying paste
455 ml (16 fl oz) rice vinegar
225 ml (8 fl oz) water
Salt and sugar to taste
Toasted sesame seeds

METHOD

1. Wash cucumbers and quarter lengthwise. Remove cores and cut into 4 cm lengths. Then cut each piece into two, lengthwise. Rub with salt and leave overnight.
2. Rinse, squeeze lightly and dry. Place cucumber on a large bamboo tray to dry in the sun for 3–4 hours. Set aside.
3. Peel shallots and blanch in **A** for 1 minute. Drain well. Bring mixture to the boil again and blanch cucumber for 1 minute. Drain.
4. Fry **B** and **C** with oil over moderate heat till fragrant. Remove.
5. Put vinegar and water into an enamel saucepan and bring to a boil. Add salt and sugar to taste and boil over low heat for 5 minutes. Set aside and leave to cool completely.
6. Combine cucumber, shallots, **B** and **C** in a large bowl. Pour in the cooked vinegar.
7. Sprinkle with sesame seeds and store in bottles or porcelain jars for at least 2 days before serving.

Clockwise: Cucumber Pickle, Beef Rendang, Sambal Telor, Spicy Fried Chicken

SAMBAL TELOR

INGREDIENTS

10 hard-boiled eggs
140 g (5 oz) *chilli garam* paste★
1 level teaspoon sugar
¼ teaspoon msg
  A pinch of salt
4 tablespoons water
4 tablespoons No. 1 milk
  Oil for frying

METHOD

1. Shell boiled eggs and soak in slightly salted water for 20 minutes. Dry eggs on a tray.

2. Deep-fry the eggs in hot smoking oil till light brown, stirring in pan till surface of eggs is slightly blistered all over. Remove to a plate.

3. Remove oil from pan and fry thawed paste over low heat till oil bubbles through. Add the rest of the ingredients, stir well for 1 minute and pour over eggs. Serve hot or cold.

★See page 185.

SPICY FRIED CHICKEN

INGREDIENTS

1.14 kg (2½ lb) chicken, cut into pieces

2 thick stalks lemon grass, lightly bashed 2 thick slices galangal, lightly bashed 2 pieces dried tamarind 1 teaspoon salt 1 teaspoon sugar 1 teaspoon msg	**A**
2 cloves garlic ½ thumb-sized piece turmeric 7 candlenuts 7 shallots	**B** *pounded roughly*

METHOD

1. Season chicken with **A** and **B** and leave for 1 hour. Place chicken in a saucepan, add 225 ml (8 fl oz) boiling water and boil, covered, for 15–20 minutes, over moderately high heat. Stir occasionally.

2. Remove pan from heat and remove chicken to a large plate. Reserve gravy.

3. Heat oil and fry chicken till golden brown. Place fried chicken on a large serving plate. Remove some oil from pan leaving 4 tablespoons. Remove lemon grass and galangal from marinade. Cook marinade in the oil till almost dry. Pour over chicken and serve.

Note:
Use a small saucepan to cook the chicken so that it is completely immersed in the water. Add more water if needed. Water should come up to 2.5 cm (1 inch) above the level of the meat.

Nasi Lontong and Sambal Goreng

BEEF SERONDENG
(BEEF WITH FRIED GRATED COCONUT)

INGREDIENTS

6 slices galangal	
14 shallots	
4 tablespoons coriander seeds	
1 teaspoon cumin seeds	
4 slices ginger	**A**
3 cloves garlic	
2 slices turmeric	
1 teaspoon pepper	

565 g (20 oz) rump or Scotch steak, cut into pieces
6 tablespoons oil

1 tablespoon salt	
5 tablespoons sugar	
3 tablespoons grated palm sugar	**B**
55 g (2 oz) tamarind in 8 tablespoons water, squeezed and strained	

565 g (20 oz) coconut, white, coarsely grated

METHOD

1. Pound **A** to a paste.
2. Let beef pieces simmer in 115 ml (4 fl oz) water and one-third of paste till tender and almost dry.
3. Heat 4 tablespoons oil, stir-fry remaining paste till fragrant. Add **B**, stir-fry for a minute and remove to a dish. Rub fried paste into the grated coconut.
4. Heat 2 tablespoons oil in a pan. Add the coconut mixture and the beef. Stir-fry over a low heat till moist and fragrant. Keep stirring constantly to prevent the coconut from burning.

NASI LONTONG
(COMPRESSED RICE CAKES)

INGREDIENTS

625 g (22 oz) No. 1 Thai rice

½ teaspoon salt
6 screw pine leaves, tied into a knot

METHOD

1. Wash and soak the rice overnight. Drain before use.
2. Wet two 10 cm × 20 cm (4 in × 8 in) cloth bags and fill each with half the rice. Stitch to seal the open end.
3. Boil 1.2 litres (2 pints) water in a heavy-bottomed aluminium saucepan. Add salt and screw pine leaves.
4. Place the cloth bags in the saucepan. The water should be 8 cm (3 in) above the bags. Add boiling water when necessary. Boil for 2 hours and remove.
5. Wrap the bags with a dry towel and place a bread board and a weight on top. Leave until the rice is firm and cold, at least 8–10 hours.
6. Unstitch the bags to remove the rice. Cut into long strips with a wet knife and again into thin squares, using a thick white thread.

(10 servings)

Note:
It is best to cook the rice in the evening and leave it pressed overnight.

Place an enamel plate in the saucepan before putting in the bag of rice to prevent it from sticking to the pan.

SAMBAL GORENG

INGREDIENTS

225 g (8 oz) beef liver, cubed
½ teaspoon salt
½ teaspoon msg
285 g (10 oz) grated coconut, white

    Oil for frying

55 g shallots or onions, sliced thinly ⎤
4 slices garlic, sliced thinly   ⎬ **A**
3 red chillies, seeded, sliced thinly ⎦

1 thick piece galangal, bashed (pounded finely)

1 teaspoon shrimp paste ⎤ **B** *pounded*
6 dried chillies   ⎦   *finely*

285 g (10 oz) small prawns, shelled and cleaned
2 large pieces soya bean cake, cut into small cubes, fried
2 packets *tempe*, cut into small pieces, fried

METHOD

1. Marinate beef liver with salt and msg.
2. Squeeze grated coconut for No. 1 milk. Set aside. Add 170 ml (6 fl oz) water and squeeze for No. 2 milk. Set aside.
3. Heat oil in an aluminium kuali. Fry **A** separately till light golden brown. Remove to a plate.
4. Pour oil from pan, leaving 3 tablespoons to fry liver for 5–6 minutes till liver is cooked. Remove to a plate.
5. In a clean pan, heat 2 tablespoons oil to fry bashed galangal for 1 minute. Add **B** and fry over moderate heat for another minute.
6. Add half of No. 1 milk and stir till it comes to a boil. Put in prawns, soya bean cake, liver and *tempe*. Cook over low heat for 2 minutes.
7. Pour in No. 2 milk and cook for 5 minutes then pour in No. 1 milk and fried ingredients **A**. Stir to mix well and simmer till gravy coats ingredients and is almost dry. Serve hot or cold.

SAYOR LODAY
(MIXED VEGETABLES IN SPICY COCONUT GRAVY)

INGREDIENTS

625 g (21 oz) grated coconut
6 soya bean cakes, cut into quarters and fried
310 g (11 oz) green egg-plants, cut into wedges and soaked in salt water. Drain before use.
    Oil
2 cloves garlic, thinly sliced
8 shallots, thinly sliced
2 tablespoons chilli paste

115 g (4 oz) shallots ⎤
1 clove garlic   ⎮
1½ tablespoons shrimp paste ⎮
½ thumb-sized piece turmeric ⎬ **A**
2 candlenuts   ⎮
5 dried chillies or 1 tablespoon paste ⎦

625 g (21 oz) cabbage, cut into small pieces ⎤
625 g (21 oz) long beans, cut into short lengths ⎬ **B**
310 g (11 oz) Chinese turnip, cut into thick short strips ⎮
4 tablespoons dried prawns, pounded finely ⎦

1 tablespoon salt ⎤
3 tablespoons sugar ⎬ **C**
1 teaspoon msg ⎦

METHOD

1. Pound **A** to a fine paste.
2. Add 225 ml (8 fl oz) water to the grated coconut and squeeze for No. 1 milk.
3. Add another 2 litres (4 pints) water to the grated coconut and squeeze again for No. 2 milk. Pour into a saucepan. Add **A**, **B** and **C** and bring to the boil.
4. Boil gently for ½ hour, add the fried soya bean cakes and egg-plants and cook for another 5–7 minutes. Remove from heat.
5. Heat 6 tablespoons oil and fry the sliced garlic and shallots till light brown.
6. Add chilli paste and stir-fry for ½ minute. Pour in the No. 1 milk and keep stirring till it comes to a boil. Add boiled vegetables and stir for another 2–3 minutes.

ACHAR
(MIXED VEGETABLE PICKLE)

INGREDIENTS

3.8 kg (8¼ lb) cucumbers
140 g (5 oz) salt
20 green chillies
20 red chillies
1 teaspoon lime paste

310 g (11 oz) shallots
55 g (2 oz) turmeric
30–40 dried chillies or 6–8 tablespoons chilli | **A**
   paste
5 red chillies

570 ml (20 fl oz) oil
1 thumb-sized piece ginger, thinly shredded

570 ml (20 fl oz) rice vinegar
570 ml (20 fl oz) water | **B**
455 g (16 oz) sugar
4 tablespoons salt

900 ml (32 fl oz) water
900 ml (32 fl oz) vinegar | **C**
2 tablespoons sugar
2 tablespoon salt

795 g (28 oz) cauliflower, cut into florets
2 carrots, peeled and cut into strips
935 g (2 lb) cabbage, cut into small pieces
455 g (1 lb) roasted peanuts, pounded
8 tablespoons roasted sesame seeds

METHOD

1. Wash the cucumbers and cut off the ends. Halve each cucumber lengthwise and cut into two or three pieces lengthwise. (Remove the seeds and soft centres.)

2. Cut again into 5 cm (2 in) lengths. Make a slit half-way down each piece.

3. Place the cucumber strips in a basin, sprinkle the salt, mix well and leave to season for 4–5 hours. Rinse, drain and squeeze in handfuls, using a piece of muslin. Set aside.

4. Slit the centre of the chillies to remove the seeds. Soak the chillies in a bowl of water with 1 teaspoon lime paste for 2–3 hours. Drain in a colander. (Do not wash after soaking in lime water.) Stuff chillies (see instructions.)

5. Pound **A** to a fine paste.

6. Heat oil in wok to fry the shredded ginger till light brown.

7. Add the paste (Method 5) and stir-fry till fragrant and oil comes up to the surface.

8. Add **B** and bring to the boil. Boil for a minute and remove to a bowl to cool completely.

9. Boil **C** rapidly and blanch the cucumbers, cauliflower, carrots and cabbage separately. Spread out to cool on large trays.

10. Heat an iron wok and stir-fry the vegetables separately for ½ minute with a little oil from the vinegar mixture. Spread on trays to cool.

To mix the pickle:
Place the fried vegetables, paste, pounded nuts, and sesame seeds in a large mixing bowl. Mix well and add the stuffed chillies. Leave overnight. Store in dry, clean bottles.

To stuff chillies:
5 candlenuts
10 shallots | **A**
1 teaspoon shrimp paste

225 ml (8 fl oz) oil
¼ teaspoon salt
2 tablespoons sugar
225 g (½ lb) dried prawns, pounded finely

1 medium-sized green papaya, skinned, finely grated and dried in the sun [optional]

METHOD

1. Pound **A**.

2. Pour oil into a heated frying pan. Stir-fry the pounded paste till fragrant.

3. Stir in the salt and sugar.

4. Add the dried prawns and papaya and stir till well mixed. Fry for 5 minutes over a low heat. Cool on a tray before stuffing the chillies.

Note:
1. *Bring the vinegar water back to a rapid boil each time to blanch the vegetables. Spread the vegetables to cool to keep them crunchy.*

2. *Lime paste here refers to the white chalky edible lime that is used by betel-nut chewers. It can be bought from any Indian grocer. The crispness of the chillies can only be obtained by soaking them in the 'lime' water.*

Clockwise: Satay Ayam Panggang, Achar, Dhal Char, Nasi Minyak

DHAL CHAR

(MUTTON RIBS WITH VEGETABLES IN SPICY GRAVY)

INGREDIENTS

285 g (10 oz) mutton ribs, cut into small pieces

½ teaspoon salt
½ teaspoon pepper   **A**
½ teaspoon msg
1 teaspoon ginger juice

285 g (10 oz) grated coconut
170 g (6 oz) lentils, washed and soaked for ½ hour
 6 tablespoons oil

½ thumb-sized piece ginger, thinly shredded
2 cloves garlic, thinly shredded   **B**
8 shallots or 1 small onion, thinly sliced

2 teaspoons curry powder
½ tablespoon cumin seeds   **C**
½ tablespoon aniseed

Seasoning for gravy:
1–1½ teaspoons salt
  1 teaspoon msg
  1 teaspoon sugar

115 g (4 oz) long beans, cut into 2.5 cm lengths
 3 brinjals, cut into pieces
 6 green chillies, slit halfway lengthwise
 3 red chillies, slit halfway lengthwise
55 g (2 oz) onions, thinly sliced

 5 cm (2 in) length cinnamon bark
 2 segments star anise
10 cardamoms, lightly bashed   **D**
 6 cloves
 1 sprig curry leaves

 1 tablespoon tamarind, mixed with
 4 tablespoons water, strained

METHOD

1. Marinate ribs with ingredients **A** for ½ hour.
2. Squeeze coconut for No.1 milk in a bowl. Set aside. Add 340 ml (12 fl oz) water to coconut and squeeze for No. 2 milk. Set aside.
3. Boil mutton ribs with 340 ml (12 fl oz) water for 1–1½ hours or till tender. Add 225 ml (8 fl oz) water and the lentils and continue boiling over low heat till lentils are tender. Set aside.
4. Heat 3 tablespoons oil in wok and fry **B** till lightly browned, add **C** and stir for a moment only. Pour in the No. 2 milk and gravy seasoning and bring to the boil. Put in the long beans and cook for 5 minutes, then add the long beans, brinjals and the chillies and continue cooking over moderate heat till vegetables are tender. Set aside.
5. Heat 3 tablespoons oil and fry the sliced onions till lightly browned, add **D** and fry for ½ minute. Remove to a bowl.
6. Bring mutton ribs to the boil, add ingredients from Methods 4 and 5. Add No. 1 milk, and boil for 2 minutes. Lastly add the tamarind water, simmer for 5 minutes. Remove from heat.

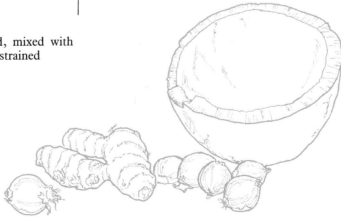

NASI MINYAK
(GHEE RICE)

INGREDIENTS

605 g (21 oz) briani rice
140 g (5 oz) white ghee

55 g (2 oz) onions, thinly sliced
1 cinnamon bark, 8 cm (3 in) long **A**
6 cloves
15 cardamoms, lightly bashed

1 tablespoon chopped ginger
1 tablespoon chopped garlic

850 ml (30 fl oz) boiling water
4 drops rose essence **B**
170 ml (6 fl oz) fresh milk
1½ teaspoons salt

2 tablespoons crispy shallots★

METHOD

1. Wash and drain rice.

2. Heat ghee in a non-stick or aluminium wok and fry **A** till onions turn light brown. Add ginger and garlic and stir-fry for 1 minute or until it turns light brown.

3. Add the rice; stir in pan for 1 minute, bring **B** to nearly boiling point in a saucepan and pour into pan to cook with the rice, then transfer to a rice cooker. Loosen rice when cooked and remove from heat. Sprinkle crispy shallots over rice. Serve hot.

★*See "Helpful Hints".*

SATAY AYAM PANGGANG

INGREDIENTS

1 chicken, 1.14 kg (2½ lb)

55 g (2 oz) shallots or onions
1 teaspoon shrimp paste
10 dried chillies
2 fresh red chillies, seeded **A**
3 stalks lemon grass, thinly sliced
4 slices galangal
1 candlenut

2 tablespoons sugar
1 level teaspoon salt
1 teaspoon msg
¼ teaspoon pepper
170 g (6 oz) grated coconut, squeezed for **B**
85 ml (3 fl oz) No. 1 milk
½ teaspoon dark soya sauce
1 teaspoon lime juice
1 teaspoon coriander powder
1 tablespoon oil

4 lime leaves, thinly sliced
2 tablespoons oil with 1 tablespoon water for basting

METHOD

1. Cut chicken from the breast downwards. Use blunt end of cleaver or chopper and crack backbone and thigh bones to flatten.

2. Grind or blend **A** to a fine paste. Blend **B** to a paste in a bowl and mix well with the lime leaves and **A**.

3. With a fork, pierce chicken breast and thighs and rub the mixture all over the chicken. Leave to marinate for 1 hour.

4. Heat grill to high and grill chicken in pan till nicely browned on both sides. Baste with oil-and-water mixture to keep chicken moist. Remove from grill, cool for a while before cutting into pieces. Serve with sliced cucumber.

Note:
Line pan with tin foil to prevent the juices from burning. Pour juices over chicken before serving.

TOW YEW BAK

(STREAKY BELLY PORK IN SOYA SAUCE)

INGREDIENTS

455 g (1 lb) streaky belly pork
½ teaspoon salt
 1 tablespoon dark soya sauce
 2 tablespoons lard or oil
 2 tablespoons sugar
 2 pips star anise
 2 cloves garlic, lightly bashed
 2 tablespoons light soya sauce
½ teaspoon msg
230 ml (8 fl oz) boiling water

METHOD

1. Scrape pork skin of bristles; wash and drain. Rub salt and dark soya sauce into pork and leave for ½ hour.

2. Heat a heavy bottom aluminium saucepan with lard to fry sugar till light golden, add star anise and garlic, fry for 1 minute. Put in the pork, light soya sauce and msg and continue cooking for 2 minutes.

3. Turn pork over to cook the other side, pour in half of the boiling water and boil over moderately high heat for ½ hour. Add remaining water, cover saucepan and cook over low heat for ¾ hour or till pork is tender. Remove from heat.

To serve:
Lift pork onto a chopping board to cut into slices, place on a deep plate and pour gravy over.

FRIED ANCHOVIES AND GROUNDNUTS

INGREDIENTS

225 g (8 oz) groundnuts
225 g (8 oz) anchovies
Oil for frying

METHOD

1. Remove head of anchovies, wash, drain and leave in colander for ½ hour before frying.

2. Heat about 570 ml (20 fl oz) cooking oil and deep-fry the groundnuts over moderate heat till nuts turn light brown. Scoop out to drain on absorbent paper and leave to cool slightly. Keep in an airtight container till ready to serve.

3. Re-heat oil in pan till hot and fry the anchovies over moderate heat for 5–7 minutes. Reduce heat to low and continue frying, stirring frequently till anchovies are light brown and crispy. To test if anchovies are cooked and will remain crisp, put a few pieces on absorbent paper. Break fish when slightly cooled and test for crispness. If the centre is not crunchy, fry a few minutes more over very low heat. Drain fish in a metal colander and place on absorbent paper to cool. Keep in airtight container till ready to serve.

4. Combine anchovies and fried groundnuts on a plate and serve.

Taiwan Porridge

FRIED SALTED MUSTARD WITH MINCED PORK AND TOMATOES

INGREDIENTS

285 g (10 oz) salted mustard
  4 tablespoons lard *or* oil
  ½ thumb-sized piece ginger, shredded finely
  1 teaspoon pounded garlic
  1 teaspoon preserved soya beans, pounded
170 g (6 oz) minced pork
  2 teaspoons sugar
  ½ teaspoon msg
115 ml (4 fl oz) water
  2 tomatoes, cut into wedges
  ½ chicken cube

METHOD

1. Slice mustard finely and soak in water for 5 minutes. Drain and squeeze hard. Set aside.

2. Heat 1 tablespoon oil in an iron wok and stir-fry the mustard till limp (3 to 4 minutes). Remove.

3. In the same pan, heat the rest of the oil and lightly brown the ginger and garlic. Add the preserved soya beans, minced pork, sugar, msg and half of the water and fry till fragrant. Put in the mustard, tomatoes, the rest of the water, and the chicken cube and cook over low heat for 20 minutes. Add a little water if gravy is greatly reduced. Remove to a dish. Serve hot or cold.

STEAMED MINCED PORK WITH PRESERVED BLACK BEANS AND PENANG SALTED FISH

INGREDIENTS

55 g (2 oz) Penang salted fish, cut into strips
285 g (10 oz) lean pork with a little fat, minced

  4 tablespoons water
  ½ teaspoon msg
  ¼ teaspoon sugar   **A**
  1 teaspoon oil

  2 tablespoons preserved black beans
  ½ thumb-sized piece ginger, cut into strips

METHOD

1. Soak salted fish for ½ minute. Drain.

2. Combine pork with **A**, add the black beans, ginger and mix well. Place meat mixture on a shallow enamel plate, put salted fish on top and steam for 10–15 minutes or till pork is well cooked.

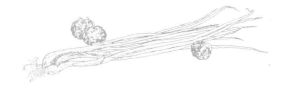

LONG BEAN OMELETTE

INGREDIENTS

115 g (4 oz) long beans, cut into very fine rounds
  1 tablespoon oil
  4 large eggs
55 g (2 oz) minced pork
55 g (2 oz) minced prawns
  4 tablespoons chopped salted preserved radish
  ½ teaspoon msg
  ¼ teaspoon salt
    Dash of pepper
    Lard *or* oil

METHOD

1. Fry the long beans in a tablespoon of oil for ½ minute. Set aside.

2. Break eggs into a large bowl, beat lightly. Add the long beans and the rest of the ingredients and beat till well mixed.

3. Heat a frying pan and pour enough oil to fry the omelette till light golden brown on both sides. Serve hot or cold.

SWEET AND SPICY FISH

INGREDIENTS

455 g (1 lb) fish tail, Tenggiri or Snapper
  1 teaspoon salt

  3 cloves garlic, chopped finely
½ thumb-sized piece ginger, thinly sliced | **A**

  1 red chilli, seeded, sliced thinly
    lengthwise
  2 sprigs coriander, cut into pieces | **B**

150 ml fish sauce
1½ teaspoon tapioca or cornflour | **C**

To cook fish sauce:
150 ml Best Quality Thai Fish Sauce
450 ml water
 10 tablespoons sugar
  5 tablespoons vinegar | **D**
  1 teaspoon salt
  1 teaspoon dark soya sauce
  8 tablespoons lemon juice

  1 carrot, thinly shredded
  8 cloves garlic, chopped coarsely
  2 red chillies, seeded and coarsely | **E**
    chopped

Boil **D** till sugar is dissolved. Add in **E**, boil for another minute. Remove to a large bowl to cool. Keep in a dry bottle to store in fridge for future use.

METHOD

1. Remove bone from fish, rub 1 teaspoon salt both sides and let stand for ½ hour.

2. Fry fish with 4 tablespoons oil in a non-stick wok till light golden brown on both sides. Remove to a serving plate. Keep warm.

3. In the same pan, put in **A**, stir-fry for ½ minute. Reduce heat, stir in **C** mixture, pour into pan and bring to boil. Pour sauce over fish and garnish with **B**. Serve hot.

Note:
Any type of fish fillet can be used, preferably the tail end.

THREADFIN FRIED WITH SOYA SAUCE AND PEPPER

INGREDIENTS

395 g (14 oz) threadfin

  3 tablespoons dark soya sauce
  2 tablespoons light soya sauce
  1 tablespoon sugar
 ½ teaspoon msg | **A**
 ½ teaspoon pepper

  3 tablespoons oil and 3 tablespoons lard
  4 tablespoons water

METHOD

1. Wash and drain threadfin.

2. Marinate fish in **A** for ½ hour.

3. Heat oil in a non-stick wok and fry the fish over moderate heat till brown. Reserve the marinade. Turn fish over, cover pan and cook till fish is done. Remove lid, pour in the marinade and the 4 tablespoons water and cook for ½ minute. Remove to a serving plate. Serve hot or cold.

CHICKEN CURRY

INGREDIENTS

1.6kg (3½ lb) chicken cut into pieces

10 cloves garlic
1 thumb-sized piece ginger
¼ thumb-sized piece turmeric
2 tablespoons curry powder mixed
   with 4 tablespoons water

A *pounded to a fine paste*

1 teaspoon salt
1 teaspoon msg
115 g (4 oz) grated coconut

1 heaped tablespoon cumin seeds *or*
¾ tablespoon cumin powder
1 heaped tablespoon poppy seeds
   (optional)
8 cashew nuts
8 almonds

B *ground to a fine paste*

115 ml (4 fl oz) oil
285 g (10 oz) shallots, thinly sliced
8–10 dried chillies, ground to a paste
1 stalk curry leaves

Seasoning:
¾–1 teaspoon salt
1 teaspoon msg

METHOD

1. Season chicken with **A**, salt, and msg and leave for ½ hour.

2. Add 225 ml (8 fl oz) water to coconut and squeeze milk into a bowl. Mix well with **B**.

3. Heat the oil in an aluminium wok and fry three-quarters of the sliced shallots till light golden brown. Lower heat, add chilli paste, curry leaves and fry till oil turns red.

4. Add the chicken, stir well, reduce heat to moderate and cook for ½ hour with lid on. Do not uncover whilst the chicken is cooking.

5. Remove the lid, add the rest of the sliced shallots, the seasoning and the milk mixture. Stir, bring to the boil, reduce heat and simmer for another 15–20 minutes or till chicken is tender.

ROTI JALA

INGREDIENTS

225 ml (8 fl oz) milk
2 eggs
Pinch of salt
1 tablespoon oil

A

115 g (4 oz) plain flour, sifted
Non-stick frying pan or electric skillet
Lacy pancake maker

METHOD

1. Combine **A** in a bowl and beat with fork till well blended.

2. Sift flour into a mixing bowl. Add egg mixture in centre of flour and stir till batter is smooth. Strain batter through a nylon sieve to remove lumps. Set aside for 15 minutes.

3. Lightly heat a non-stick frying pan or skillet. Grease lightly with oil and run the batter in a lacy pattern into the pan from the pancake maker. Cook for ½ minute or till batter changes colour. With a spatula, fold the pancake whilst still in pan.

4. Fry till all the batter is used up. Place the folded pancakes on top of one another and cover with a tea towel or tin foil to prevent drying. Serve hot or cold with Chicken Curry.

Chicken Curry and Roti Jala

Dim Sum

Bak Pow

Char Siew Pow

Fried Wan Tan

Har Kow

Hum Sui Kok

Kee Chang

Prawn Fritters

Kuey Chang Babi

Siew Mai

Steamed Beef Balls

Stuffed Mushrooms

Yam Puff

Tan Tart

Clockwise: Yam Puffs, Har Kow, Prawn Fritters, Fried Wan Tan

BAK POW
(MEAT BUNS)

INGREDIENTS

Filling:
1.2 kg (42 oz) pork, cut into thin pieces
2 pairs Chinese sausages, cut into small
  pieces

Marinade:
2 teaspoons dark soya sauce
1 teaspoon light soya sauce
2 teaspoons oyster sauce
1 teaspoon pepper
1½ level teaspoons salt
4 heaped teaspoons sugar
1 teaspoon sesame oil
4 tablespoons peanut butter
3 tablespoons cornstarch *or* corn flour
2 tablespoons lard
2 teaspoons msg
1 teaspoon coarsely chopped spring onions

METHOD

Place pork slices and Chinese sausages in a
bowl. Add the marinade and mix well and
allow to rest for 1 hour before filling.

Making The Bun:

INGREDIENTS

2 tablespoons baking powder
455 g (1 lb) self-raising flour
85 g (3 oz) castor sugar
200 ml (7 fl oz) hot water
55 g (2 oz) lard

METHOD

1. Put flour in a bowl, make a well in the
   centre and put in the sugar.
2. Pour in the hot water and stir to dissolve
   the sugar.
3. Bring in half of the flour from the sides to
   mix with the sugar. Rub in the rest of the
   flour with the lard and mix till well
   blended. Leave to stand for 15 minutes.

CHAR SIEW POW
(STEAMED ROAST PORK BUNS)

INGREDIENTS

Filling:
285 g (10 oz) roast pork strips (*char siew*)
2 tablespoons lard or oil
2 cloves garlic, chopped finely
55 g (2 oz) onions, chopped finely

5 teaspoons sugar
½ teaspoon pepper
1 teaspoon sesame oil   **A** *mixed together*
1 teaspoon dark soya sauce
1 teaspoon light soya sauce
115 ml (4 fl oz) water

1 heaped tablespoon plain flour mixed with
  2 tablespoons oil

METHOD

1. Cut roast pork into very small cubes. Heat
   oil in frying pan to fry garlic till light
   brown, add chopped onions and cook till
   transparent. Pour in **A** and bring to boil
   over medium heat.
2. Put in the roast pork, stir for a moment and
   add flour and oil mixture. Mix well, cook
   for ½ minute and remove to a plate to cool.
   Chill in fridge before filling.

4. Divide dough into 3 parts and cut each into
   8 pieces, about the size of a small egg.
5. Roll each piece into a ball, press to flatten,
   place filling and seal by pleating the edge.
   Put bun on a square piece of grease-proof
   paper and leave for 10 minutes in a warm
   place. Steam over rapidly boiling water for
   10 minutes. Do not lift lid whilst steaming.
   Serve hot.

FRIED WAN TAN
(FRIED MEAT DUMPLINGS)

INGREDIENTS

½ teaspoon sesame oil
½ teaspoon salt
½ teaspoon sugar
 1 teaspoon light soya sauce
   Dash of pepper   **A**
½ teaspoon msg
 1 tablespoon oil
½ egg yolk

170 g (6 oz) minced lean pork, with some fat
 55 g (2 oz) minced prawn meat
20–30 dumpling (*wan tan*) skins
    Oil for deep frying

METHOD

1. Put **A** in a bowl and stir well. Add minced pork and prawns and, using chopsticks, mix till well blended.

2. Place 1 teaspoon of meat mixture on one corner of skin, fold and roll to centre of skin. Wet the two ends, twist the folded meat and press the ends together to seal. Repeat with the rest of the meat. Place dumplings apart on a large tray to retain its shape.

3. Heat oil for deep frying in an aluminium wok or small saucepan. Put in as many dumplings as possible, leaving space for skin to expand whilst frying, and fry to a light golden colour. Scoop out gently with a large wire mesh ladle and drain on absorbent paper. Serve while hot and crunchy.

Note:
Dumpling skins are sold in different sizes in most markets. For fried dumplings, select the small thin skins.

HAR KOW
(STEAMED SHRIMP DUMPLINGS)

INGREDIENTS

Skin:
170 g (6 oz) non-glutinous flour
 1 teaspoon salt   **A**
 1 teaspoon msg

170 ml (6 fl oz) boiling water
 30 ml (1 fl oz) cold water
 1 tablespoon lard

Pour boiling water over **A**, add cold water, lard and mix well in a bowl. Knead.

Filling:
 2 tablespoons lard
 55 g (2 oz) pork, finely minced
225 g (8 oz) prawn meat, cut into big pieces
 30 g (1 oz) boiled pork fat, chopped finely
½ teaspoon sugar
½ teaspoon msg
½ teaspoon sesame oil
¼ teaspoon pepper
 2 teaspoons light soya sauce
 1 tablespoon corn flour
 1 tablespoon ginger juice
 4 tablespoons finely chopped bamboo shoots
 1 teaspoon sherry

METHOD

1. Fry pork and prawn with lard for ½ minute. Remove to a bowl, add the rest of the ingredients, mix well and chill in refrigerator.

2. Roll dough into a thin log and cut into 35 pieces. Cover with damp cloth. Flatten each piece and spoon 1–1½ teaspoons filling in centre and fold. Seal by pleating from underside of dough to form a neat pouch.

3. Place on greased tin and steam over rapidly boiling water for 6–8 minutes. Serve hot.

HUM SUI KOK
(CHINESE CURRY PUFFS)

INGREDIENTS

Filling:
    1 tablespoon oil
115 g (4 oz) lean pork, diced
115 g (4 oz) prawn meat, diced
 55 g (2 oz) pork fat, boiled and diced
 55 g (2 oz) roast pork, diced
    2 tablespoons dried prawns, diced
    8 water chestnuts, diced

Seasoning:
    ½ teaspoon salt
    1 teaspoon msg
 1½ teaspoons sugar
    2 teaspoons dark soya sauce   **A**
    1 teaspoon sesame oil
Dash of pepper
115 ml (4 fl oz) water

    1 tablespoon oil blended with 1 tablespoon plain
    flour (thickening)

Heat 1 tablespoon oil and fry pork for ½ minute, add the prawns and the rest of the ingredients, and then the seasoning **A**. Cook till sauce is almost dry, add the thickening, stir well and remove to a dish to cool.

Pastry:
115 g (4 oz) non-glutinous flour
115 g (4 oz) castor sugar
255 g (9 oz) glutinous rice flour mixed with 225 ml
    (8 fl oz) water
115 g (4 oz) glutinous rice flour
115 g (4 oz) lard
 55 g (2 oz) sesame seeds

METHOD

1. Mix 170 ml (6 oz) boiling water with the non-glutinous flour in a large basin, stir with chopstick, cover with cloth and leave for 5 minutes.

2. Knead the dough for 1 minute, add the sugar, the wet glutinous rice flour and knead well for 3 minutes. Add the glutinous rice flour and the fat and knead again till smooth.

3. Roll dough into a cylindrical shape, cut into equal parts — the size of a small egg — and set aside. Flatten each part into an oval, put filling in centre, fold and seal by pressing the edges of dough together. Brush dough lightly with water, roll in sesame seeds and deep fry in hot oil till light golden brown. Remove and leave to drain on absorbent paper. Serve hot.

Note:
Ground roasted groundnuts mixed with sugar and roasted sesame seeds, or grated coconut cooked with palm sugar can also be used for the filling.

KEE CHANG
(GLUTINOUS RICE DUMPLINGS)

INGREDIENTS

1.2 kg (42 oz) glutinous rice, remove transparent
    grains
    1 teaspoon salt
    4 tablespoons alkaline water⋆
   60 bamboo leaves (fresh or dry), washed and
    drained
40–50 long strands of straw for tying (to be soaked
    overnight and tied together in equal lengths)

    1 teaspoon salt
    1 teaspoon *pheng say* (available at Chinese   **A**
    medicine shops)

METHOD

1. Wash glutinous rice till water runs clear. Drain. Put the glutinous rice in a porcelain container, add 1 teaspoon salt and 2 tablespoons of alkaline water, mix well and add water to cover up to 2.5 cm (1 in) above level of glutinous rice. Soak overnight or for 12 hours at least.

2. Drain the glutinous rice in a colander. Transfer to an enamel or porcelain basin and pour in the rest of the alkaline water. Mix well by hand so that the alkaline water and the glutinous rice are evenly mixed. Set aside for ½ hour.

To wrap and boil the dumplings:

1. Take 1 broad long leaf or 2 narrow leaves and fold into a cone. Put in 3 tablespoons glutinous rice. Fold the leaf over the rice to form a triangular shape. Use straw to tie securely around the dumpling. Tie dumplings in groups of 20.

2. Fill half a large saucepan with water and bring it to a rapid boil over high heat.

3. Add **A**. Put in the dumplings and boil for 3–4 hours. To test whether dumplings are cooked, unwrap one after 3 hours, cut into half and see whether the glutinous rice is smooth to the touch. The number of hours in boiling depends on the size of the bundles of dumplings.

4. When dumplings are cooked, remove from saucepan, cut off protruding leaves and tie into neat bundles of 10. Leave to hang till cool. Remove leaves and cut dumplings into thin slices. Serve with screw pine flavoured syrup made by boiling sugar and water with screw pine leaves till fairly thick or with coarsely grated young coconut and palm sugar syrup.

To boil the syrup:

Grate the palm sugar, add sugar, water, screw pine leaves and boil in a saucepan for 10 minutes till syrup is fairly thick.

Note:
Add boiling water if water in saucepan evaporates. Boil over moderately high heat throughout.

When using dried bamboo leaves, soak them overnight in cold water, then boil in a basin or wok for 15 minutes. Drain. Adding phreng say and salt to the boiling water prevents the leaves from sticking to the dumplings.

Cool dumplings for at least 8–10 hours so that they will be firm before cutting into pieces to serve.

*See page 199.

PRAWN FRITTERS

INGREDIENTS

10 large prawns
 1 tablespoon ginger juice
   Pinch of salt
   Dash of pepper

70 g (2½ oz) self-raising flour
 1 teaspoon Bird's eye custard powder
   Pinch of salt   **A**
 ½ teaspoon bicarbonate of soda
70 ml (2½ fl oz) water
 1 tablespoon oil

1.14 litres (2 pints) oil for deep-frying
Cucumber
Tomatoes

METHOD

1. Shell prawns, leaving tail unshelled. Slit prawns halfway lengthwise and remove dark veins. Season with 1 tablespoon ginger juice, a pinch of salt and a dash of pepper. Set aside.

2. Combine **A** in a bowl and mix till well blended. Stand for 5 minutes.

3. Heat oil in an aluminium wok. Dip each prawn into batter and fry till light golden brown. Remove to absorbent paper to drain oil and place on a serving dish. Arrange cucumber and tomato slices around edge of plate and serve.

KUEH CHANG BABI
GLUTINOUS RICE DUMPLING

INGREDIENTS

2.1 kg (4.5 lb) glutinous rice
3 tablespoons salt
510 ml (18 fl oz) water
3 level teaspoons pepper
425 g (15 oz) lard
30–35 large screw pine leaves (8 cm × 55 cm)

Filling Ingredients:
1.2 kg (2.5 lb) lean pork
115 g (4 oz) pork fat
55 g (2 oz) dried Chinese mushrooms
225 g (8 oz) preserved sugared winter melon
200 ml (7 fl oz) lard or oil
55 g (2 oz) garlic, pounded finely
225 g (8 oz) shallots, pounded finely
1 rounded teaspoon salt
395 g (14 oz) sugar
2 tablespoons pepper
4 tablespoons dark soya sauce
6 tablespoons roasted ground coriander seeds

METHOD

To Prepare Rice:

1. Soak glutinous rice overnight. Drain and divide into three parts. Steam each part over rapidly boiling water for 20 minutes. Make steam holes before steaming.

2. Remove glutinous rice to a saucepan. Dissolve 1 tablespoon salt in 170 ml (6 fl oz) of water. Add 1 teaspoon pepper and pour around the steamed glutinous rice. Mix well. Cover for 10 minutes and mix lard evenly with rice. Keep warm in a saucepan with a tight fitting lid. Repeat with remaining glutinous rice.

To Prepare Filling:

3. Place the pork and pork fat in a saucepan. Pour in 850 ml (30 fl oz) water and bring to the boil. Boil over moderately high heat for 20 minutes then remove pork and fat. Cool, dice and set aside pork and fat. Continue boiling stock till it is reduced by half.

4. Soak Chinese mushrooms and cut into tiny cubes. Dice sugared melon.

5. Heat oil in wok and fry the pounded garlic and shallots adding pork, salt, sugar, pepper and dark soya sauce. Stir in pan till pork changes colour. Add stock, mushrooms, sugared melon and fat. Continue cooking over medium heat for ½ hour.

6. Now add the coriander powder and stir well. Reduce heat and simmer till filling is almost dry. Remove to a large bowl to cool. Keep overnight before filling.

To Wrap Dumplings:

7. Take 1 broad or two narrow screwpine leaves. Fold from the centre to form a cone. Take a fistful of glutinous rice and line the sides.

8. Put 2–3 tablespoons of pork filling over rice and cover neatly with more glutinous rice. Fold leaf over and tie tightly with raffia or string.

9. Tie dumplings in groups of ten and boil in rapidly boiling water for 3 to 3½ hours. Add 2 tablespoons of salt to the water.

Note:
Unwrap one dumpling to see if glutinous rice is cooked and smooth. Otherwise, continue boiling for another 30 to 45 minutes. Hang dumplings for 1 to 2 hours after cooking to drip dry, thus preventing sogginess.

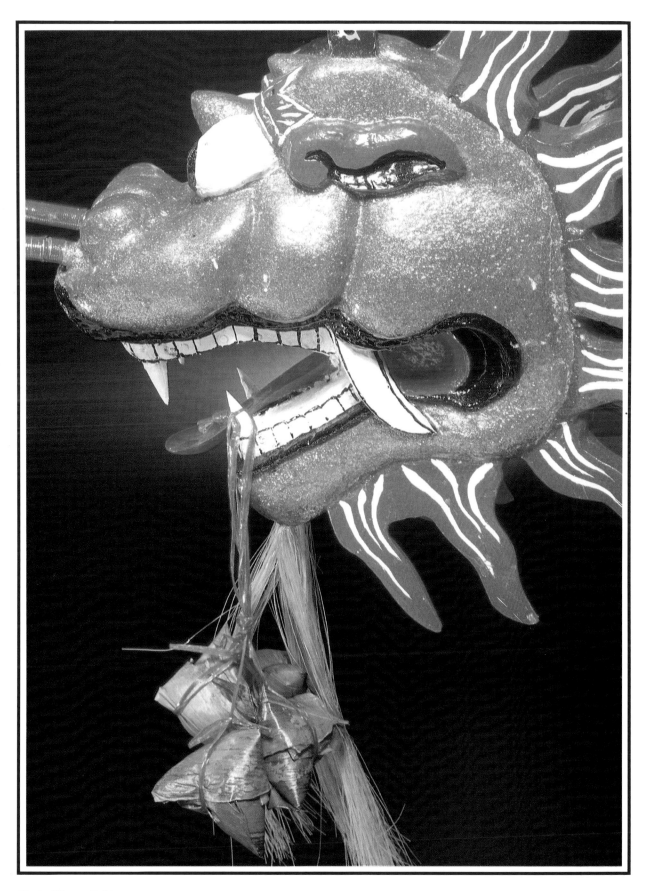

Kueh Chang Babi

SIEW MAI
(MEAT SAVOURIES)

INGREDIENTS

1 teaspoon msg	
1 teaspoon sherry	
2 tablespoons light soya sauce	
½ teaspoon salt	
1 teaspoon sugar	
½ teaspoon sesame oil	**A**
2 teaspoons cornflour	
1 tablespoon ginger juice	
1 small egg	
½ teaspoon pepper	
1 tablespoon chopped spring onions	

285 g (10 oz) minced pork
225 g (½ lb) prawns, shelled, deveined and cut
55 g (2 oz) boiled pork fat, finely cubed **B**
4 tablespoons boiled bamboo shoots, chopped finely

115 g (4 oz) square egg skins ('wan tan' skins), obtainable from local markets

METHOD

1. Mix **A** in a bowl. Add **B**. Mix well.

2. Cut off the four corners of the egg skins. Place a tablespoon of the meat mixture in the centre of each skin. Enclose filling with egg skin, so that the top filling is seen. Flatten base of each siew mai.

To steam:

Brush steamer rack with oil. Space siew mai on rack.

Steam over rapidly boiling water for 5–7 minutes or till cooked.

Serve hot with chilli sauce and mustard.

(Makes 30–40 'siew mai')

STEAMED BEEF BALLS

INGREDIENTS

115 ml (4 fl oz) water
1½ tablespoons cornflour **A**
1½ tablespoons water chestnut flour

455 g (16 oz) topside beef, minced finely
1 teaspoon alkaline water★

½ teaspoon salt
1½ teaspoons msg
3 tablespoons sugar **B**
1 teaspoon sesame oil
Dash of pepper

115 g (4 oz) pork fat, cut into very small squares
4 sprigs Chinese parsley, chopped finely **C**
½ teaspoon dried orange peel, chopped finely

Pepper

METHOD

1. Blend **A** in a bowl.

2. Place minced beef and alkaline water in a mixing bowl and mix thoroughly by hand. Slap beef on to sides of bowl. Knead till it is sticky, about 10 minutes. Leave to stand for 2 hours.

3. Transfer beef paste to a large mixing bowl. Add **A** (Method 1) and **B**. Use palms of hands to rub and knead till beef is pasty and sticky, about 10 minutes.

4. Add **C** and dash of pepper. Mix well. Grease palms of hands. Roll mixture into balls (each the size of a small egg). Place beef balls on a greased plate.

5. Steam for 10 minutes over rapidly boiling water. Serve hot.

★*See page 122.*

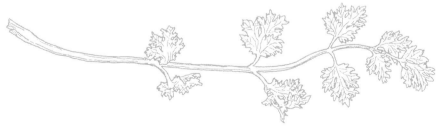

STUFFED MUSHROOMS

INGREDIENTS

680 ml (24 fl oz) water ⎫
  1 teaspoon sugar   ⎬ **A**
  ½ teaspoon salt |
  1 tablespoon lard   ⎭

225 g (8 oz) Chinese mustard
15 big Chinese mushrooms soaked in hot water

  1 egg white, lightly beaten ⎫
  ½ teaspoon msg |
  ¼ teaspoon salt |
  1 teaspoon light soya sauce ⎬ **B**
  1 tablespoon cornflour |
  Dash of pepper |
  1 tablespoon lard |
  ¼ teaspoon sesame oil   ⎭

225 g (½ lb) minced pork with a little fat ⎫
455 g (1 lb) prawns, shelled, deveined and |
  finely chopped   ⎬ **C**
  4 water chestnuts, finely chopped |
  1 tablespoon spring onions, finely chopped ⎭

1. Boil **A**. Add Chinese mustard, cut into pieces. Boil for ½ minute. Drain.

2. Dust underside of mushrooms with cornflour.

3. Mix **B** in a bowl. Add **C**. Mix well.

4. Spread mixture on to dusted side of mushrooms. Steam mushrooms, meat side up, on a greased plate for 7–10 minutes.

Gravy: (A)
¼ teaspoon salt, ½ teaspoon msg, ½ teaspoon sugar, 2 teaspoons light soya sauce, 225 ml (8 fl oz) chicken stock

  1 clove garlic, finely chopped

2 teaspoons cornflour ⎫
                   ⎬ **B**
2 tablespoons water   ⎭

1. Mix **A** in a bowl.

2. Heat 1 tablespoon lard in a hot pan. Fry chopped garlic. Pour in **A** and bring to the boil. Reduce heat to low.

3. Add **B** to pan. Stir till it boils. Pour over stuffed mushrooms, meat side up on the boiled mustard. Serve hot.

YAM PUFF

INGREDIENTS

115 g (4 oz) non-glutinous wheat flour
570 g (1¼ lb) yam, steamed and mashed
  2 teaspoons sesame oil

115 g (4 oz) lard   ⎫
  ½ teaspoon salt |
  4 teaspoons fine sugar   ⎬ **A**
  ¾ teaspoon pepper |
  1 level teaspoon msg   ⎭

Filling for yam puff:
  2 teaspoons oil
  1 teaspoon pounded garlic
115 g (4 oz) prawn meat, deveined and cubed
455 g (1 lb) lean meat, cut into small cubes
  55 g (2 oz) canned button mushrooms, cut into small pieces
  1 egg, lightly beaten
  2 tablespoons cornflour, mixed with
    2 tablespoons water

Seasoning:
½ teaspoon salt, ½ teaspoon msg, ¾ teaspoon pepper, 3 teaspoons fine sugar, 1 teaspoon black soya sauce, 1 teaspoon oyster sauce

METHOD

To prepare yam paste:
1. Blend the wheat flour with 115 ml (4 fl oz) boiling water in a small enamel basin.

2. Add mashed yam in small amounts with sesame oil and knead till smooth. Add in **A**. Mix well.

3. Divide dough into 4 parts and cut each part into small equal pieces, the size of a walnut.

4. Flatten each piece, place filling in centre, fold and seal edges.

5. Deep-fry puffs in a big, flat wire mesh ladle till golden brown. Remove to an absorbent paper to drain. Serve hot.

To cook filling:
Heat oil in pan and fry garlic till lightly browned. Add prawns, pork, mushrooms and stir-fry for 1 minute. Put in beaten egg, stir and pour in the cornflour mixture. Stir well and add seasoning.

TAN TART
(CHINESE EGG CUSTARD TARTLETS)

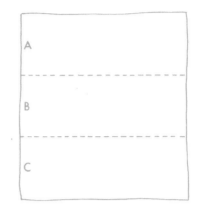

INGREDIENTS

Lard Dough Ingredients:
115 g (4 oz) lukewarm lard
140 g (5 oz) plain flour
½ teaspoon salt

METHOD

1. Mix ingredients together well in a bowl. Line a 13 × 15 cm tray with tin foil and pour on the lard mixture to spread evenly. Refrigerate overnight.

Plain Dough Ingredients:
170 g (6 oz) plain flour
½ teaspoon fine salt
2 teaspoons sugar
130 g (4½ oz) frozen butter
1 egg yolk
3 tablespoons iced water

METHOD

1. Combine plain flour, salt and sugar in a bowl. Cut frozen butter into 1.5 cm (½ in) squares. Put flour and butter into a food processor and use a steel blade cutter to process till mixture resembles breadcrumbs.

2. Beat the egg yolk with iced water. Remove flour mixture into a mixing bowl and make a well in the centre. Pour egg mixture gradually in centre and combine to form a dough.

3. Remove dough to a lightly floured flat work surface. Knead till dough is smooth. Flatten dough and keep in fridge for ½ hour.

To Roll Pastry:
4. Roll plain dough on a lightly dusted surface to a rectangular 20 × 25.5 cm (8 in × 11 in) shape. Mark dough in 3 equal parts: A, B and C. (see diagram)

5. Place lard dough on parts A and B. Bring part C over to cover B. Then fold A over to cover B and C. Press open edges firmly to seal and prevent lard from spilling. Cool in fridge for 45 minutes.

6. Place dough with narrow side facing you. Use rolling pin to press lightly at intervals to roll to a rectangular 20 × 25.5 cm. Fold bottom third of dough over and bring top third down. Press narrow edges firmly to seal and cool in fridge for 30 minutes. This is first rolling.

7. Repeat step (6) twice. Cool in fridge after each rolling.

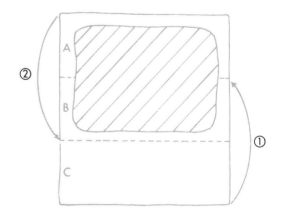

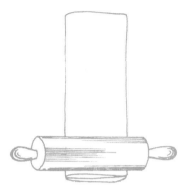

1. Mix custard powder with 1 tablespoon water. Add beaten egg and vanilla. Beat till well blended. Set aside.

2. Combine sugar, 455 ml (16 fl oz) water and condensed milk in a small saucepan. Cook till sugar is dissolved and milk is heated through. Pour the hot milk gradually into the beaten egg mixture and stir well. Cook over low heat for 3 minutes, stirring all the time. Cool before use to prevent bubbles forming while baking. Pour into pastry shells just before baking.

8. Place dough on a lightly floured surface. Roll till 3 mm (0.1 in) thick. Use a round cutter to cut shapes slightly larger than fluted tartlet tins.

9. Grease tartlet tins lightly and line with pastry. Press lightly on the sides to get impression from the fluted tins. Prick with sharp metal skewer if bubbles appear at base of pastry.

To Bake Custard Tartlets:

1. Preheat oven to 230°C (450°F). Place lined tartlets on a baking tray. Pour in custard to ½ fill the shells. Bake on high heat for 15 minutes, then reduce to 135°C (275°F) to continue baking for another 25–30 minutes or till custard sets and pastry turns light brown.

2. When done, remove from oven to cool for a moment. Place tartlets on paper cups. Serve hot.

Custard Ingredients:
    2 rounded teaspoons custard powder (Bird's eye brand)
    Water
    4 large eggs, lightly beaten
    1 teaspoon vanilla essence
225 g (8 oz) sugar
    4 tablespoons condensed milk

Note:
Do not overfill pastry with custard. This will cause the pastry to become soggy and soft.

Savoury Snacks

Beef Curry Puffs

Bun Susi

Cheese Straws

Chee Cheong Fun

Cheesey Beef Patties

Chwee Kuey

Kueh Pie Tee

Lemper Ayam

Minced Pork and Prawn Toast

Morokoo

Prawn Sambal Sandwiches

Rissoles

Pork Rolls

Spicy Prawn Rolls

Soon Kuey

Steamed Fish and Milk Sauce Sandwiches

Clockwise: Kueh Chang Babi, Soon Kuey, Chwee Kuey, Chee Cheong Fun

BEEF CURRY PUFFS

INGREDIENTS

Pastry:

225 g (8 oz) pastry margarine
1 egg
2 tablespoons castor sugar
2 tablespoons lemon juice
1 teaspoon salt
3–5 drops of yellow food colouring
170 ml (6 fl oz) iced water
455 g (16 oz) flour, sifted
115 g (4 oz) butter

METHOD

1. Cut pastry margarine into 2 cm (¾ in) cubes.

2. Mix egg, sugar, lemon juice, salt and food colouring in a bowl. Beat lightly with a fork. Pour in the iced water and stir till well mixed. Chill in a refrigerator.

3. Rub butter into the flour till mixture resembles breadcrumbs. Add the margarine cubes and mix lightly with the flour. Add the egg mixture and mix with both hands to form a dough. Do not knead. Chill dough in refrigerator for 1 hour.

4. Divide dough into two portions. Place one portion on a floured board or flat surface; dredge flour over; flatten and roll out into a rectangle. Fold into three, bringing down one-third of the pastry from the top to fold over the centre. Make a half turn so that the open edges on both ends face you and the fold is at your right. Roll out.

5. Repeat the folding and rolling three more times. Dust board with flour, roll out pastry to 0.5 cm (¼ in) thickness and use a fluted-edged cutter to cut pastry into rounds.

6. Repeat process with the other portion.

7. Place a tablespoonful of filling in the centre of each round. Moisten half the edge with water and bring the other half over to seal.

8. Space curry puffs on a greased tray. Brush with glaze and bake in a very hot oven at 230°C (450°F) or Regulo 10 to 10 minutes. Bake on centre shelf of oven. Reduce heat to 205°C (400°F) or Regulo 8 and bake for another 20 minutes till golden brown. Lift curry puffs on to a wire rack to cool.

To Glaze:

Beat one egg with 2 drops of yellow food colouring.

Filling:

Oil for frying
340 g (12 oz) onions, diced
340 g (12 oz) potatoes, diced
¼ teaspoon salt

1 teaspoon chopped ginger
2 cloves garlic, sliced thinly
8 shallots, sliced thinly
455 g (1 lb) minced beef
4 heaped tablespoons curry powder
225 g (8 oz) grated coconut, to 125 ml (4 fl oz) water, squeezed and strained

Seasoning for curry filling:

2 tablespoons sugar
2 teaspoons salt
1 teaspoon msg

METHOD

1. Heat an iron wok. When very hot, add 4 tablespoons oil and fry onions till transparent. Remove to a plate leaving oil in wok.

2. Add 2 tablespoons oil, stir-fry potatoes with ¼ teapoon salt over a high heat for 5 minutes. Sprinkle 115 ml (4 fl oz) water, stir and cover. Cook over a moderate heat till potatoes are done. Remove and set aside.

3. In a clean iron wok, heat 4 tablespoons oil to brown ginger, sliced garlic, and shallots. Add minced meat and stir-fry for 5 minutes over a moderate heat. Add the curry powder and stir-fry for another 5 minutes. Add the fried onions and cooked potatoes. Mix well then add the coconut milk and the seasoning.

4. Reduce the heat, and cook till meat mixture is almost dry, stirring occasionally. Remove to a large plate to cool.

BUN SUSI
(MEAT BUNS)

INGREDIENTS

Buns:
 30 g (1 oz) or 2 tablespoons fresh yeast
115 g (4 oz) castor sugar
455 g (16 oz) flour, sifted
170 ml (6 fl oz) hot milk
115 g (4 oz) soft butter
 5 egg yolks
 1 egg white, lightly beaten
½ teaspoon salt
225 g (8 oz) bread dough, from bakery
 Flour for dusting

METHOD

1. Dissolve yeast in 3 tablespoons warm water, 1 teaspoon sugar, and 1 tablespoon flour. Let stand for 10 minutes or till frothy.

2. Place hot milk in a mixing bowl, add the butter, egg yolks, egg white, salt, sugar, and 225 g (8 oz) of the flour. Stir till well mixed.

3. Break bread dough into small portions in a big bowl. Add the yeast mixture and the milk mixture.

4. Claw mixture with hand for 5 minutes. Add the rest of the flour to form a dough. Place dough on a flat surface and knead till dough is smooth and leaves palm of hand clean. Place dough in a greased bowl. Cover with a damp cloth and allow to rise in a warm place till double its size.

5. Remove dough to a floured board, dust with some flour and knead for 2 minutes.

6. Divide dough into four parts and shape each into a long roll. Cut into equal walnut-sized pieces. Flatten each piece lightly with the palm of hand, making a well in the centre. Fill with meat filling and shape the dough to form a small bun.

7. Space buns out on a greased tray, allowing room for expansion. Leave to rise in a warm place for 20–30 minutes. Glaze and bake in oven at 205°C (400°F) or Regulo 8 for 10 minutes. Reduce heat to 150°C (300°F) or Regulo 4 and bake for a further 10–15 minutes till golden brown. Cool on a rack.

Filling:

1 teaspoon msg	
¾ teaspoon salt	
3 tablespoons sugar	**A**
2 tablespoons dark soya sauce	
4 tablespoons water	

 3 tablespoons lard or oil
 8 shallots, sliced thinly
 1 tablespoon pounded garlic
680 g (24 oz) minced pork
 2 teaspoons pepper
285 g (10 oz) potatoes, diced and fried
¼ piece grated nutmeg
 3 tablespoons crispy shallots

Thickening:
2 tablespoons cornflour with 4 tablespoons water

METHOD

1. In a very hot pan, heat 3 tablespoons lard or oil to fry the sliced shallots and garlic till brown. Add the minced pork and pepper, stir-fry for 5 minutes. Add the potatoes, cook for 5 minutes.

2. Mix **A** in a bowl for the seasoning.

3. Pour in the seasoning, stir-fry in pan till meat mixture is almost dry. Sprinkle with nutmeg and crispy shallots. Pour in the cornflour mixture and cook for 1 minute. Cool on tray before use.

To Glaze:
Beat 1 egg and 1 egg yolk with 1 tablespoon milk, a pinch of salt, 1 teaspoon sugar and 2–3 drops of yellow food colouring.

Note:
An electric dough hook can be used to knead the dough. Use speed No. 1 or No. 2 for about 15 minutes, or till dough leaves inside of bowl clean.

CHEESE STRAWS

INGREDIENTS

225 g (8 oz) cheese, finely grated |
¾ teaspoon salt |
½ teaspoon pepper | **A**
1 tablespoon granulated sugar |

170 g (6 oz) butter
225 g (8 oz) flour
2 egg yolks, beaten
1 egg white, lightly beaten for glaze

METHOD

1. Rub butter into flour. Add **A**. Mix well.

2. Pour the beaten egg yolks into the flour mixture. Knead lightly with hand to form a soft dough. Chill dough in refrigerator for ½ hour.

3. Roll dough on a floured pastry board to 0.5 cm (¼ in) thickness.

4. Cut pastry with a pastry wheel into 5 cm (2 in) blocks. Cut each block into strips, so that each strip is 5 cm long by 0.5 cm wide (2 in × ¼ in).

5. Glaze whole blocks of cheese strips with egg white. Place on baking trays and bake in oven at 190°C (375°F) or Regulo 7 for about 20–25 minutes till light brown. Store in an airtight container when cool.

CHEE CHEONG FUN

INGREDIENTS

½ teaspoon salt | **A**
2 tablespoons oil |

140 g (5 oz) rice flour
2 tablespoons sago flour
570 ml (20 fl oz) water
4 tablespoons toasted sesame seeds
Crispy shallots

METHOD

1. Mix the two types of flour with 255 ml (9 fl oz) of the water. Add **A** and mix well. Set aside.

2. Bring the rest of the water to the boil and add gradually to the flour mixture, stirring as you pour.

To steam:
1. Grease two 23 cm (9 in) round sandwich trays with oil. Place trays on a perforated rack in an iron wok of rapidly boiling water. Cover trays and heat for 2 minutes. Keep water in wok below the level of the rack at all times during steaming.

2. Stir flour mixture, and pour a ladlespoon or 115–140 ml (4–5 fl oz) of it into the trays. Tilt trays so that the mixture spreads evenly, before steaming. Cover wok and steam for about 1–1½ minutes or till mixture turns transparent.

3. Remove trays from wok and put over a shallow basin of cold water for 1 minute. Use spatula to remove cooked paste. Form into a roll and place on a plate. Repeat with the rest of the mixture.

To serve:
Cut *chee cheong fun* into pieces, sprinkle with crispy shallots and sesame seeds and serve with mushroom soya sauce (*see recipe*) and chilli sauce. Sliced roast pork strips or steamed small prawns can be added if desired.

To make *chee cheong fun* mushroom soya sauce:
 1 tablespoon oil
 4 slices ginger
 2 tablespoons sugar
55 g (2 oz) mushroom soya sauce
55 ml (2 fl oz) water
 1 teaspoon msg

In a saucepan, heat oil, sugar and ginger till sugar turns a light brown. Pour in the mushroom soya sauce, water and msg. Bring to the boil and boil for 5 minutes. Serve when cool.

CHEESEY BEEF PATTIES

INGREDIENTS

500 g (18 oz) top-side beef, minced
115 g (4 oz) onions, chopped finely, fried in
    a little oil till soft   **A**
  ¼ cup Chinese celery, chopped finely

Seasoning:
(Beaten together)
 1 teaspoon fine salt
 1 teaspoon pepper
 1 teaspoon msg

15 g (½ oz) cheddar cheese, finely cubed
 1 kg (2¼ lb) potatoes
  Self-raising flour
 1 egg, beaten
 1 cup dry breadcrumbs
  Oil for deep frying

METHOD

1. Place **A** in a large bowl. Add cheese and seasoning; mix till well combined. Divide into 12 portions, shape into flat patties and chill in refrigerator for ½ hour.

2. Wash potatoes and cut deep slits in each to boil gently till tender. Peel skin and mash well whilst hot, adding ½ teaspoon each of fine salt and pepper. Mix well. Divide potato into 12 portions and cover to keep warm.

3. Pat potato around meat patties. Roll patties in self-raising flour; dip in beaten egg and coat with breadcrumbs. Keep in refrigerator for an hour.

4. Heat oil for deep frying. Fry patties till golden. Remove to absorbent paper and serve hot with tomato sauce.

Note:
Make large portions of Cheesey Beef Patties and keep in freezer in a plastic container. Minced pork can be used instead of beef.

CHWEE KUEY
(STEAMED RICE CAKES WITH PRESERVED SALTED RADISH)

INGREDIENTS

565 ml (20 fl oz) water
140 g (5 oz) rice flour
 1 heaped tablespoon sago flour
 ½ teaspoon salt
 2 tablespoons oil
170 g (6 oz) lard
 2 cloves garlic, lightly bashed
115 g (4 oz) chopped, preserved, salted radish
 ½ teaspoon msg
  Dash of pepper

METHOD

1. Mix well 225 ml (8 fl oz) of the water with the two types of flour and salt in a bowl. Add the oil and beat well with a fork till well blended. Set aside.

2. Bring the rest of the water to the boil and pour gradually into the rice mixture, stirring all the time to prevent lumps forming.

3. Arrange the moulds on a steamer tray over boiling water and steam empty moulds over moderate heat for 5 minutes.

4. Pour rice mixture into each mould and steam for 10–15 minutes or till well cooked. Remove the rice cakes from steamer and allow to cool for about 10 minutes, before taking them out of the moulds.

To cook the radish:
Dice the lard, wash and drain. Cook lard and garlic in a small saucepan till lard turns light brown. Discard garlic and lard, leaving oil to cook radish, msg and pepper, over low heat for ½ hour. Stir occasionally to prevent burning. Place a spoonful of cooked radish on top of the steamed rice cakes and serve. Sweet chilli sauce can be added if desired.

Note:
You can buy the chopped preserved salted radish from any supermarket or grocer's.

KUEH PIE TEE
(SHREDDED BAMBOO SHOOTS IN PATTY CASES)

INGREDIENTS

Patty cases:

1 large egg, lightly beaten 225 ml (8 fl oz) water A pinch of salt	**A**

115 g (4 oz) plain flour, sifted
Oil for deep-frying

METHOD

1. Mix **A** in a bowl.
2. Pour mixture gradually into the flour to form a smooth batter. Sieve into a bowl. Leave to stand for ½ hour.
3. Heat oil for deep-frying.
4. Heat the special patty mould in the hot oil for 2 minutes. Remove the mould, dip it in batter and deep-fry till patty case is light brown and can retain its shape when it slips away from the mould.
5. Place patty cases on absorbent paper. Cool and store in an air-tight container immediately to retain crispness.

Filling:

1.2 kg (43 oz) tender, boiled bamboo shoots 310 g (11 oz) Chinese turnip	**A**

½ teaspoon·salt ½ teaspoon msg 2 tablespoons sugar 2 tablespoons preserved brown soya beans, pounded	**B**

455 g (1 lb) streaky pork
A pinch of salt
225 g (½ lb) small prawns
225 ml (8 fl oz) water
4 tablespoons lard or oil
2 tablespoons pounded garlic

2 big soya bean cakes, cut into thin strips and fried

METHOD

1. Cook pork in 455 ml (16 fl oz) water and a pinch of salt for ½ hour. Remove and slice pork thinly. Cut again into fine strips. Set aside stock.
2. Shred **A** finely.
3. Shell and devein prawns. Pound prawn shells. Add water and mix well. Strain and set aside stock.
4. Heat lard or oil in an iron wok. Fry garlic till brown, add **B**. Stir-fry for ½ minute. Add shredded ingredients, prawn stock and pork stock. Cook for ¾ hour over a moderate heat.
5. Add prawns, pork and soya bean strips. Stir and cook till almost dry. Cool on tray before filling.

Garnish:
225 g (½ lb) steamed crab meat
225 g (½ lb) prawns, fried with a pinch of salt and cut into small pieces
3 bundles of Chinese parsley, without roots, washed and drained
4 tablespoons pounded garlic, fried crisp
2 eggs, fried into thin pancakes and shredded

To serve:
Fill patty cases with filling. Top with bits of garnish. Serve with chilli sauce.

Note:
Dip shredded turnip in cold water to remove the starch. Drain in colander before cooking.

(50–60 patty cases)

LEMPER AYAM
(STEAMED GLUTINOUS RICE WITH
SPICED SHREDDED CHICKEN)

INGREDIENTS

40 g (1½ oz) shallots ⎫
1 stalk lemon grass ⎪ **A**
2 slices ginger ⎪
30 g (1 oz) candlenut ⎭

1½ teaspoons salt ⎫
2 tablespoons sugar ⎪ **B**
2 teaspoons pepper ⎪ *mixed*
2 rounded tablespoons roasted ground ⎪ *in a*
   coriander seeds ⎪ *bowl*
2 tablespoons condensed milk ⎭

605 g (21 oz) glutinous rice, soaked overnight
570 g (20 oz) grated coconut
¾ tablespoon salt
1 level tablespoon sugar
Banana leaves

Filling:
285 g (10 oz) chicken breast
   Pinch of salt

3 tablespoons oil
55 ml (2 fl oz) No. 1 milk (*from To prepare glutinous rice, Step 3*)

To prepare glutinous rice:
1. Wash banana leaves. Cut into 30 cm × 10 cm (12 in × 4 in) pieces, and soak in a basin of boiling water for 10 minutes to soften.
2. Drain glutinous rice.
3. Squeeze coconut for 200 ml (7 fl oz) No. 1 milk. Stir in salt and sugar till dissolved. Set aside 55 ml (2 fl oz) to cook the filling. Add 170 ml (6 fl oz) water to coconut and squeeze for 140 ml (5 fl oz) No. 2 milk.
4. Make steam holes in glutinous rice and steam over rapidly boiling water for 20 minutes. Transfer glutinous rice to a saucepan, pour in the No. 2 milk, stir and leave in saucepan, covered, for 5 minutes.

5. Return glutinous rice to steamer, make steam holes and re-steam for 7 minutes. Transfer into saucepan again and pour in the No. 1 milk. Stir and leave in pan for 5 minutes. Re-steam for another 5 minutes. Remove from heat and keep steamed glutinous rice warm.

To cook filling:
1. Boil chicken breast gently with a pinch of salt and 455 ml (16 fl oz) water for ½ hour. Remove chicken to cool. Boil stock till it is reduced by half.
2. Bash chicken with side of chopper and shred finely.
3. Heat oil and fry paste **A** over moderate heat till fragrant and light brown. Add the No. 1 milk, stock and **B**. Stir well, put in the shredded chicken and cook over low heat till mixture is moist. Cool before use.

To fill *lemper*:
1. Oil hands with boiled coconut oil, put 340 g (12 oz) warm glutinous rice on a banana leaf. Flatten into a rectangular shape 1 cm (½ in) thick.
2. Place 115 g (4 oz) filling in the centre of the glutinous rice lengthwise. Roll glutinous rice to cover filling. Roll banana leaf tightly over glutinous rice and press firmly to flatten. Cut into pieces 5 cm (2 in) long. Wrap with grease-proof paper and staple ends.

Note:
Wrapped lemper *can be pan-fried over moderate heat (without oil) if preferred.*

MINCED PORK AND PRAWN TOAST

INGREDIENTS

225 g (½ lb) minced pork
225 g (½ lb) prawns, shelled, deveined and chopped
115 g (4 oz) chopped pork and ham (mashed)
 1 egg
 2 small boiled potatoes, mashed
 2 tablespoons chopped spring onions   **A**
⅛ teaspoon salt
 1 teaspoon sugar
½ teaspoon msg
½ teaspoon pepper

 1 big loaf of bread (French loaf), cut into 1 cm (½ in) thick slices
 Oil for deep-frying
 1 egg, beaten with a pinch of salt

METHOD

1. Mix **A** well into a pasty mixture using a wooden spoon.

2. Spread meat mixture on to slices of bread.

3. Dip only the meat side of the bread in the beaten egg. Deep-fry over a moderate heat, meat-side down, for 2 minutes.

4. Turn over once, fry for just half a minute till light golden brown. Remove and place on absorbent paper. Serve hot with tomato sauce or salad cream.

MOROKOO
(BLACK BEAN FLOUR AND COCONUT CRISPS)

INGREDIENTS

455 g (16 oz) rice flour
115 g (4 oz) black bean flour
 2 teaspoon oom seeds (available at Indian grocery shops)
 4 teaspoons cumin seeds, whole   **A**
½ teaspoon turmeric powder
 2 level teaspoons salt
55 g (2 oz) grated coconut, white

1.2 kg (2½ lb) grated coconut, white
 2 litres (4 pints) oil for deep frying

METHOD

1. Squeeze the 1.2 kg grated coconut for 455 ml No. 1 milk. Set aside.

2. Put **A** into a large mixing bowl. Stir by hand till evenly combined. Pour the No. 1 milk gradually into mixture and knead to form a smooth semi-firm dough. Allow to rest for ½ hour.

3. Put dough in morokoo presser to test for texture. It should flow easily showing a clear pattern.

3. Fill presser with dough and press dough into heated oil in wok. Fry over moderately high heat till golden brown.

PRAWN SAMBAL SANDWICHES

INGREDIENTS

 4 tablespoons oil
 4 tablespoons chopped onions
2–4 tablespoons dried chilli paste
140 g (5 oz) rempah sambal udang (See page 186)
55 ml (2 fl oz) No. 1 milk from 140 g (5 oz) grated coconut
55 g (2 oz) tamarind and 6 tablespoons water, squeezed and strained for juice
 3 tablespoons sugar
170 g (6 oz) dried prawns, pounded very finely
20 lime leaves, sliced very finely

METHOD

1. Heat 4 tablespoons oil in an aluminium pan and fry onions till light brown. Add chilli paste, rempah udang and coconut milk and stir over moderate heat for 1 minute.

2. Pour in the tamarind juice and sugar, and stir. Add the dried prawns and keep stirring over low heat till mixture is fragrant and almost dry. Mix lime leaves and cool before making sandwiches.

RISSOLES
(MEAT ROLLS)

INGREDIENTS

Batter:

170 g (6 oz) plain flour
  2 tablespoons cornflour   **A**
  3 tablespoons powdered milk

  6 eggs, lightly beaten
425 ml (15 fl oz) lukewarm water   **B**
  A pinch of salt
  3 tablespoons oil

1. Sieve **A** in a bowl.

2. Beat **B** lightly with a fork and pour gradually into flour to make a smooth batter. Strain and leave to stand for 20 minutes.

3. Heat a 20 cm (8 in) base frying pan till very hot. Remove from the heat, grease base of pan with oil once only.

4. Pour in batter, tilting pan to spread batter evenly. Turn pancake out when edges begin to curl. Pile pancakes on a plate.

Filling:

115 g (4 oz) steamed crab meat
225 g (8 oz) boiled bamboo shoots, diced
  6 tablespoons boiled green peas
  3 tablespoons light soya sauce
  1 tablespoon oyster sauce
  1 teaspoon sherry   **A**
  ¾ teaspoon salt
  1 teaspoon msg
  1 teaspoon pepper
  2 teaspoons sugar

  1 rounded tablespoon cornflour   **B**
  6 tablespoons water

  6 tablespoons lard or oil
  1 teaspoon garlic, pounded
  1 onion, diced small
455 g (1 lb) prawns, shelled, deveined and chopped
455 g (1 lb) minced pork
  2 tablespoons spring onions, chopped finely

1. Heat oil in pan, fry garlic till light brown. Add the diced onion stirring till transparent. Add the prawns and cook for 1 minute. Add the minced pork and stir-fry till cooked.

2. Add **A**. Stir well and cook over a moderate heat for 5 minutes.

3. Mix **B** and add to mixture in pan. Stir and cook for 1 minute, then add the chopped spring onions. Stir and remove to a tray to cool.

To make rolls:

1 egg
  A pinch of salt
  Meat filling
  'Paxo' brand golden breadcrumbs
  Oil

METHOD

1. Beat egg lightly with salt. Set aside.

2. Place 2 tablespoonfuls of meat filling on each pancake and roll.

3. Brush roll with beaten egg and coat with breadcrumbs. Deep-fry in hot oil for half a minute over a high heat. Place rolls on absorbent paper. Serve hot or cold.

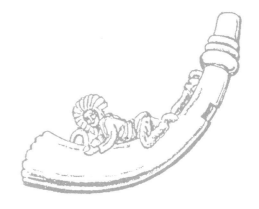

PORK ROLLS

INGREDIENTS

1 tablespoon tomato sauce
½ tablespoon Chinese wine
¾ level teaspoon salt
½ teaspoon Lea & Perrins sauce   **A**

Gravy:
1 tablespoon sugar
1 tablespoon tomato sauce
½ teaspoon Lea & Perrins sauce
½ teaspoon msg   **B**
1 teaspoon light soya sauce
½ dark soya sauce
½ teaspoon sago flour in 2 tablespoons water

455 g (1 lb) pork chop meat

115 g (4 oz) pork fat
115 g (4 oz) pig or chicken liver   *boiled and cut into strips*
115 g (4 oz) bamboo shoots

55 ml (2 fl oz) oil
1 tablespoon lard
A few lettuce leaves

METHOD

1. Cut pork chops into 5 cm strips. Slice each strip horizontally but without cutting through completely.

2. Mix **A** in a bowl and marinate pork for ¾ hour.

3. Spread open each piece of sliced pork on a wooden chopping board. Cut pork fat, liver and bamboo shoots the same length as the pork; put a piece each of these ingredients at one end of pork and roll tightly for frying.

4. Heat a frying pan till hot. Add 55 ml (2 fl oz) oil to fry rolls till brown. Remove.

5. In a clean pan, heat 1 tablespoon lard till very hot. Put in rolls and pour in **B**. Cover pan immediately for ½ minute. Remove from heat and spoon rolls on cut lettuce in serving plate. Pour remaining gravy over rolls. Serve hot.

SPICY PRAWN ROLLS

INGREDIENTS

6 candlenuts
1 thumb-sized piece turmeric   **A**
1 teaspoon shrimp paste

8 tablespoons sugar
½ tablespoon salt
3 tablespoons tamarind in 140 ml (5 fl oz)   **B**
water, squeezed and strained
340 g (12 oz) dried prawns, soaked and finely pounded

115 g (4 oz) green chillies
115 g (4 oz) red chillies
115 g (4 oz) garlic   **C**
225 g (8 oz) shallots
10 stalks lemon grass, sliced slantwise

285 ml (10 fl oz) oil
50 pieces Spring Roll skins

Filling:
1. Pound ingredients **A** to a paste. Add **B** and mix thoroughly.

2. Slice **C** finely.

3. Heat an iron wok, then add oil. When oil is heated through, fry the sliced ingredients (**C**) separately till light brown. Set aside.

4. With the same oil, fry the dried prawn mixture over low heat till almost dry. Stir constantly to prevent burning.

5. Add all the fried ingredients and stir-fry for 5 minutes. Remove to a tray and cool.

To Make Prawn Rolls:
1. Cut the Spring Roll skin into quarters. Take one square of skin and scoop 1 teaspoon spicy prawn filling on it. Roll, wrap and seal with flour and water mixture. Repeat with remaining ingredients.

2. Heat oil for deep frying. Put rolls in to fry over moderate heat till lightly browned. Scoop out with a wire mesh ladle onto absorbent paper to drain oil.

3. Store in an air-tight container whilst still lukewarm.

SOON KUEY

INGREDIENTS

300 g (10½ oz) rice flour
570 ml (20 fl oz) water
 ½ teaspoon salt
    Pinch of *pheng say* (available at Chinese
    medicine shops)
 70 g (2½ oz) sago flour
 55 ml (2 fl oz) oil

1. Mix 2 tablespoons rice flour with 170 ml (6 fl oz) water in a cup.
2. Boil the rest of the water in a saucepan with the salt and *pheng say*. Reduce heat, pour in the flour mixture from Method 1 and stir well. Add the rest of the rice flour, and stir with wooden spoon till mixture is smooth. Remove from heat.
3. Transfer to a large basin or tray, add sago flour, oil and knead for 5 minutes.
4. Divide dough into egg-shape sizes, flatten and put in 2 tablespoons filling. Fold dough over filling and seal by pinching the edges together to resemble a curry puff. Place *soon kuey* on an oiled steamer tray and steam for 10–12 minutes. Serve hot with chilli sauce.

Filling:

 1 teaspoon pounded preserved soya bean
 1 teaspoon sugar
 ½ teaspoon msg
 ½ teaspoon salt

A

455 g (1 lb) Chinese turnip
 3 tablespoons lard *or* oil
 1 tablespoon pounded garlic
 55 g (2 oz) small dried prawns, washed

1. Cut turnip into thin strips, immerse in water and drain.
2. Heat oil in pan and fry garlic till light brown, add **A** and fry for short while. Pour in 115 ml water, add dried prawns and bring to the boil.
3. Put in the turnip, stir in pan and cook over moderate heat till almost dry. Cool before use.

Note:
170 g (6 oz) fresh prawns can also be added together with the dried prawns.

STEAMED FISH AND MILK SAUCE SANDWICHES

INGREDIENTS

225 g (8 oz) fish (threadfin)
 5 slices ginger
 1 teaspoon butter
 1 teaspoon light soya sauce
 2 tablespoons butter for frying shallots
 2 shallots or 1 small onion, thinly sliced
1½ tablespoons plain flour
115 ml (4 fl oz) milk
 1 tablespoon spring onions, cut finely
 1 hard boiled egg, mashed

Seasoning:
½ teaspoon salt
 1 teaspoon sugar
½ teaspoon msg
    Dash of pepper

METHOD

1. Cut fish into two; clean. Place ginger slices in an enamel plate, put fish over and dab with butter and soya sauce. Steam fish over high heat for 10 minutes or till fish is cooked. Remove ginger. Set aside fish and fish stock.
2. Heat butter in a non-stick pan to fry sliced shallots till light brown. Add flour and fry for short while. Reduce heat to low, pour in milk and fish stock. Cook for 1 minute and remove to a plate to cool.
3. Flake fish and mix well with flour mixture. Lastly, add spring onions and mashed egg. Stir in seasoning and cool.

Note:
Keep sandwiches covered with a damp cloth till ready to serve.

Sambals, Pickles and Sauces

Chilli Sauce — Hot

Chilli Sauce — Sweet

Chilli Garam Paste

Dried Chilli Paste

Garam Assam Paste

Luak Chye

Rempah Sambal Udang

Salt Fish Sambal

Sambal Belimbing

Sambal Tempe Udang

Sambal Tumis

Sambal Lengkong

Sambal Udang Kering Goreng

Achar (page 148)

CHILLI SAUCE — HOT

INGREDIENTS

625 g (22 oz) red chillies
 55 g (2 oz) dried chillies
  8 cloves garlic
  1 thumb-sized piece ginger, skinned and sliced
  5 tablespoons salt
455 g (16 oz) sugar
170 ml (6 fl oz) rice vinegar

METHOD

1. Remove stems from chillies.

2. Boil the dried chillies in a saucepan, using a little water, for 2 minutes. Leave to soak for 5 minutes. Wash chillies till the water is clear. Drain in a colander.

3. Put half of the chillies in a electric blender. Pour in 285 ml (10 fl oz) water and turn the control to high to blend chillies till very fine. Remove and set aside. Repeat process with the other half of the chillies, adding the garlic and ginger.

4. Combine the liquidized chilli mixture and the remaining water in an enamel saucepan. Add the salt and bring to boil over a moderate heat, stirring constantly for 10 minutes.

5. Stir in the sugar. Bring chilli sauce to the boil. Lower the heat and continue simmering for 1½ hours, stirring occasionally.

6. Add the vinegar, stir and continue boiling for 5 minutes. Remove from the heat. Cool before storing in dry, clean bottles.

CHILLI SAUCE — SWEET

INGREDIENTS

115 g (4 oz) dried chilli paste or 55 g (2 oz).   ⎫
 dried chillies
  1 tablespoon shrimp paste   **A**
 55 g (2 oz) whitish pale raisins
 85 g (3 oz) ginger, sliced thinly
  6 cloves garlic, skin removed   ⎭

455 g (1 lb) fresh red chillies
1.12 litres (39 fl oz) water
340 g (12 oz) coarse sugar
  4 level tablespoons salt
170 ml (6 fl oz) vinegar

METHOD

1. Remove stems from fresh chillies, wash and drain.

2. Blend **A** and half of the chillies in an electric blender till very fine. Add some water if paste thickens. Keep the paste rotating in bowl.

3. Remove from blender. Repeat process with the rest of the chillies.

4. Pour the rest of the water, sugar and salt into a non-stick saucepan or a heavy aluminium saucepan and bring to the boil. Add the chilli mixture and boil over moderate heat for 20 minutes, stirring occasionally to prevent it from sticking and burning at bottom of pan.

5. Lower heat, continue to cook for 1 hour, stirring occasionally till sauce thickens. Pour mixture into an enamel saucepan. Add the vinegar and boil for another 10 minutes. Leave to cool completely before storing in very dry bottles.

Note:
Fill each bottle to the top with chilli sauce and screw on the plastic cover tightly before storing.

If metal cap is used, line it with a piece of wax paper to prevent rust.

Store in a cool place or refrigerator.

CHILLI GARAM PASTE

INGREDIENTS

605 g (21 oz) fresh red chillies
85 g (3 oz) shrimp paste, cut into tiny pieces
225 ml (8 fl oz) oil
2¼ tablespoons salt
2 tablespoons sugar
85 ml (3 fl oz) water

METHOD

1. Pound chillies and shrimp paste together coarsely.
2. Heat oil in pan. Put in the chilli paste and fry over moderate heat till oil bubbles through and smells fragrant. Add the salt, sugar, water and stir-fry till moist and oily. Leave to cool. Cool completely before packing into a plastic container and store in freezer.

Note:
When the chilli paste hardens, cut into cubes of 4 cm (1½ in), then put it back into the freezer. You can then thaw the amount you need each time.

DRIED CHILLI PASTE

INGREDIENTS

225 g (8 oz) dried chillies

METHOD

1. Remove stems from chillies.
2. Place chillies in a saucepan, three-quarters filled with cold water.
3. Bring to a boil and cook for 5 minutes. Cover pan and leave chillies to soak for 10 minutes. Drain. Place chillies in a large basin, wash till water is clear. Drain in a colander.
4. Using an electric blender, blend half of the chillies with 225 ml (8 oz) water till very fine. Remove paste and repeat process with the other half of the chillies and water.
5. Store chilli paste in a plastic container. Keep in freezer until needed.

Note:
Keep chilli paste rotating whilst blending. Add spoonfuls of water if paste is not rotating.

(Makes approximately 32 tablespoonfuls of chilli paste.)

GARAM ASSAM PASTE

INGREDIENTS

340 g (12 oz) sliced galangal
340 g (12 oz) sliced lemon grass
285 g (10 oz) candlenut
455 g (1 lb) shrimp paste } **A**

680 g (1½ lb) fresh red chillies
1.4 kg (3 lb) onions
40 g (1½ oz) turmeric powder
30 g (1 oz) chilli powder *or* dried chillies ground to a fine paste
710 ml (25 fl oz) oil for frying

METHOD

1. Grind or blend **A** to a very fine paste.
2. Pound fresh chillies and onions separately into rough pieces.
3. Combine everything and mix thoroughly till well blended.
4. Heat an aluminium or iron wok till very hot. Heat oil till smoking hot, add half of the mixture and fry over moderately high heat till oil bubbles through, stirring constantly to prevent paste burning. Add the rest of the paste and keep stirring.
5. Lower heat and keep frying till paste is fragrant and almost dry. Cool completely before packing in 455 g (1 lb) packets in plastic bags or containers. Store in freezer for future use.

LUAK CHYE
(MIXED VEGETABLE PICKLE IN MUSTARD SEASONING)

INGREDIENTS

85 g (3 oz) young ginger
1 carrot   **A**
2 radishes

115 ml (4 fl oz) vinegar
85 ml (3 fl oz) water   **B**
4 tablespoons sugar
¾ level teaspoon salt

3 teaspoons salt
1 tablespoon sugar
455 g (1 lb) green mustard, thinly sliced
2–3 tablespoons French mustard

METHOD

1. Slice **A** thinly. Season with 1 teaspoon salt and 1 tablespoon sugar, and set aside for ½ hour. Put vegetables into a wire sieve, rinse with water and squeeze dry with a piece of muslin.
2. Spread vegetables on a tray and leave to air in a sunny place for 1 hour.
3. Repeat process with the green mustard, using 2 teaspoons salt.
4. Boil **B** in an enamel saucepan for 1 minute. Remove from heat to cool.
5. Blend a few spoonfuls of the vinegar mixture with the French mustard, then pour in the rest of the vinegar.
6. Mix the sliced vegetables together, put them into a large porcelain jar or glass bottle, pour in the vinegar and stir well. Leave uncovered for 4–6 hours and store in refrigerator for future use. Keep for 1 day before serving.

REMPAH SAMBAL UDANG
(FROZEN SPICY PASTE)

INGREDIENTS

140 g (5 oz) dried chillies
115 g (4 oz) fresh red chillies   **A**
905 g (2 lb) shallots *or* onions
4 small cloves garlic

455 g (1 lb) grated coconut, white
340 ml (12 fl oz) oil

METHOD

1. Remove stems from chillies, soak dried chillies in hot water for ½ hour to soften. Drain.
2. Grind or blend **A** in an electric blender or food processor to a very fine paste. Remove to a bowl.
3. Use muslin to squeeze coconut for No. 1 milk. Set aside 170–200 ml (6–7 fl oz) in a bowl.
4. Heat an iron or aluminium wok till very hot. Heat the oil, pour in the paste and stir-fry till oil bubbles through and smells fragrant. Add the No. 1 milk and stir for 5 minutes over high heat. Remove paste to a large basin to cool completely. Pack in plastic bags or container when completely cool and store in refrigerator for use.

Note:
Chill in refrigerator or freezer to hasten the cooling process for packing. Stir well so that oil is evenly distributed with paste before packing. This rempah *can be used for fish, prawns and cuttlefish.*

SALT FISH SAMBAL

INGREDIENTS

6 cloves garlic
4 shallots
1 teaspoon shrimp paste
5 red chillies, seeded **A**

140 g (5 oz) Penang salt fish
170 ml (6 fl oz) oil for frying salt fish
10 red and 10 green chilli padi, stems removed
2 red tomatoes, cut into thin slices
4 tablespoons water

Seasoning:
2 teaspoons sugar
½ teaspoon msg
1 teaspoon vinegar

METHOD

1. Cut salt fish into thin slices; immerse in cold water for 1 minute. Remove to a colander and drain for 10 minutes.

2. Heat oil in a small aluminium pan. Put in salt fish and fry till pale brown. Remove to a wire sieve to drain and cool (approximately 5 minutes).

3. Reheat the oil till very hot. Return fish and stir in pan for 2 to 3 minutes till light golden brown. Drain oil from fish on absorbent paper and keep in container when cooled. Reserve oil for frying sambal.

4. Pound **A** coarsely. Bash chilli padi very lightly.

5. Heat 3 tablespoons oil reserved from (3) till hot. Stir-fry the pounded mixture till fragrant and lightly browned. Add sliced tomatoes and chilli padi to fry till oil bubbles through. Add 4 tablespoons water, seasoning and cook over moderate heat till mixture is thick and oily. Lastly, put in salt fish just before serving.

Note:
Both fried fish and sambal can be prepared ahead and stored. To serve, reheat sambal and add salt fish.

SAMBAL BELIMBING

INGREDIENTS

115 g (4 oz) shallots, sliced thinly
55 g (2 oz) garlic, sliced thinly
4 red chillies, sliced thinly slantwise
4 green chillies, sliced thinly slantwise **A**

1 teaspoon shrimp paste
2 candlenuts
1 stalk lemon grass, sliced thinly **B** *pounded to a fine paste*

455 g (1 lb) sour star fruit (belimbing)
2 level teaspoons salt
455 g (1 lb) small prawns
455 g (1 lb) grated coconut, white
Oil for frying

Seasoning:
1 teaspoon salt
1½ teaspoons sugar
½ teaspoon msg

METHOD

1. Remove stems of sour star fruit and slice into thin rounds.

2. Rub salt into fruit and marinate for 1 hour. Rinse and squeeze lightly and set aside.

3. Shell and clean prawns. Set aside.

4. Squeeze grated coconut for approximately 225 ml (8 fl oz) of No. 1 milk. Set aside.

5. Heat oil in kuali. Fry **A** separately till light brown. Remove to a plate.

6. In a clean kuali, heat 4 tablespoons of oil and fry **B** till fragrant.

7. Add fruit and half of No. 1 milk with 4 tablespoons water. Cook for 10 minutes over low heat.

8. Add seasoning, prawns and cook till prawns change colour. Pour and stir in remainder of No. 1 milk.

SAMBAL TEMPE UDANG
(SPICY PASTE WITH FERMENTED SOYA BEAN CAKE AND PRAWNS)

INGREDIENTS

115 g (4 oz) shallots or onions
   (preferably shallots)
 55 g (2 oz) garlic   **A**
115 g (4 oz) red chillies, sliced slantwise
115 g (4 oz) green chillies, sliced slantwise
   4 stalks lemon grass, thinly sliced

Seasoning:
  2 tablespoons sugar
  1 teaspoon msg   **B**
  1 teaspoon salt

  2 tablespoons tamarind, mixed with   **C**
    4 tablespoons water and strained

285 g (10 oz) very small prawns
 10 fermented soya bean cakes (5 packets)
  4 large soya bean cakes
340 ml (12 fl oz) oil
285 g (10 oz) long beans, cut into 3 cm (1¼ in)
    lengths, slantwise
    Pinch of salt
  1 teaspoon sugar
  4 tablespoons oil
2–3 tablespoons dry chilli paste
605 g (21 oz) grated coconut, squeezed for 225 ml
    (8 fl oz) No. 1 milk

METHOD

1. Wash prawns, cut sharp points and tail; drain.
2. Cut fermented soya bean cake into cubes, approximately 1.5 cm (½ in). Immerse in slightly salted water and drain immediately. Set aside. Cut soya bean cake into the same size as the fermented soya bean cake and repeat process. Set aside.
3. Heat 225 ml (8 fl oz) oil in a non-stick frying pan till hot. Fry soya bean cake, fermented soya bean cake and the contents of **A** separately and in order till lightly browned. Set aside in a plate.
4. Add 115 ml (4 fl oz) oil in pan and fry prawns with a pinch of salt till shells are crisp and almost dry. Drain in a colander. Pour oil away, leaving 2 tablespoons to fry the long beans till soft (approximately 2 minutes). Add a pinch of salt and 1 teaspoon sugar. Mix well and remove to a plate.
5. In a clean wok, heat 4 tablespoons oil to fry the chilli paste for ½ minute, add in the No. 1 milk, seasoning (**B**) and tamarind water (**C**). Keep stirring over moderate heat till mixture boils, then put in all the fried ingredients.
6. Increase heat, stir well in pan and cook till almost dry. Spread on to a large tray to cool.

SAMBAL TUMIS
(BASIC SAMBAL)

INGREDIENTS

15 shallots
30 dried chillies *or* 3 tablespoons chilli paste*   **A**
 1 tablespoon shrimp paste
 1 clove garlic

 1 teaspoon sugar
½ teaspoon salt
  Pinch of msg   **B**
 1 tablespoon tamarind with 55 ml (2 fl oz)
   water, squeezed and strained

 6 tablespoons oil
115 g (4 oz) grated coconut squeezed with 55 ml
   water for milk

METHOD

1. Grind **A** to a paste.
2. Heat oil and fry paste over moderate heat till oil bubbles through.
3. Add half of the coconut milk and stir for 2 minutes. Add **B**. Cover and cook for another 2 minutes. Add the rest of the coconut milk. Stir for 1 minute and serve.

*See page 185.

SAMBAL LENGKONG
(CRISPY FISH GRANULES)

INGREDIENTS

340 g (12 oz) shallots
8 candlenuts
3 red chillies, seeded   **A**
14 slices galangal, weighing 55 g (2 oz)
6 stalks lemon grass, finely sliced

1.2 kg (43 oz) grated coconut
225 ml (8 fl oz) water
1.2 kg (2 lb 11 oz) wolf-herring, washed
2 teaspoons salt
5 tablespoons sugar, mixed with
    3 tablespoons hot water
10 lime leaves

METHOD

1. Pound **A** to a fine paste.

2. Use a piece of muslin to squeeze the coconut for No. 1 milk. Add water to the grated coconut and squeeze for No. 2 milk.

3. Place fish in a deep plate. Pour in the No. 2 milk and steam over a high heat till fish is cooked. Remove and put aside.

4. Mix the fish stock with the No. 1 milk and the paste. Add salt.

5. Debone and flake fish very finely. Add to the fish stock and mix well.

6. Heat an iron wok. Pour in the fish mixture to fry over a moderate heat till almost dry, stirring all the time. Reduce the heat to very low and sprinkle the sweetened water. Add the lime leaves and fry until the fish granules are crispy and light brown in colour, stirring constantly.

Note:
To test if the fish granules are crispy, press them between thumb and finger. They should be grainy. Cool before storing in an airtight bottle. Steamed fish should be mashed till fine whilst still hot. A mincer may also be used.

SAMBAL UDANG KERING GORENG
(FRIED DRIED PRAWNS)

INGREDIENTS

6 candlenuts
1 thumb-sized piece turmeric   **A**
1 teaspoon shrimp paste

6 tablespoons sugar
½ tablespoon salt
3 tablespoons tamarind with 140 ml   **B**
    (5 fl oz) water, squeezed and strained
340 g (12 oz) dried prawns, soaked and
    pounded till fine

115 g (4 oz) green chillies
115 g (4 oz) red chillies
115 g (4 oz) garlic   **C**
225 g (8 oz) shallots
10 stalks lemon grass

285 ml (10 fl oz) oil

METHOD

1. Pound **A** to a paste. Add **B** and mix thoroughly.

2. Slice **C** finely. (The lemon grass should be sliced slantwise.)

3. Heat oil in wok. Fry sliced ingredients separately till light brown. Remove.

4. Leave oil in wok and fry the dried prawn mixture over a low heat till almost dry. Add all the fried ingredients.

5. Stir-fry for 5 minutes and remove to a tray to cool.

Note:
Stir the dried prawn mixture constantly when cooking to prevent it from burning. This dish can be kept for months if stored in a refrigerator. When using an electric blender, do not soak or wash the dried prawns. Blend a little at a time.

Nonya Kueh

Apom Berkuah

Abok-Abok Sago

Kueh Bangket

Kueh Bengka Ambon

Kueh Bengka Ubi Kayu

Kueh Bolu

Savory Kueh Bolu

Kueh Dadar

Kueh Khoo

Kueh Ko Chee

Kueh Ko Swee

Kueh Lapis Batavia

Kueh Lapis Almond

Kueh Lapis Beras

Kueh Lompang

Kueh Pulot Bengka

Kueh Lopis

Kueh Pisang

Kueh Sarlat

Kueh Talam Pandan

Jemput-jemput

Onde Onde

Pulot Panggang

Pulot Tarpay

Pulot Tartar

Sar-sargon

Seray-kaya

Clockwise: Kueh Ko Chee, Bengka Ambon, Apom Berkuah with Sauce

APOM BERKUAH

INGREDIENTS

¾ teaspoon dry yeast (ground to a fine
    powder) or ½ teaspoons fresh yeast
4 tablespoons plain flour   **A**
1 teaspoon castor sugar
5 tablespoons coconut water, lukewarm

340 g (12 oz) rice flour
  2 tablespoons glutinous rice flour   **B**
  1 level teaspoon fine salt
310 ml (11 fl oz) cold water

1.6 kg (3½ lb) coconut, white
285 ml (10 fl oz) coconut water, lukewarm
½ teaspoon lime juice
    Few drops of food colouring

METHOD

1. Squeeze coconut for No. 1 milk. Measure
   285 ml (10 fl oz) for the batter and another
   340 ml (12 fl oz) for the sauce. Put in separate bowls. Add 1.1 litre (2 pints) water to
   the grated coconut and squeeze for No. 2
   milk. Measure 370 ml (13 fl oz) for the batter and another 735 ml (26 fl oz) for the
   sauce. Put in separate bowls and set aside.

2. Mix **A**, stir lightly and set aside for 4–
   6 minutes till frothy.

3. Heat the 285 ml No. 1 milk gently over low
   heat till it turns creamy and thick, stirring
   all the time. Do not overboil. Set aside.

4. Combine **B** in a bowl and pour in the
   370 ml No. 2 milk and **A**. Beat with palm
   of hand till mixture turns to a smooth batter. Add in the 285 ml lukewarm coconut
   water and continue beating for 2 minutes,
   then pour in the creamy No. 1 milk from
   Method 3. Beat till well blended.

5. Cover bowl and leave to stand in a warm
   place for 1–2 hours. Beat lightly with a
   wooden spoon at intervals of 10 minutes.
   To test if batter is ready, take a tablespoon
   of batter and fry in a slightly greased pan.
   Batter is only ready when the cake breaks
   into bubbles and forms holes all over.

6. Pour 140 ml (5 fl oz) of the batter in a cup,
   stir in the food colouring and lime juice. Set
   aside.

To fry the apom (using a special apom berkuah pan)

1. Heat pan till very hot, remove from heat
   and slightly grease each patty pan with oil.
   Return pan to moderately high heat. Stir
   batter well and pour white batter to fill up
   all the patty pans. Take ½ teaspoon of the
   coloured batter and spread in a circular motion over the white batter immediately before it starts to bubble. Reduce heat when
   the cake bubbles and breaks into tiny holes
   all over.

2. Sprinkle water all over pan, cover with lid
   and cook for another 4–5 minutes. Loosen
   cake with edge of knife and place on a cake
   rack to cool. Oil pan each time before you
   fry the rest of the batter.

Sauce for the apom:

  55 g (2 oz) rice flour
    3 tablespoons plain flour   **A**
225 ml (8 fl oz) No. 2 milk

225 g (8 oz) palm sugar, finely grated
140 g (5 oz) coarse sugar
115 ml (4 fl oz) water   **B**
  8 screw pine leaves, cut into short lengths
  ¾ teaspoon salt

10 bananas (pisang rajah)
510 ml (18 fl oz) No. 2 milk
340 ml (12 fl oz) No. 1 milk

METHOD

1. Steam the bananas for 7 minutes. Leave to
   cool. Slice.

2. Blend **A** till smooth. Set aside. Combine **B**
   in a saucepan and bring to boil. Boil for
   5 minutes, then add 510 ml No. 2 milk and
   bring to boil again. Strain into a heavy aluminium saucepan.

3. Reduce heat, pour the flour mixture into
   saucepan gradually, stirring all the time.
   Allow to boil gently before adding the 340
   ml No. 1 milk. Add the sliced bananas and
   stir till just boiling. Do not overboil or
   sauce will turn oily and lose its richness.
   Remove the screw pine leaves.

4. Remove from heat, pour sauce into a large
   mixing or china bowl. Stand bowl in a basin
   of cold water to cool, stirring for a moment.

ABOK ABOK SAGO

INGREDIENTS

115 g (4 oz) pearl sago
170 g (6 oz) grated palm sugar
  2 tablespoons coarse sugar
¾–1 teaspoon fine salt
285 g (10 oz) coarsely grated coconut, white
    Few drops of blue food colouring
  4 screw pine leaves, tied into a knot

METHOD

1. Wash and soak pearl sago in cold water for 15 minutes. Drain.
2. Mix the grated palm sugar with the sugar.
3. Sprinkle salt over coconut, mix evenly and combine with the pearl sago in a bowl.
4. Mix one-third of the sago mixture with a few drops of blue food colouring. Put aside.
5. Place the white sago mixture in a shallow oval or round heatproof dish, sprinkle the sugar evenly over it and cover sugar with the blue sago mixture. Place the screw pine leaves on top.
6. Steam over rapidly boiling water for 15–20 minutes.

Using banana leaves to steam:
Wash and scald 10 pieces banana leaves 22 cm × 15 cm (9 in × 6 in). Fold into a cone and staple the edge. Fill with sago mixtures as in Method 5. Put a small piece of screw pine leaf on top before folding over. Secure with stapler and steam for 15–20 minutes.

Note:
Leave a 1.25 cm (½ in) margin round sides of sago mixture when you sprinkle the grated sugar. This will prevent the sugar from melting down the sides of the bowl.

KUEH BANGKET

INGREDIENTS

225 g (8 oz) rice flour
455 g (1 lb) tapioca flour

455 g (1 lb) grated coconut, white, squeezed for 225 ml (8 fl oz) No. 1 milk
  5 eggs
395 g (14 oz) sugar
¾ teaspoon salt

METHOD

To prepare the flour:
1. Stir rice flour and tapioca flour separately in a dry iron wok over low heat till very light and fluffy.
2. Mix and sift the two types of flour together into a basin. Leave overnight.

To make biscuits:
1. Using a piece of muslin, squeeze coconut for No. 1 milk. Set aside.
2. Beat eggs and sugar till thick and creamy. Add the salt and No. 1 milk. Beat till well blended.
3. Set aside 115 g (4 oz) of the sifted flour for dusting and 1 teacup of the egg mixture.
4. Mix the remaining egg mixture into the flour to form a dough. Take a handful of the dough and place it on a dusted board or a marble table top. (Keep the rest of the dough covered with a damp cloth.)
5. Flatten the dough with palm of hand. Dust with flour and roll dough out to 0.5 cm thickness.
6. Cut dough with a round pastry cutter. Pinch biscuit, using a jagged-edged pair of pincers (usually used for pineapple tarts), to form a pattern.
7. Mix leftover dough cuttings with another lot of new dough and a little of the beaten egg mixture each time. Mix to a smooth texture before rolling out and repeating process.
8. Place biscuits on greased trays and bake in a moderate oven at 175°C or Regulo 6 for 20–30 minutes. Cool biscuits on a rack before storing in an airtight tin.

KUEH BENGKA AMBON
(HONEYCOMB CAKE)

INGREDIENTS

30 g (1 oz) fresh yeast or
  1 tablespoon dry yeast
2 teaspoons sugar   A
55 g (2 oz) flour
115 ml (4 fl oz) warm water

680 g (1½ lb) grated coconut, white
  6 screw pine leaves, tied into a knot
340 g (12 oz) sugar
170 g (6 oz) sago flour *or* corn flour
  6 eggs, lightly beaten
½ teaspoon vanilla essence
½ teaspoon salt
  2 drops yellow food colouring

METHOD

1. Combine **A** in a bowl. Stir till batter is smooth and leave in a warm place till frothy (about 15 minutes).

2. Squeeze coconut in small handfuls through a piece of muslin for 340 ml (12 fl oz) No. 1 milk. Set aside in a bowl.

3. Cook coconut milk, screw pine leaves and sugar over very low heat till sugar is dissolved. Stir to prevent burning at the bottom of the pan. Cool. Do not allow the milk to boil. Remove the screw pine leaves.

4. Put sago flour in a mixing bowl. Add beaten eggs, vanilla essence and salt and mix by hand to form a smooth batter. Add the coconut milk mixture, yellow food colouring and stir till well combined.

5. Add the risen yeast dough. Mix till well blended. Rinse mixing bowl with boiling water. Wipe dry and pour batter into bowl. Cover bowl. Put in a warm place and leave for 4-5 hours.

To bake ambon:
Heat brass cake mould over charcoal fire. Brush with corn oil or boiled coconut oil. Stir the batter, fill three quarters of mould and cook over moderate heat till cake bubbles right through to the surface, resembling a honeycomb.

To brown top of cakes:
Place all the cakes on a tray. Put tray 10 cm (4 in) from the heat under a hot grill for 3–5 minutes to brown the surface of the cakes. Cool on a wire rack.

Note:
Bengka ambon can also be baked in a single heavy brass mould or brass 'kueh bolu' mould, uncovered. Charcoal fire is better as the heat is more evenly distributed than in electric or gas rings.

Note: (Coconut oil)
To make oil for greasing patty tins for extra fragrance:– Boil 1 cup oil with 115 g (4 oz) grated coconut and 4 screw pine leaves cut into pieces till coconut turns light brown. Strain and cool before use. When using desiccated coconut, dampen slightly before boiling. Keep in refrigerator for future use.

KUEH BENGKA UBI KAYU
(NONYA TAPIOCA CAKE)

INGREDIENTS

1.4 kg (3lbs) tapioca, finely grated
905 g (2 lbs) grated coconut, white

480 g (17 oz) castor sugar
  3 teaspoons sago or cornflour
  3 eggs, beaten lightly   A
  1 tablespoon butter, melted
1½ teaspoons vanilla essence
1½ level teaspoons salt

METHOD

1. Preheat oven to 177°C. Add 1 cup cold water to grated tapioca and squeeze water out with a piece of muslin into a small saucepan. Set tapioca aside and allow tapioca water to stand for tapioca starch to settle at the bottom of pan. After approximately half hour, pour water away carefully to collect starch. Mix tapioca starch with grated tapioca.

2. Squeeze coconut for No. 1 milk. Measure 455 ml (16 fl oz) into a bowl and set aside. Add 170 ml (6 fl oz) water to coconut and squeeze out 170 ml of No. 2 milk. Set aside.

3. Combine Ingredients **A** with No. 2 milk and whisk lightly till blended. Pour mixture into a heavy aluminium saucepan and cook over moderate heat till heated through and sugar dissolves. Add No. 1 milk and cook for another minute.

4. Put grated tapioca into a large mixing bowl. Pour in the hot egg and coconut mixture and stir till well blended.

5. Grease a square baking tin (20 × 20 × 4 cm) on base and sides. Cut a strip of grease proof paper to line the sides of the tin, allowing ½ cm clearance from sides. Grease paper and dust tin with flour.

6. Put tapioca mixture into tin and bake for 10-15 minutes or till cake turns light brown. Reduce heat to 135°C and cook for another 1-1¼ hour or till cake is golden brown.

7. Remove from oven and allow to cool for 10 minutes. Remove cake from tin and allow to cool completely before cutting.

KUEH BOLU
(NONYA SPONGE CUP CAKE)

INGREDIENTS

170 g (6 oz) plain flour
1½ teaspoons baking powder
 5 eggs
155 g (5 oz) castor sugar

METHOD

1. Preheat oven to 205°C (400°F). Sift flour and baking powder twice. Divide into two equal parts. Set aside.

2. Beat eggs and sugar till very thick and creamy. Divide into two portions.

3. Sift one portion of the flour over one portion of the egg mixture. Fold very lightly as for sponge sandwich.

4. Spoon batter into greased and heated Kueh Bolu pans till ¾ filled. Bake in 205°C for 5 minutes then reduce heat to 150°C (300°F) till cake turns golden brown. Remove to cooling rack with fork.

5. Repeat with remaining egg and flour. Wait till temperature reaches 205°C before baking. Bake at once when batter is spooned into the moulds. Do not leave to stand.

6. Cool cakes completely before keeping in an air-tight container.

SAVORY KUEH BOLU
(NONYA SPONGE CAKE WITH MINCEMEAT FILLING)

INGREDIENTS

285 g (10 oz) lean pork
 55 g (2 oz) shallots, chopped finely
 1 clove garlic, chopped finely
 2 level teaspoons roasted coriander seeds, ground
 4 tablespoons oil
 Pork stock, approx. 225 ml (8 oz)

Seasoning:
½ teaspoon salt
 3 rounded tablespoons sugar
½ teaspoon pepper
 1 teaspoon msg
2–3 teaspoons black sauce

 2 large eggs
 55 g (2 oz) castor sugar
 70 g (2½ oz) plain flour (sifted twice)
 2 tablespoons evaporated milk

METHOD

1. Boil whole piece of pork with 285 ml (10 fl oz) water, ¼ teaspoon each of salt and msg for 20 minutes. Remove pork and keep stock. Dice pork into very small pieces.

2. Heat the oil in pan to fry the garlic and shallots till lightly browned. Add in the pork and seasoning, stir well and cook for 2 minutes. Add in the coriander and a third of the pork stock. Stir over moderate heat for 10 minutes.

3. Pour in the rest of the stock and cook till mixture is dry and oily.

4. Beat eggs and sugar till very thick and creamy about 15–20 minutes. Add in the evaporated milk and beat for ½ a minute.

5. Fold in sifted flour gently till blended. Heat bolu pan for 5 minutes, brush with oil and spoon batter to fill ⅔ of each mould. Add in a teaspoon filling and cover filling with batter. Bake in a heated oven for 5–6 minutes till golden brown.

KUEH DADAR
(COCONUT ROLLS WITH COCONUT SAUCE)

INGREDIENTS

Batter:
- ½ teaspoon salt
- 2 tablespoons oil
- 4 large eggs, lightly beaten } **A**
- 225 g (8 oz) flour
- 1 tablespoon sago flour

565 g (20 oz) grated coconut, white, for No. 1 milk
Different shades of food colouring

METHOD

1. Extract 225 ml (8 fl oz) No. 1 milk from grated coconut. Set aside. Add 455 ml (16 fl oz) water to grated coconut and squeeze again to obtain 225 ml (8 fl oz) No. 2 milk. Set aside.

2. Blend the two types of coconut milk together with **A** and mix till smooth. Strain into another bowl. Divide batter into three or four portions. Add a few drops of different shades of food colouring to each portion. Stir well. Let stand for ½ hour.

3. Heat an omelette pan. When hot, remove pan from the heat and grease base. Pour just enough batter to cover the base of the pan thinly. Fry pancake till edges curl slightly upwards. Pile pancakes on a plate to cool before filling.

4. Fill each pancake with 2 tablespoonfuls of coconut filling. Fold to enclose filling, then roll.

Filling:
- 3 tablespoons sugar
- 285 g (10 oz) grated palm sugar } **A**
- 3 tablespoons water
- 6 screw pine leaves

565 g (20 oz) grated coconut, white
1 tablespoon sago flour mixed with 2 tablespoons water

Boil **A** to dissolve sugar. Add coconut, lower heat, stirring till almost dry. Add flour and cook for 5 min. Cool.

Sauce:
- 680 g (24 oz) grated coconut, white
- 455 ml (16 fl oz) water
- 3 tablespoons plain flour
- 55 g (2 oz) wet rice flour *or* 3 tablespoons rice flour
- 1 teaspoon salt
- 1 tablespoon sugar
- 6 screw pine leaves, tied into a knot

METHOD

1. Squeeze grated coconut for No. 1 milk. Set aside. Add 455 ml (16 fl oz) water to grated coconut and squeeze again for No. 2 milk. Measure milk and add water to bring it up to 855 ml (2 pints).

2. Mix 225 ml (8 fl oz) of the No. 2 milk with the two types of flour. Set aside.

3. Bring the rest of the No. 2 milk together with the salt, sugar and screw pine leaves to nearly boiling point in a saucepan.

4. Remove saucepan from heat. Add the flour mixture gradually to the hot milk, stirring all the time. Add No. 1 milk.

5. Return saucepan to the heat and allow mixture to boil over a very low heat, stirring constantly. Remove and pour sauce into a large bowl to cool.

6. Serve with coconut rolls.

Wet rice or glutinous rice flour:
To 22 oz of fine rice or glutinous rice flour, gradually add 15–17 oz of cold water and stir till it becomes a firm paste. Use the amount required for each recipe and keep the remainder in the freezer for future use. The paste will keep in the freezer for 1–2 months if stored in plastic bags flattened to one inch thick slabs. Recommended brands: "Superior Quality Thai Rice and Glutinous Rice Flour" (Three Elephant Heads trade mark); "Fine Rice Flour" (Sea Gull trade mark); freshly ground wet rice or glutinous rice flour obtainable from Singapore markets, e.g. Joo Chiat Market.

Note:
For the pancakes, use an omelette pan with a 16.5 cm (6½ in) base.

(22 pieces)

KUEH KHOO

(STEAMED GLUTINOUS RICE PASTE
WITH SWEET GREEN BEAN FILLING)

INGREDIENTS

2 tablespoons sugar
2 tablespoons oil   **A**
½ teaspoon salt

115 g (4 oz) sweet potato
680 g (1½ lb) grated coconut, white
455 g (1 lb) glutinous rice flour
   Red food colouring
20 pieces of banana leaves, cut to fit size of mould

METHOD

1. Peel sweet potato, cut into pieces and boil gently. When tender press through a ricer whilst still hot.

2. Squeeze coconut through muslin for No. 1 milk. Set aside 285 ml (10 fl oz) in a bowl. Add 170 ml (6 fl oz) water to the coconut and squeeze for 170 ml (6 fl oz) No. 2 milk. Add **A** and set aside in a small bowl.

3. Combine the sweet potato with 285 g (10 oz) of the glutinous rice flour in a large mixing bowl. Set aside.

4. Bring the No. 2 milk mixture to the boil in a small saucepan. Add a few drops of red food colouring and remove from heat. Pour in the rest of the glutinous rice flour and stir well.

5. Remove hot dough to flour and sweet potato mixture in mixing bowl. Pour in the No. 1 milk gradually and mix well to form a dough. Place dough on a lightly floured board (using glutinous rice flour for dusting) and knead lightly to form a smooth dough. Put dough in a bowl and cover with a damp cloth till ready for filling.

Filling:
565 g (20 oz) skinned green beans, washed, soaked overnight and drained
  8 screw pine leaves, tied into a knot
625 g (22 oz) coarse sugar

METHOD

1. Steam the green beans till soft (20 minutes) and pass through the ricer whilst hot. Set aside.

2. Boil 140 ml (5 fl oz) water in an iron wok. Add the screw pine leaves and sugar and boil over a low heat till the sugar turns syrupy.

3. Add the mashed beans, mix well and cook mixture until almost dry, stirring all the time. Remove the screw pine leaves and let the mixture cool.

4. Form the sweet filling into 20 small balls and place them on a tray till ready for filling.

To mould kuey khoo:
1. Pour 115 ml (4 fl oz) corn or boiled coconut oil (*see page 194*) into a cup. Oil palms of hands and divide dough into 20 equal parts. Roll each part into a ball, make a well in each ball to hold a piece of sweet filling and bring up the sides to cover.

2. Oil palms of hands again and roll cakes till well-rounded. Place each cake in centre of mould and press cake firmly till it fills the mould to obtain a deep impression of the pattern. Turn out each cake on to a piece of banana leaf. Repeat process with the rest of the dough.

To steam kueh khoo:
1. Place the kueh khoos on a perforated steamer tray and steam over medium heat for 7–10 minutes. The water in the steamer must be boiling gently, or cakes will not retain its pattern. Wipe lid of steamer to prevent water dripping down to the cakes.

2. Remove cakes to a rack. Brush cakes lightly with oil whilst still hot. Cover with a big piece of banana leaf till ready to serve. This will keep the cakes soft and moist.

KUEH KO CHEE
(STEAMED GLUTINOUS RICE PASTE
WITH COCONUT FILLING)

INGREDIENTS

20 banana leaves, 20 cm (8 in) in diameter
455 g (1 lb) grated coconut, white
115 g (4 oz) sweet potato
395 g (14 oz) glutinous rice flour
   Pinch of salt
  2 tablespoons sugar
  2 tablespoons oil (corn or refined oil)
  2 drops blue food colouring

METHOD

1. Wipe banana leaves with a wet cloth and scald in a saucepan of boiling water for 1 minute. Drain in a colander.

2. Squeeze coconut for 200 ml (7 fl oz) No. 1 milk. Set aside. Add 115 ml (4 fl oz) water to coconut and squeeze for No. 2 milk. Set aside.

3. Boil sweet potato gently till cooked and pass through a potato ricer or mash till smooth. Mix well with 225 g (8 oz) of the flour and set aside.

4. Boil the No. 2 milk, salt, sugar and oil in a saucepan. Add the 2 drops of blue food colouring, remove from heat, and add the remaining flour. Stir lightly. Cool for 1 minute.

5. Put the sweet potato-and-flour mixture in a saucepan, add the No. 1 milk and stir with wooden ladle till it forms a paste. Add mixture from Method 4 and rub the paste lightly to form a smooth firm dough. Add a little flour if dough is too soft.

6. Divide dough into 4 parts and cut each part into 16 pieces. Roll each piece into a ball, put in a knob of coconut filling and seal. Fold each banana leaf into a cone, put in the filled paste, and fold the top over to form a triangle. Staple the ends to secure. Repeat with the rest of the paste and steam over moderately high heat for 15 minutes.

Filling:
  3 tablespoons sugar
285 g (10 oz) grated palm sugar   **A**
  3 tablespoons water
  6 screw pine leaves

565 g (20 oz) grated coconut, white
  1 tablespoon pearl sago, mixed with 2 tablespoons water

METHOD

1. Boil **A** in an iron wok until the sugar turns syrupy.

2. Add grated coconut and lower the heat. Stir mixture constantly till almost dry.

3. Add the sago mixture. Stir thoroughly. Cook for another 5 minutes. Remove to a tray to cool.

Note:
A simpler way of bundling kueh ko chee is to put filling in centre of each piece of paste, cover to form a ball, put on a square piece of softened banana leaf and fold into a neat bundle. Staple the ends and steam.

Store leftover filling in a plastic container in freezer for future use.

KUEH KO SWEE
(RICE CUP CAKES)

INGREDIENTS

285 g (10 oz) wet rice flour★
285 g (10 oz) sago flour
570 ml (1¼ pints) cold water   **A**
  3 tablespoons alkaline water

455 g (16 oz) palm sugar
225 g (8 oz) coarse sugar
 10 screw pine leaves, cut into 5 cm (2 in) **B**
   lengths
455 ml (16 fl oz) water

455 g (16 oz) grated coconut, white, mixed with a pinch of fine salt

METHOD

1. Mix **A** in a bowl.

2. Boil **B** for 10 minutes.

3. Strain the hot boiled syrup gradually into the flour mixture, stirring with a wooden spoon till well mixed.

4. Steam small empty cups for 5 minutes. Fill cups with flour mixture and steam over a high heat for 7 minutes. Cool and remove cake from each cup. Roll cakes in grated coconut before serving.

To make alkaline water:
625 g (22 oz) white alkaline crystal balls, obtainable from local markets
680 ml (24 fl oz) hot water

1. Place alkaline crystal balls in a porcelain jar. Add the hot water and stir with a wooden spoon till the crystal balls dissolve. Allow to stand overnight.
2. Strain alkaline water through fine muslin. Store the alkaline water in a bottle for future use.

Note:
Prepared alkaline water can be kept for almost a year. Store in a bottle.

★See page 196.

KUEH LAPIS BATAVIA
(INDONESIAN LAYER CAKE)

INGREDIENTS

455 g (1 lb) butter
  1 teaspoon mixed spice (see recipe)
115 g (4 oz) flour
  17 egg yolks
   5 egg whites
255 g (9 oz) sugar
  2 tablespoons brandy

To prepare batter:
1. Beat butter till creamy.
2. Sift mixed spice and flour together.
3. Place egg yolks and egg whites in two separate bowls.
4. Beat egg yolks with 200 g (7 oz) sugar till thick.
5. Beat egg whites with the remaining sugar till thick.

6. Fold in alternately, the egg yolk mixture and the egg white mixture to the creamed butter, adding a little flour each time. Lastly, add the brandy.

To bake the cake:
1. Grease bottom and sides of tin with butter.
2. Cut a piece of greaseproof paper in to fit base of tin exactly. Place paper in and grease with butter.
3. Heat grill till moderately hot. Place greased tin under grill for 1 minute. Remove and place in one ladleful of cake mixture. Spread mixture evenly and bake for 5 minutes or till light brown. Remove tin from grill and, using a fine sharp skewer or satay stick, prick top of cake to prevent air bubbles from forming.
4. Add another ladleful of cake mixture. Bake and repeat process as for the first layer, till the cake mixture is used up. Remove cake from tin at once. Turn it over, top side up, on to a cooling rack to cool for ½ hour.

MIXED SPICE

INGREDIENTS

30 g (1 oz) cinnamon bark
20 cloves
 1 star anise
20 pieces green cardamom

METHOD

1. Wash cinnamon bark, cloves and star anise. Air in the sun till very dry.
2. Remove the rounded tips from the cloves.
3. Place all the dried ingredients in a heated frying pan to fry over a low heat for 20 minutes.
4. Remove the whitish covering from the cardamom to extract the seeds.
5. Pound the spices together till very fine. Pass them through a fine sieve and store in a clean dry bottle.

KUEH LAPIS ALMOND

INGREDIENTS

85 g (3 oz) SoftasSilk flour
1 teaspoon mixed spice★
255 g (9 oz) castor sugar
375 g (13 oz) butter
2 tablespoons condensed milk
15 egg yolks
5 egg whites
¼ teaspoon cream of tartar
2½ tablespoons brandy
100 g (4 oz) almond powder

METHOD

1. Sift flour and spice 3 times. Divide sugar into 3 portions.

2. Cream butter with 1 part sugar till creamy. Add condensed milk and beat till well blended. Whisk egg yolks with 2nd portion sugar till creamy and thick.

   Whisk egg white with 3rd portion sugar till frothy. Sprinkle cream of tartar and continue to beat till soft peaks form.

3. Scoop butter mixture into a large bowl, fold egg white and flour alternately with the brandy. Fold in almond powder.

4. Grease an 18 cm (7 in) square tin at base and sides with butter. Cut a piece of grease-proof paper to fill base exactly. Dust with extra flour at sides of tin.

5. Heat oven to moderately high. Heat tin for 2 minutes. Scoop about ½ cup of the batter into tin, use spoon to spread evenly then place tin in oven to bake for 5 minutes till light golden brown. Remove tin. Use satay stick to prick holes around cake. Repeat process with the rest of the batter.

6. Remove cake from oven, turn over to cool on cake rack for 20 minutes. Turn over again and cool completely. Cut into pieces to serve.

Note:
Spread batter evenly with a small flattened tablespoon before baking. Piercing holes in cake helps each layer to merge with the next. This will prevent the cake from splitting when cut into thin pieces.

★See page 199.

KUEH LAPIS BERAS
(RAINBOW LAYER CAKE)

INGREDIENTS

680 g (24 oz) grated coconut, white
340 g (12 oz) wet rice flour★
225 g (8 oz) sago flour
¼ teaspoon salt
455 g (16 oz) coarse sugar

8 screw pine leaves, tied into a knot
Different shades of food colouring

METHOD

1. Add 570 ml (20 fl oz) water to the grated coconut and squeeze for milk, using a piece of muslin. Add water to bring it to 855 ml (30 fl oz).

2. Place the two types of flour and salt in a bowl; add the coconut milk a little at a time and mix till smooth. Set aside.

3. Boil the sugar with 285 ml (10 fl oz) water and the screw pine leaves for 10 minutes over a moderate heat. Strain the syrup into a bowl. Measure it and add hot water if necessary to bring it to 425 ml (15 fl oz).

4. Pour the hot boiled syrup gradually into the flour mixture, stirring all the time till it is well blended.

5. Divide the flour mixture into four portions. Set aside one portion to remain uncoloured and add a few drops of different shades of food colouring to the other three portions. (Set aside 140 ml (5 fl oz) of the uncoloured mixture to be coloured dark red for the top layer.)

6. Grease an 18 cm (7 in) diameter × 5 cm (2 in) deep cake tin with oil. Place tin in steamer of rapidly boiling water. Pour 140 ml (5 fl oz) of different coloured batters for each layer and steam for 5–6 minutes each time, till mixture is used up.

7. For the final top layer, use the dark red batter. Remove cake to cool for at least 7–8 hours before cutting.

★See "Wet Rice Flour" on page 196.

KUEH LOMPANG

(STEAMED RICE CAKES WITH GRATED COCONUT TOPPING)

INGREDIENTS

140 g (5 oz) rice flour
  1 heaped tablespoon tapioca flour
285 g (10 oz) coarse sugar
  8 screw pine leaves, knotted
   A selection of food colouring
455 g (16 oz) coarsely grated coconut, mixed with a
  pinch of table salt

METHOD

1. Mix the rice and tapioca flour in 75 ml (3 fl oz) water. Stir well.

2. Boil sugar and screw pine leaves in 425 ml (15 fl oz) water for 5 minutes or till sugar dissolves. Pour the syrup gradually through a strainer into the flour mixture, stirring all the time.

3. Divide the mixture into 3 or 4 portions. Put one or two drops of food colouring into each portion to make light pastel shades. (The colour deepens on steaming so colour sparingly).

4. Place small Chinese tea cups in a steamer over rapidly boiling water to heat for 5 minutes. Fill cups with coloured flour mixture and steam for 10 minutes. Wipe condensation off lid after 5 minutes' steaming.

5. Remove cups and allow cakes to cool for about 20 minutes before removing with a blunt knife. Roll the cakes in the grated coconut and serve.

Note:
To facilitate filling of small cups, pour mixture from a teapot. Stir mixture well for an even consistency.

KUEH PULOT BENGKA

(GLUTINOUS RICE CAKE)

INGREDIENTS

  A 20 cm (8 in) square banana leaf, for lining cake tin
680 g (24 oz) grated coconut, white, for No. 1 milk
395 g (14 oz) coarse sugar
  4 screw pine leaves tied into a knot
510 g (18 oz) wet glutinous rice flour★
115 g (4 oz) wet rice flour
½ teaspoon salt
340 g (12 oz) coarsely grated coconut, white

METHOD

1. Grease the sides and base of a square cake tin, and line it with the banana leaf.

2. Extract 285 ml (10 fl oz) No. 1 milk from the grated coconut. Set aside.

3. Cook the sugar, No. 1 milk and the screw pine leaves in a heavy-bottomed aluminium saucepan over a low heat. Keep stirring all the time till the sugar dissolves. Remove from the heat.

4. Place the two types of wet flour in a basin.

5. Add the sugary mixture gradually to the flour. Mix till well blended. Return the mixture to the saucepan, and cook over a very low heat, stirring all the time, till the mixture becomes thick and gluey (half-cooked). Remove from the heat, stir in salt and the coarsely grated coconut.

6. Pour mixture into cake tin and bake in oven at 190°C (375°F) or Regulo 7 for 15 minutes. Reduce heat to 175°C (350°F) or Regulo 6 and bake for 1–1½ hours or till cake is cooked. Leave cake in tin for 20 minutes before turning it on to a cake rack to cool before cutting.

★*See "Wet Rice Flour" on page 196.*

KUEH LOPIS
(GLUTINOUS RICE WITH GRATED COCONUT AND PALM SUGAR SYRUP)

INGREDIENTS

455 g (1 lb) glutinous rice
  2 tablespoons alkaline water★
285 g (10 oz) palm sugar
  2 tablespoons coarse sugar
  5 screw pine leaves cut into pieces
455 g (1 lb) tender grated coconut, white
  Pinch of salt

METHOD

1. Wash glutinous rice till water runs clear, place in a container and add water to cover 5 cm (2 in) above level of rice. Add the alkaline water, mix well and evenly and leave to soak for 4 hours.

2. Rinse rice, then drain well, using colander. Set aside for 20 minutes.

3. Make two cloth bags by cutting two pieces of white material measuring 30 cm × 20 cm (12 in × 8 in). Fold the material into halves lengthwise and use running stitch to sew it 0.5 cm from the edge. Use a string to tie one end of the bag 5 cm away from the edge.

4. Pack ½ the rice firmly in 1 bag and tie to resemble a large sausage. Repeat process with the other bag.

5. Put a low steaming rack at bottom of a large saucepan. Add 170 ml (6 fl oz) water and bring to boil. Put in the 2 bags, and boil over constant high heat for 3 hours. Water level in saucepan should always be 8–10 cm above the bags. (Add boiling water when necessary.)

6. Remove bags to cool overnight. Untie bags and use thick thread to slice *lopis* fairly thickly.

To boil the syrup:
Grate the palm sugar, add sugar, water, screw pine leaves and boil in a saucepan for 10 minutes till syrup is fairly thick.

To serve:
Mix the salt evenly with the grated coconut. For each serving, put 2 slices of *lopis* on a plate, and 2 tablespoons of grated coconut on top. Pour some syrup and serve.

★*See page 199.*

KUEH PISANG
(BANANA CAKE)

INGREDIENTS

625 g (22 oz) grated coconut, white, for milk
6–8 bananas (pisang rajah)
  1 packet green bean flour
¾ teaspoon salt
310 g (11 oz) sugar

METHOD

1. Squeeze grated coconut for No. 1 milk. Add 455 ml (16 fl oz) water to grated coconut and squeeze again. Mix both together and add water so that it measures 1 litre (2 pints).

2. Steam bananas with skin on till cooked (about 10–12 minutes). Cool, remove skin and slice bananas (1 cm thick).

3. Place the green bean flour in a heavy-bottomed aluminium saucepan. Add 1 teacup of the measured coconut milk and salt. Stir to blend. Set aside.

4. Cook the sugar and the rest of the coconut milk over a low heat, stirring constantly till nearly boiling. Remove.

5. Stir flour mixture in the saucepan, pour in the hot coconut milk gradually, stirring all the while. Cook it gently over a very low heat till it boils. Let it boil for ½ minute, stirring all the time. Remove from the heat.

6. Add the sliced bananas and mix well.

7. Rinse a square 23 cm (9 in) × 5 cm deep tin. Pour in the mixture to set. Chill in refrigerator.

KUEH SARLAT

(GLUTINOUS RICE CAKE WITH
CUSTARD TOPPING)

Coconut milk:

1.6 kg (3½ lb) grated coconut, white
1½ teaspoons salt
  1 tablespoon castor sugar

1. Using a piece of muslin, squeeze grated coconut to obtain approximately 625 ml (22 fl oz) No. 1 milk. Set aside 455 ml (16 fl oz) for the custard topping.

2. Pour the remaining 170 ml (6 fl oz) No. 1 milk into a separate jug for the glutinous rice. Add the salt and castor sugar and stir till dissolved. Set aside. Add 340 ml (12 fl oz) water to grated coconut and squeeze for No. 2 milk. Measure 225 ml (8 fl oz) and set aside.

Custard topping:

  1 tablespoon flour
  1 tablespoon cornflour
 10 screw pine leaves, pounded to a fine pulp
370 g (13 oz) coarse sugar
 10 eggs, beaten lightly
  1 teaspoon green food colouring

1. Mix 4 tablespoons from 455 ml (16 fl oz) of the No. 1 milk with two types of flour till smooth.

2. Add the rest of the milk to the pounded screw pine leaves. Mix well and squeeze with a fine muslin.

3. Blend the milk with the flour mixture. Set aside.

4. Cook the sugar and beaten eggs in a heavy-bottomed aluminium saucepan over a very low heat. Stir constantly till sugar dissolves.

5. Remove from the heat. Add the flour mixture and green food colouring. Stir well and set aside.

Glutinous rice:

625 g (22 oz) glutinous rice, washed and soaked overnight
  6 screw pine leaves, tied into a knot

1. Drain and steam glutinous rice with screw pine leaves over rapidly boiling water for 15 minutes. Make steam holes in glutinous rice using handle of wooden spoon before steaming.

2. Remove glutinous rice to a saucepan, pour in the No. 2 milk. Mix well and cover for 5 minutes.

3. Return glutinous rice to the steamer. Steam for another 7 minutes. Remove to saucepan and mix well with the salted No. 1 milk. Steam again for another 5 minutes.

4. Remove glutinous rice to a round tray, 30 cm (12 in) in diameter and 5 cm (2 in) deep. Press down firmly with a banana leaf or a thick piece of soft plastic.

To steam kueh sarlat:

1. Steam tray of glutinous rice over boiling water for 15 minutes.

2. Re-heat the egg mixture for 2 minutes, stirring all the time. Pour it over the glutinous rice. Cover and steam over a moderately high heat for 15 minutes or till mixture changes colour and sets, forming slight ridges on the surface.

3. Reduce heat to very low and continue steaming for ¾ hour, or till a knife comes out clean when inserted into the centre of top green layer. Remove and place tray on a wire rack to cool completely before cutting.

Note:
Make steam holes each time using a chopstick when re-steaming glutinous rice. From time to time, wipe water collected on the underside of lid of iron wok. Any droplet will cause discolouration of the cake. Add boiling water to iron wok when necessary.

KUEH TALAM PANDAN

INGREDIENTS

Green base layer:

25 g (1 oz) wet rice flour★	
55 g (2 oz) tapioca flour or cornflour	
28 g (1 oz) grean bean flour (Hoen Kwe Flour)	**A**
½ teaspoon alkaline water★★	
½ teaspoon green food colouring	

170–225 g (6–8 oz) sugar

  5 screw pine leaves, shredded
  4 tablespoons SANTAN powder dissolved
    in 400 ml (14 fl oz) water for milk

METHOD

1. Liquidise screw pine leaves with 115 ml (4 fl oz) of milk, squeeze and mix with **A** till smooth.

2. Bring to boil the remaining milk and sugar till sugar is dissolved. Remove from heat.

3. Pour boiling syrup into flour mixture, stirring as you pour.

4. Return flour mixture to cook over low heat till almost boiling. Keep stirring to prevent flour sticking at bottom of pan. Remove and set aside.

5. Place round tray or small cups in steamer for 5 minutes over rapidly boiling water.

6. Pour green mixture into tray or cups (half filled) and steam over high heat for 7–10 minutes. Remove lid, pour in white topping and return to steam for further 6 minutes. Remove to cool completely before cutting.

Note:
Wipe steam from under lid from time to time.

1 tablespoon SANTAN powder is equivalent to 4 oz grated coconut.

Coconut Creme Topping
  ½ 30 g packet SANTAN dissolved in 85 ml
    (3 fl oz) water for No. 1 milk
  2 tablespoons SANTAN dissolved in 255 ml
    (9 fl oz) water for No. 2 milk

1½ rounded tablespoons tapioca flour or cornflour	
1½ rounded tablespoons plain flour	**A**
1½ rounded tablespoons green bean flour	
2 tablespoons rice flour	

  ¾ teaspoon salt
  ½ teaspoon sugar
  2 pieces screw pine leaves, tied into a knot
    (optional)

METHOD

1. Combine **A** with 85 ml of No. 2 milk till well blended, in a non-stick saucepan.

2. Bring the remaining No. 2 milk to nearly boiling point in a saucepan. Remove from heat. Stir flour mixture before pouring in the hot milk.

3. Return mixture over very low heat and keep stirring till nearly boiling point. Add the No. 1 milk, sugar, salt and screw pine leaves.

4. Keep stirring till mixture begins to thicken. Remove from heat and set aside.

★*See page 196.* ★★*See page 199.*

JEMPUT-JEMPUT
(BANANA FRITTERS)

INGREDIENTS

200 g (7 oz) grated coconut, white
  4 eggs
225 g (8 oz) sugar
½ teaspoon salt
340 g (12 oz) self-raising flour
115 g (4 oz) grated coconut, white
10 – 12 bananas, (pisang rajah) mashed
    Oil for deep-frying

METHOD

1. Using a piece of muslin, squeeze the coconut for No 1 milk.

2. In a large bowl, beat eggs and sugar to a thick cream. Add salt.

Top: Kueh Khoo

On Plate: (Clockwise) Seray-kaya, Onde Onde, Pulot Tartar

3. Stir in the flour gradually. Add the white grated coconut, mashed bananas and No 1 milk. Mix very lightly.

4. Heat oil for deep-frying till hot.

5. Drop a few spoonfuls of the batter into the hot oil and fry till light brown. Repeat process till batter is used up.

6. Remove fritters to absorbent paper to cool.

Note:
Turn fritters once over only when one side is brown. Do not pile the fritters when they are still hot.

ONDE ONDE

INGREDIENTS

8 screw pine leaves

300 g (10 oz) glutinous rice flour
1 heaped tablespoon tapioca flour or corn flour
Pinch of salt

Few drops of green food colouring
285 g (10 oz) grated coconut, mixed with a pinch of salt
150 g (5 oz) palm sugar, finely grated and mixed with 1 tablespoon castor sugar

METHOD

1. Pound screw pine pieces till fine, add enough water to bring it to 210 ml (7 fl oz). Add salt and green colouring. Strain and set aside.

2. Boil tapioca flour with 85 ml (3 fl oz) water over low heat, stirring till almost transparent.

3. Pour the tapioca mixture immediately into the glutinous rice flour in a large bowl. Still till well absorbed and gradually add in the screw pine water to form a paste.

4. Place paste on a flat surface. Rub well to form a firm smooth dough. If dough is too soft, add in a little flour. Divide dough in 4 parts. Roll each part into a longish roll and cut into 12 pieces. Keep uncut dough covered with a piece of cloth.

5. Bring a big saucepan of water to the boil. Take 1 piece of cut dough and roll with palms of hands till well rounded. Fill with 1½ teaspoons of the grated sugar in centre.

Put into the boiling water. Repeat process with the remaining dough and boil till each ball surfaces. Keep boiling for 2 minutes to dissolve the sugar.

6. Remove each ball with a tea strainer, dab strainer over dry cloth and roll onde onde in grated coconut. Repeat with the rest of the dough.

Note:
It is very important to keep the balls well sealed to prevent cracking whilst boiling. When onde onde floats to the surface keep boiling for at least 2–2½ minutes.
This will keep the onde onde soft and at the same time turns the grated sugar syrupy.

PULOT PANGGANG
(GRILLED GLUTINOUS RICE WITH DRIED PRAWN FILLING)

INGREDIENTS

Glutinous rice:
35–40 banana leaves, 12 cm × 16 cm (5 in × 6 in)
570 g (1¼ lb) grated coconut, white
2 teaspoons salt
1½ tablespoons castor sugar
905 g (2 lb) glutinous rice, washed and soaked overnight
8 screw pine leaves, tied into a knot

METHOD

1. Scald the banana leaves in a basin of boiling water for 2 minutes and allow to soak for further two minutes before wiping dry.

2. Squeeze coconut for 225 ml (8 fl oz) No. 1 milk. Stir in salt and sugar till dissolved. Set aside. Add 225 ml water to coconut for No. 2 milk. Set aside.

3. Place glutinous rice in a steamer with the screw pine leaves. Make steam holes with handle of wooden spoon and steam over rapidly boiling water for 20 minutes.

4. Remove glutinous rice to a saucepan. Pour in No. 2 milk. Mix well and cover for 5 minutes.

5. Return rice to steamer, make steam holes and steam for another 7 minutes. Remove and mix glutinous rice with No. 1 milk in a

saucepan, cover for 5 minutes and re-steam for 5 minutes. (Make steam holes before steaming.) Remove steamer from heat and leave glutinous rice in the steamer. Cover with kitchen towel to keep warm.

Filling:

170 g (6 oz) grated coconut, white
 85 g (3 oz) dried prawns, pounded finely
  8 tablespoons oil

55 g (2 oz) shallots or onions
 8 candlenuts   *pounded to a fine paste*
 1 stalk lemon grass, thinly sliced

4 tablespoons sugar
2 teaspoons pepper
1 tablespoon roasted ground coriander

55 ml (2 fl oz) water
 1 tablespoon cornflour   *thickening, mixed in a bowl*
 2 teaspoons dark soya sauce

To cook filling:

1. Heat an iron or aluminium wok till very hot. Fry coconut over low heat till light brown in colour. Add dried prawns and continue frying for further 20 minutes. Remove to a plate.

2. Heat 8 tablespoons oil in a pan and fry paste till fragrant and lightly browned. Add the sugar, pepper and coriander and stir in pan. Add the fried coconut, dried prawns and the thickening. Stir well so that the fried paste is well mixed with the coconut mixture. Remove to a plate to cool.

To wrap:

1. Wet hands with cool boiled water. Squeeze a small handful of the warm glutinous rice lightly to form a firm oval shape. Use index finger to make a tunnel along the length to hold the filling. Fill and make sure that filling is in the centre. Seal both edges to form a cylindrical shape and wrap with banana leaf. Staple both ends of leaf. Repeat with the rest of the glutinous rice.

2. Heat grill. Put glutinous rice cakes 5 cm (2 in) below grill and grill for 7–8 minutes to brown on all sides. Alternatively, grill over charcoal fire on a satay burner.

Note:
Mixed colours of blue and white glutinous rice can be used. Mix one-third of steamed glutinous rice with a few drops of blue food colouring and 1 teaspoon lime juice. Mix the blue glutinous rice with the white to create a marbling effect.

PULOT TARPAY
(FERMENTED GLUTINOUS RICE)

INGREDIENTS

1.2 kg (42 oz) glutinous rice
140 g (5 oz) rock sugar, pounded finely
170 ml (6 fl oz) hot water
225 ml (8 fl oz) water
1½ pieces *ragi* (Malaysian dry yeast cake) pounded very finely

METHOD

1. Wash glutinous rice and soak overnight.

2. Put the pounded sugar in a bowl. Pour 170 ml (6 fl oz) hot water and stir to dissolve.

3. Drain and steam glutinous rice over rapidly boiling water for 20 minutes. Remove to a saucepan; pour in 225 ml (8 fl oz) water, stir till well mixed, and cover pan for 5 minutes.

4. Return glutinous rice to steamer and steam for another 8 minutes, then remove to a large tray.

5. Set aside 4 tablespoons pounded yeast.

6. Sprinkle the rest of the yeast with the syrup evenly over the warm glutinous rice and mix thoroughly by hand.

7. In a clean dry enamel container or large glass bottle, sprinkle 2 tablespoons of the yeast evenly on base of container. Put the glutinous rice into the container and sprinkle the rest of the yeast evenly on top. Cover container tightly to ferment the glutinous rice. Keep in a warm dark place for 5–6 days.

To serve:
Serve in individual small bowls with chipped ice.

Note:
Separate all the transparent glutinous rice from the chalky rice before steaming. The transparent glutinous rice is harvested before maturity and will leave hardened bits when the tarpay is ready. Do not remove the lid until after the fourth day of fermentation. Keep for a day or two more if it is not fermented.

PULOT TARTAR
(COMPRESSED STEAMED GLUTINOUS RICE WITH COCONUT CREME SAUCE)

INGREDIENTS

605 g (21 oz) glutinous rice
605 g (21 oz) grated coconut, white
   1 tablespoon fine sugar
1½ teaspoons fine salt
   6 screw pine leaves, tied into a knot
Softened banana leaves

1. Soak rice overnight. Drain.

2. Squeeze coconut through a piece of muslin for 200 ml (7 fl oz) No. 1 milk. Stir in the sugar and salt. Set aside. Add 170 ml (6 fl oz) water to coconut and squeeze for No. 2 milk. Set aside.

3. Pour the rice into a colander to drain well before steaming. Steam glutinous rice with the screw pine leaves over rapidly boiling water for 20 minutes. Make steam holes in rice with handle of wooden spoon before steaming.

4. Transfer steamed rice to a saucepan, pour in No. 2 milk, mix well and cover for 5 minutes. Return glutinous rice to steamer, make steam holes and steam for 7 minutes.

5. Stir No. 1 milk to dissolve the sugar and salt and repeat Method 4 using No. 1 milk. Steam for 5 minutes.

6. Line two 10 cm × 15 cm × 10 cm (4 in × 6 in × 4 in) rectangular tins with softened banana leaves. Put half of the glutinous rice into each of the lined tins. Use a piece of banana leaf to press the rice till it is firm and tightly packed in the tin. Leave for 2–4 hours or till completely cool.

7. Cut into slices and serve with coconut creme. Sprinkle castor sugar over if desired.

To make coconut creme sauce:
680 g (24 oz) grated coconut, white
   2 heaped tablespoons plain flour
   4 tablespoons rice flour
   6 screw pine leaves, tied into a knot
   1 teaspoon sugar
   1 level teaspoon fine salt

1. Squeeze grated coconut for approximately 225–285 ml (8–10 fl oz) No. 1 milk. Set aside in a cup. Add 680 ml (24 fl oz) water to the grated coconut and squeeze for No. 2 milk. Set aside.

2. Mix the two types of flour with 225 ml (8 fl oz) of the No. 2 milk. Pour the remaining No. 2 milk into a saucepan, put in the screw pine leaves and cook till nearly boiling point. Add sugar and salt. Stir till dissolved and remove from heat. Stir flour mixture till well blended and pour gradually into saucepan, stirring as you pour. Add No. 1 milk. Stir well.

3. Return saucepan to cook over low heat till sauce comes to the boil, stirring constantly. Remove and pour into a large bowl to cool.

Note:
Mixed colours of blue and white glutinous rice can be used. Mix one-third of steamed glutinous rice with a few drops of blue food colouring and 1 teaspoon lime juice. Mix the blue glutinous rice with the white to create a marbling effect. Stir sauce in pan over a basin of iced water to cool and to prevent it from turning oily.

SAR-SARGON

(CRISPY GROUND RICE AND
COCONUT GRANULES)

INGREDIENTS

605 g (21 oz) No. 1 Thai rice, milled
½ teaspoon fine salt
¼ teaspoon lime paste
3 coconuts, white, coarsely grated
2 eggs, lightly beaten
225–340 g (8–12 oz) sugar

METHOD

1. Wash and soak rice overnight. Drain and
dry in sun. When very dry, grind till very
fine.
2. Rub salt and lime paste into grated coconut
in a large bowl. Pour the eggs over the
coconut and mix lightly by hand. Add the
rice flour a little at a time and rub between
finger and thumb lightly till evenly mixed.

To fry:
1. Heat a wok, pour in the coconut mixture
and fry over moderate heat till dry and brittle. Keep stirring to prevent browning.
2. When mixture becomes grainy and free
from lumps, reduce heat and stir till it is
very crunchy.
3. Add the sugar, stir for 2 minutes and remove from heat. Leave to cool in wok.
Taste a spoonful for desired sweetness and
add sugar if necessary.

Note:
*Charcoal fire and a bronze or brass wok is more suitable for this
recipe as it allows the sargon to remain very pale and off-white in
colour, yet keeps it very brittle and crunchy as it should be.
However if you do not possess a brass or bronze wok, use an iron
or thick aluminium wok to fry over charcoal fire.*

*Lime paste must be very smooth and pasty otherwise it will not
mix well with the coconut.*

*Ready packed ground rice can be substituted for the No. 1 Thai
rice.*

SERAY-KAYA

(RICH EGG CUSTARD)

INGREDIENTS

905 g (32 oz) grated coconut, white
10 eggs, approx. 565 g (20 oz) in weight
565 g (20 oz) coarse sugar
2 screw pine leaves, tied into a knot

METHOD

1. Using a piece of muslin, squeeze grated
coconut to obtain 400 ml (14 fl oz) No. 1
milk.
2. Beat eggs and sugar till well mixed.
3. Heat egg mixture and screw pine leaves in
an enamel container over a very low heat to
dissolve the sugar (about 10 minutes). Keep
stirring all the time with a wooden spoon.
Remove from heat. Take away the screw
pine leaves.
4. Add the No. 1 milk to the egg mixture.
Strain into an enamel container.
5. Stand container of egg mixture on a rack in
a saucepan of rapidly boiling water. Keep
stirring with a wooden spoon until the egg
mixture turns thick like custard cream
(¾ hour).

To steam seray-kaya:
1. Wrap lid of container with a dry tea-towel.
Place container, with lid on, on rack in a
saucepan.
2. Add hot water to saucepan to measure
2.5 cm (1 in) from base of container. Cover
saucepan and steam for 3 hours over moderate heat. Do not stir.
3. Dry the underlid of the cover of the saucepan from time to time to prevent discolouration of the seray-kaya.

Desserts

Agar-Agar Cordial

Agar-Agar Delight

Agar-Agar Talam

Au Nee

Almond Creme

Almond Jelly

Bubor Terigu

Bubor Cha Cha

Chendol

Green Beans with Pearl Sago

Groundnut Creme

Kueh Kuria

Lek-Tow-Suan

Len-Chee-Suan

Lotus Seed Fluff

Lotus Seed Paste Mooncake

Mock Pomegranate

Pearl Sago with Mixed Fruit

Red Beans with Coconut Creme Topping

Sago Pudding

Sweet Red Bean and Lotus Seed Soup

Sweet Lotus Seeds and Dried Longan Soup

Agar-Agar Cordial

AGAR-AGAR CORDIAL

INGREDIENTS

  1 packet agar-agar powder (Rose brand)
  8 screw pine leaves, knotted
85 g (3 oz) sugar

285 g (10 oz) sugar
285 ml (10 fl oz) water   **A**
  8 screw pine leaves

  ½ teaspoon red food colouring
  ¼ teaspoon rose essence

METHOD

1. Dissolve agar-agar powder in 8 tablespoons cold water.

2. Bring 1 litre water and the agar-agar solution to a boil with the screw pine leaves over moderate heat. Add in sugar, boil till dissolved and continue boiling for 5 minutes.

3. Rinse a mould or square tin. Pour the agar-agar through a nylon sieve into the mould and allow to set. Keep in refrigerator till ready for use.

4. To make syrup, bring **A** to a boil in a saucepan for 15 minutes. Put in red colouring and boil for another minute. Remove from heat. Allow to cool before adding rose essence. Pour syrup into a jar through a piece of muslin.

5. To serve, cut agar-agar into slabs and grate into long strips with a coarse grater. Put agar agar strips into glasses and add syrup. Dilute with cold water to taste. Serve with ice chips.

AGAR-AGAR DELIGHT

INGREDIENTS

  ½ packet agar-agar powder (Rose brand)
115 g (4 oz) sugar
  3 tablespoons condensed milk
225 ml (8 fl oz) evaporated milk
  1 tablespoon vanilla
    A few drops green or pink food colouring
  2 egg yolks, lightly beaten
  3 egg whites, beaten with 1 teaspoon sugar till stiff (but not dry)
  1 tin fruit cocktail

METHOD

1. Stir agar-agar in 455 ml (16 fl oz) cold water till dissolved. Bring to the boil and boil for 1 minute. Add in the sugar and cook till sugar dissolves. Keep warm.

2. In another saucepan, bring the condensed and evaporated milk and 400 ml (14 fl oz) water to almost boiling point.

3. Pour 1 cup of the milk mixture gradually into the beaten egg yolks and stir well. Pour this mixture to combine with the agar-agar mixture. Stir and simmer till boiling, stirring occasionally. Add vanilla essence and 2 to 5 drops of food colouring. Simmer for 1 minute.

4. Pour in the egg white, cook gently for ½ minute. Cut to separate the large pieces of egg white. Leave to cook for 10 seconds. Remove from heat.

5. Rinse a shallow, rectangular glass dish and pour agar-agar into the dish allowing the egg white to float evenly. Allow to cool and set before chilling. To serve, cut into small pieces. Garnish with fruit cocktail and serve cold.

Note:
Use ½ of 15 g packet agar-agar powder.

AGAR-AGAR TALAM
(FROSTED AGAR-AGAR)

INGREDIENTS

Bottom layer:
15 g (½ oz) agar-agar, soaked and cut into small pieces
1.4 litres (3 pints) water
6 screw pine leaves, tied into a knot
395 g (14 oz) coarse sugar
A few drops of red food colouring
3 drops of rose essence

METHOD

1. Press soaked agar-agar lightly to fill one cup.
2. Boil the water and screw pine leaves in a saucepan. Dissolve agar-agar in it. Add sugar and boil till dissolved.
3. Remove from the heat. Stir in the red food colouring and the rose essence.
4. Rinse a round cake tin, 28 cm in diameter and 5 cm deep. Pour the agar-agar into the tin. Allow to set 20–30 minutes, till a thin film forms over the surface, before pouring in the coconut layer.

Coconut layer:
680 g (24 oz) grated coconut, white
1 litre (36 fl oz) water
4 screw pine leaves, tied into a knot
15 g (½ oz) agar-agar, soaked and cut into small pieces
85 g (3 oz) coarse sugar
½ teaspoon salt

1. Squeeze grated coconut for No. 1 milk. Set aside 340 ml (12 fl oz).
2. Boil the water and screw pine leaves in a saucepan. Boil agar-agar and sugar till dissolved.
3. Reduce heat to low, pour in No. 1 milk, stirring well into the agar-agar mixture. Add salt and stir until it comes to a boil.
4. Pour coconut mixture over the red layer, allowing it to run and spread over the surface.
5. Allow to cool and set on a flat surface. Chill in refrigerator. Cut and serve.

AU NEE
(SWEET YAM PASTE)

INGREDIENTS

115 g (4 oz) shelled gingko nuts
227 g (8 oz) sugar
225 g (8 oz) pumpkin cubes, approx. 2 cm
905 g (2 lbs) yam slices (5 cm sq. × 1 cm)
12 tablespoons castor sugar
6 tablespoons lard
3 shallots, sliced thinly

METHOD

1. Wash gingko nuts. Boil with half of sugar in 2 tablespoons water over low heat for 45 minutes till sugar is absorbed into the nuts. Add water a little at a time while cooking. Cool and cut gingko nuts into half, removing centre fibre if any.
2. Cook pumpkin cubes in remaining sugar and 2 tablespoons water over low heat in a heavy-bottomed saucepan. Cook till sugar is absorbed. Add a little water at a time while cooking to prevent sugar from burning. Set gingko nuts and pumpkins aside.
3. Steam yam pieces over rapidly boiling water till very soft. Use a food processor to blend half of the yam, 2 tablespoons lard and half of the sugar till paste is smooth. Remove to a bowl and repeat with remaining yam, lard and remaining sugar.
4. Heat another 2 tablespoons lard in a wok to fry the sliced shallots till very lightly browned. Put in yam paste and stir fry over low heat for ½ minute. Remove to a shallow serving bowl. Place cooked pumpkin cubes around sides of the bowl and gingko nuts over the yam. Serve hot.

ALMOND CREME

INGREDIENTS

285 g (10 oz) almonds
855 ml (30 fl oz) water
285 g (10 oz) sugar to boil in 115 ml (4 fl oz) water

Thickening:
(Mix to a smooth paste)
3–4 tablespoons rice flour
170 ml (6 fl oz) water
170 ml (6 fl oz) fresh milk

METHOD

1. Scald and skin almonds. Drain. Blend till very fine using some of the measured water. Strain through a fine sieve into a saucepan. Blend remaining bits and sieve again. Add remaining water and set aside.

2. Dissolve sugar in the 115 ml boiling water.

3. Bring the blended almonds to a boil over moderate heat, stirring till it boils. Add syrup. Stir thickening and pour gradually into mixture, stirring as you pour.

4. Reduce heat but keep boiling for 5 minutes till mixture thickens. 2 drops of almond essence may be added after removing from heat. Serve hot.

ALMOND JELLY

INGREDIENTS

1 handful of agar-agar strips
4 tablespoons sugar
455 ml (16 fl oz) fresh milk
1 tablespoon condensed milk
3 drops of almond essence

METHOD

1. Soak agar-agar strips in cold water, squeeze out water. Cut agar-agar into very small pieces. Press lightly to fill half a 225 ml (8 fl oz) measuring cup.

2. Boil 510 ml (18 fl oz) water and dissolve the agar-agar in it. Add sugar and boil till dissolved.

3. Pour in the fresh milk and condensed milk. Stir and cook for 2 minutes. Remove from the heat. Add almond essence.

4. Pour into a rinsed jelly mould to set. Cool and chill in refrigerator.

To serve almond jelly:
Place jelly in a deep bowl, add canned longans or lychees and cherries with the syrup. Add chipped ice and serve.

BUBOR TERIGU

INGREDIENTS

115 g (4 oz) coarse sugar	
285 g (10 oz) palm sugar	**A**
225 ml (8 fl oz) water	
8 screw pine leaves	

55 g (2 oz) quick cooking oats	**B**
285 ml (10 fl oz) water	

680 g (1½ lb) grated coconut (white)
¼ teaspoon salt
285 ml (10 fl oz) water
285 g (10 oz) *biji terigu* (without husk)
1.7 litres (4 pints) water

3 tablespoons flour to mix with 170 ml (6 fl oz) water | *thickening*

METHOD

1. Boil **A** for 10 minutes and strain.

2. Mix **B** and cook for 5–7 minutes.

3. Squeeze coconut for No. 1 milk. Add salt and set aside. Add 285 ml water to coconut and squeeze for No. 2 milk.

4. Soak *biji terigu* in cold water for 10 minutes; drain. Pound to break up the *terigu*. Bring it to the boil with the 1.7 litres water till *terigu* is tender and swelling. Reduce heat.

5. Pour **A**, **B** and thickening into the saucepan. Add No. 2 milk, and boil for 2 minutes. Remove from heat.

Note:
Serve in individual bowls with a topping of 2 tablespoons No. 1 milk. Serve hot.

BUBOR CHA-CHA

INGREDIENTS

905 g (32 oz) grated coconut, white
565 ml (20 fl oz) cooled, boiled water for No. 2
    milk
310 g (11 oz) diced sweet potatoes
310 g (11 oz) diced yam
225 ml (8 fl oz) water
    6 screw pine leaves, tied into a knot
140 g (5 oz) coarse sugar
310 g (11 oz) fine quality sago flour
    ½ teaspoon borax, available from Chinese dispen-
    saries
225 ml (8 fl oz) boiling water
    A few drops of red, green and blue food
    colouring
½–1 teaspoon salt

METHOD

1. Squeeze grated coconut with muslin for No. 1 milk.
2. Add the cooled, boiled water to the grated coconut and squeeze again for No. 2 milk.
3. Rinse and drain sweet potato cubes, and steam for 5–7 minutes till cooked. Set aside.
4. Steam yam cubes for 5–7 minutes till cooked. Set aside.
5. Boil the 225 ml water with the screw pine leaves and sugar for 10 minutes. Strain syrup into a bowl.

To make sago-flour triangles:
1. Sift sago flour with the borax into a basin.
2. Pour the boiling water over the sago flour. Stir with a wooden spoon to combine.
3. Knead to form a firm dough. Flour palms of hands with sago flour to prevent dough from sticking to them. Knead dough till smooth.
4. Divide dough into four parts. Leave one part uncoloured. Mix a few drops of different food colouring to the other three parts. Knead till colour blends in.
5. Roll each part into thin long strips of about 1 cm in diameter. Use a pair of scissors to cut each strip into small triangles.
6. Bring a saucepan of water to the boil. Place the sago triangles in the boiling water, stirring to keep them from sticking together. Scoop out the cooked sago triangles as soon as they float to the surface. Soak them in a basin of cold water for 10 minutes.
7. Drain and place in a bowl. Add 4 tablespoons sugar and mix to keep the cooked sago triangles separated.

To boil the coconut milk:
1. Mix syrup with No. 2 coconut milk in a saucepan. Bring to the boil over a low heat, stirring all the time.
2. Pour in the No. 1 milk and add salt. Stir well. Cook for a moment. Remove from the heat and keep stirring for a while to prevent mixture from curdling and turning oily.

To serve:
Place a tablespoonful each of cooked sweet potatoes, yam, and sago triangles in a small bowl. Add coconut milk to fill the bowl. Serve hot or cold.

Note:
Clean yam with a brush. Wipe it dry and remove the dark skin. Do not wash after removing the skin or it will be very slimy and difficult to handle. Keep diced yam dry.

Place saucepan of boiled coconut milk in a large basin of cold water and stir to release the heat to prevent curdling when cooking in big amounts.

CHENDOL

Green Bean Flour Droplets:
Basin of iced water
10 screw pine leaves, pounded to a pulp
¼ teaspoon salt
1 teaspoon green food colouring
1 packet green bean flour, 'Flower' brand

1. Prepare a basin of iced water.
2. Mix the pounded screw pine leaves with 1.2 litres (2 pints) water. Squeeze and strain liquid. Add the salt and food colouring.
3. Blend 225 ml (8 fl oz) of the screw pine liquid with the green bean flour in a bowl. Set aside.
4. Bring the remaining screw pine liquid to the boil in a saucepan. Remove from heat. Stir the green bean flour mixture and pour gradually into the saucepan, stirring all the time.
5. Cook over a low heat till it boils, stirring constantly. Remove from the heat immediately when it boils. Leave to stand for 5 minutes.
6. Place the frame for making green bean flour droplets (see diagram) over the basin of iced water. Pour the hot green pea flour mixture on to the frame. Using a flat Chinese frying slice, press mixture in long, downward strokes.
7. Leave droplets to set in the iced water till firm. Add ice to the water to set droplets faster.
8. Drain in colander. Cool droplets in refrigerator till ready to serve.

Palm Sugar Syrup:

625 g (22 oz) palm sugar, grated 6 tablespoons sugar 225 ml (8 fl oz) water 6 screw pine leaves, tied into a knot	**A**

1. Boil **A** for ½ hour.
2. Strain syrup and set aside till ready to serve.

Coconut Milk:
2 kg (4½ lb) grated coconut
910 ml (32 fl oz) cooled, boiled water
1–1½ teaspoons salt

1. Add water to the grated coconut. Squeeze in small handfuls, using a piece of muslin.
2. Add salt to milk. Stir till thoroughly dissolved and cool in refrigerator.

To serve coconut milk mix:
Spoon green bean flour droplets into glasses, add some crushed ice and pour coconut milk to fill glasses. Serve with palm sugar syrup according to taste. Add salt if necessary.

(20–30 servings)

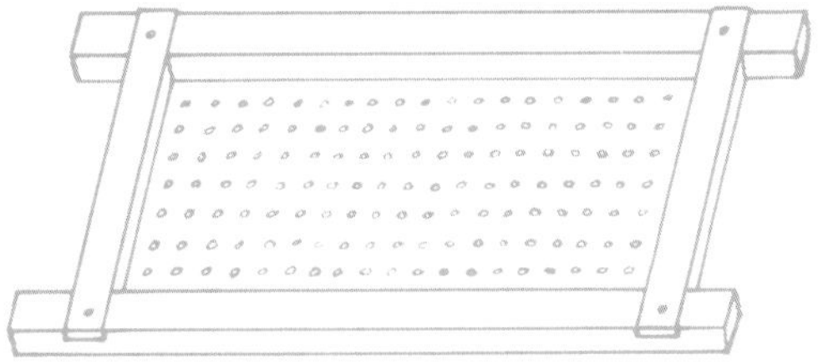

Frame for green bean flour droplets.

GREEN BEANS WITH PEARL SAGO

INGREDIENTS

455 g (1 lb) grated coconut
 85 g (3 oz) pearl sago
605 g (21 oz) green beans
340 g (12 oz) coarse sugar
225 g (8 oz) palm sugar
 6 screw pine leaves tied into a knot
 1 teaspoon salt

METHOD

1. Squeeze grated coconut for approximately 200 ml (7 fl oz) No. 1 milk. Add 455 ml (16 fl oz) water and squeeze for No. 2 milk.

2. Soak pearl sago for 10 minutes. Drain.

3. Boil green beans with 1.14 litres (2 pints) cold water for 20 minutes over high heat.

4. Add 2.27 litres (4½ pints) of cold water and bring to the boil. Reduce heat to moderate and continue boiling till beans are tender and swollen.

5. Put in pearl sago and cook till sago turns transparent. Add No. 2 milk, the two types of sugar and screw pine leaves and cook till it comes to a boil. Add No. 1 milk, salt and cook for 2 minutes. Remove from heat and serve.

GROUNDNUT CREME

INGREDIENTS

625 g (22 oz) groundnuts, shelled
 2 tablespoons rice, washed and drained
 2 litres (4 pints) water
310 g (11 oz) sugar

METHOD

1. Roast groundnuts till light brown. Remove skin.

2. Using an electric blender, blend rice and half of the groundnuts with 455 ml (16 fl oz) water till very fine. Add two or three tablespoonfuls of water if necessary to keep the mixture moving and rotating. Pour into a bowl and set aside.

3. Repeat process using the other half of the groundnuts with another 455 ml (16 fl oz) water.

4. Place the blended groundnuts, sugar and remaining water in a heavy-bottomed aluminium saucepan. Bring to the boil over a moderate heat. Stir mixture all the time with a wooden spoon. Let simmer for 5 minutes, stirring continuously. Remove from the heat. Serve hot or cold.

KUEH KURIA
(TAPIOCA DOUGHNUTS)

INGREDIENTS

455 g (16 oz) grated tapioca, skinned and with
  centre vein removed
170 g (6 oz) grated coconut, white **A**
  3 tablespoons glutinous rice flour or sago
    flour
  ¾ teaspoon salt

For the sugar coating:
 55 ml (2 fl oz) water
225 g (8 oz) coarse sugar
  4 screw pine leaves

METHOD

1. Mix **A** in a bowl.
2. Form mixture into small balls, flatten, and make a hole in the centre as for American doughnuts.
3. Heat oil in iron wok for deep-frying. Fry tapioca rings till golden brown. Remove to absorbent paper.
4. Drain oil from wok. Do not wash. Add the water, sugar and screw pine leaves. Boil till syrup is thick and sticky.
5. Reduce heat to very low and add the tapioca rings. Stir for a minute till they are well-coated with the syrup. Remove wok from heat and keep tossing the tapioca rings in wok till the sugar is dry. Let rings cool on a rack before serving.

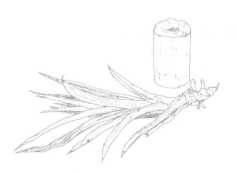

LEK-TOW-SUAN
(GREEN BEAN SOUP)

INGREDIENTS

605 g (21 oz) shelled, split green beans or
  4 packets each of 255 g (9 oz)
  ready-soaked green beans

680 g (1½ lb) coarse sugar
285 ml (10 fl oz) water **A**
  8 screw pine leaves

115 g (4 oz) sweet potato flour

1.7 litres (4 pints) water
10 screw pine leaves tied into a knot **B**

METHOD

1. Wash and soak beans overnight *or* for 5–6 hours. Remove loose skin from beans and drain. Bring beans to the boil and boil for 10 minutes. Drain in a colander, immerse in cold water and drain again immediately.
2. Place the beans in a steamer and steam till beans swell and are tender. Do not steam until beans split. Spread beans to cool on a large tray.
3. Boil **A** in a saucepan over moderately high heat for about 10 minutes till sugar turns syrupy.
4. Mix the sweet potato flour with 340 ml (12 fl oz) water. Strain into a saucepan.
5. Boil **B** for 15 minutes. Pour **B** (still boiling) gradually into sweet potato mixture stirring as you pour. Add the syrup, bring to the boil, add the steamed beans, and continue cooking over low heat till mixture boils. Serve hot in small bowls with slices of crispy Chinese crullers.

Note:
Do not oversoak the beans as this will harden the beans and prevent them from being tender when steamed. Ready-soaked beans are much easier to use and can be bought from any supermarket.

LOTUS SEED FLUFF

INGREDIENTS

55 g (2 oz) pearl barley, washed and drained
115 g (4 oz) gingko nuts, blanched and skinned
  (remove centre fibre)

Dried soya bean strips (*see notes on preparation*)
  6 screw pine leaves
510 g (18 oz) sugar
8–10 eggs, beaten with 4 tablespoons water and
  1 tablespoon sugar
Lotus seeds (*see notes on preparation*)

METHOD

1. Bring 3.2 litres (6 pints) water to the boil.
   Add pearl barley and gingko nuts. Boil
   gently for ½ hour.
2. Add the prepared soya bean strips and
   screw pine leaves and let simmer for
   ½ hour. Add the sugar and cook for
   10 minutes.
3. Increase heat to high. Pour in the beaten
   egg mixture gradually, stirring till egg floats
   to the surface. Remove from heat. Lastly,
   add the prepared lotus seeds. Remove screw
   pine leaves. Serve hot.

To prepare dried soya bean strips:
170 g (6 oz) dried soya bean strips
1.4 litres (2 pints) cold water
½ teaspoon bicarbonate of soda

1. Soak soya bean strips in cold water for
   10 minutes. Add bicarbonate of soda, mix
   and allow to soak for 20 minutes.
2. Rinse and soak again in cold water. Drain
   just before use.

To prepare dried lotus seeds:
115 g (4 oz) dried lotus seeds, skinned
¼ teaspoon bicarbonate of soda
2 screw pine leaves
115 g (4 oz) sugar

1. Soak lotus seeds in 595 g (21 fl oz) water
   for 20 minutes. Split lotus seeds and remove
   green centres, if any.
2. Add bicarbonate of soda and allow lotus
   seeds to soak for 3 hours.
3. Rinse and drain lotus seeds and bring to the
   boil with 340 ml (12 fl oz) of the water and
   two screw pine leaves. Let simmer for
   ½ hour. Add remaining water and 115 g
   sugar and cook for another 10 minutes.

LEN-CHEE-SUAN
(LOTUS SEED SOUP)

INGREDIENTS

285 g (10 oz) lotus seeds
  8 screw pine leaves, tied into a knot
170 g (6 oz) sugar

5 tablespoons sugar
2 tablespoons water ⎱ **A**

2½ tablespoons sweet potato flour, mixed with
  6 tablespoons water

METHOD

1. Soak lotus seeds in lukewarm water for
   4 hours.
2. Split lotus seeds into halves, removing
   greenish centre if any.

3. Boil 565 ml (20 fl oz) water with the lotus
   seeds and 4 screw pine leaves. Lower heat
   and simmer lotus seeds in a covered saucepan for 15–20 minutes, or till tender. Add
   the sugar, stir gently and set aside. Remove
   screw pine leaves.
4. Heat **A** in an aluminium saucepan till light
   golden brown. Add 395 ml (14 fl oz) water
   and the remaining screw pine leaves and
   allow to boil till dissolved.
5. Pour the syrup into the saucepan of lotus
   seeds and bring back to boil over low heat.
   Remove screw pine leaves. Remove from
   heat, stir the sweet potato mixture in bowl
   and pour gradually into saucepan, stirring
   gently. Return saucepan to heat and boil
   gently over low heat. Remove from heat
   and serve hot.

Note:
*To caramelise sugar, boil sugar and water till dissolved. Do not
stir at all after sugar has dissolved, and boil to the colour desired.
Too dark a caramel tastes bitter.*

LOTUS SEED PASTE MOONCAKES

INGREDIENTS

600 g (21 oz) Hongkong soft flour, available at specialist shops catering to restaurants★
170 ml (6 oz) vegetable oil
 1 tablespoon alkaline water★★
225 ml (8 fl oz) golden syrup
 2 kg (4 lb) lotus seed paste
115 g (4 oz) melon seeds
115 g (4 oz) olive seeds
 14 salted egg yolks

Glaze ingredients:
1 egg
1 egg yolk
1 tablespoon water
2 teaspoons golden syrup

METHOD

1. Sift flour into a mixing bowl. Pour oil around flour and stir lightly with a fork. Mix the alkaline water with the syrup and pour around flour mixture. Gather dough into a ball and keep covered in bowl for 1 hour.

2. Divide lotus paste into 20 equal portions. Mix seeds and divide into 20 equal portions. Grease palm of hands; take a portion of mixed seeds and knead into a portion of lotus seed paste. Wrap two yolks in each portion. Repeat with remaining ingredients. Set aside.

3. Divide dough into 20 portions. Place each portion between plastic sheets and press to flatten before rolling out thinly. Cut each portion of dough into a large circle to cover lotus seed paste completely.

4. Place a portion of lotus seed paste in your hand and lift a circle of dough to cover paste tightly and evenly, leaving no air pockets. Roll with both hands to form a smooth round ball.

5. Dust mooncake mould with flour. Knock off excess flour and place ball into mould, pressing gently into shape making sure that cake takes up impression from mould. Knock mould gently side to side to release cake. Repeat with remaining ingredients.

6. Preheat oven to moderately high. Glaze mooncakes very lightly on top and side. Place them on a baking tray to bake for 10 minutes. Remove from oven, glaze again and bake for another 10 minutes. Glaze for the third time, reduce heat to low and bake for 20–30 minutes or till golden brown. Remove to cool on a rack. Keep for 3–5 days before serving.

Note:
Glaze cakes very lightly and evenly on top and sides. Do not allow glaze to drip around cakes.
After the third glaze, remember to turn heat to low to prevent cake from cracking.
Use canned golden syrup and not the bottled variety.

★*Try the one in Lor 27, Sims Avenue.*

★★*See page 199.*

Lotus Seed Mooncakes

MOCK POMEGRANATE SEEDS IN COCONUT MILK

INGREDIENTS

455 g (1 lb) fresh water chestnuts or 565 g (1.2 lb) canned water chestnuts
    1 teaspoon red food colouring
225 g (8 oz) tapioca flour
    5 tablespoons sugar dissolved in 225 ml (8 fl oz) water
1.2 kg (3 lb) grated coconut, white
340 g (12 oz) sugar
    4 screw pine leaves
    1 level teaspoon salt

METHOD

1. Cut water chestnuts into pomegranate seed-sized bits. Add red food colouring, mixing well till colour turns deep pink.

2. Put tapioca flour and water chestnut pieces into a plastic bag. Tie up bag and shake till flour coats chestnuts evenly. Leave in bag for 10 minutes.

3. Bring large saucepan of water to boil. Put chestnuts in and boil till they come to the surface. Stir with chopstick to separate chestnut bits whilst cooking.

4. Scoop out chestnuts and put into a basin of cold water. Drain and pour in more cold water. Stir and drain in colander before putting in sugar solution till ready to serve.

5. To make coconut milk, add 855 ml (30 fl oz) boiling water to grated coconut; cover and leave for 15 minutes. Make syrup with the 340 g sugar, screw pine leaves and 225 ml (8 fl oz) water. Strain and cool.

6. Squeeze coconut for milk into a saucepan and cook over moderate heat to scalding point. Keep stirring whilst cooking. Remove from heat, pour in syrup from (5) and 1 level teaspoon salt. Stir well. Allow to cool and keep in fridge till ready to serve.

PEARL SAGO WITH MIXED FRUIT

INGREDIENTS

1 packet SANTAN instant coconut cream powder*
Diced fruit (melon/honey dew or sweet potato/yam)
90 g (3 oz) pearl sago
6 screw pine leaves, tied into a knot
100 g (3½ oz) sugar
½ teaspoon salt
3 extra screw pine leaves, tied into a knot

METHOD

1. Whisk 1 packet SANTAN with 200 ml (7 fl oz) water. Strain and set aside.

2. Chill in fridge — ½ cup each of diced water melon, rock melon and honey dew. (Alternative: Steamed sweet potato and yam cubes.)

3. Wash and soak the pearl sago for 5 minutes. Drain in colander.

4. Bring 1 litre (2 pints) water to a boil with the 6 screw pine leaves. Continue boiling gently for another 5 minutes. Pour in the pearl sago and cook till it turns transparent.

5. Lower heat, add in the sugar and stir till sugar is dissolved. Pour in the SANTAN milk and salt, stirring as you pour. Put in the extra leaves. Remove from heat and pour into a large bowl to cool.

6. Chill in fridge till ready to serve.

*One 30 g packet of SANTAN is equivalent to 1 lb white grated coconut.

To serve:
Serve the sago coconut sauce in a glass bowl with 1 cup ice chips. Arrange diced fruits over.

RED BEANS WITH COCONUT CREME TOPPING

INGREDIENTS

285 g (10 oz) red beans, washed and drained
½–¾ piece dried orange peel, cut into thin slices (optional)
6 screw pine leaves — tied into a knot (optional)
250 g (9 oz) sugar
1 can lotus seed in syrup (455 ml)

METHOD

1. Boil red beans with orange peel and screw pine leaves in 1.5 litres (3 pints) water till soft.

2. Leave to cool for 15 minutes, remove screw pine leaves, then liquidise red beans till smooth.

3. Return liquidised beans into saucepan, add sugar and bring to boil. Add lotus seed and continue to boil gently for 10 minutes.

4. Pour red bean soup into a large serving bowl, pour coconut creme over and serve hot.

Preparation for coconut creme:

30 g (1 oz) SANTAN instant coconut powder 350 ml (12 fl oz) water 1 tablespoon plain flour ¼ teaspoon salt 1 teaspoon sugar	**A**

3 screw pine leaves, tied into a knot (optional)

1. Blend **A** together and strain into a non-stick saucepan.

2. Put screwpine leaves into SANTAN mixture and cook over moderate heat till boiling point. Keep stirring to prevent lumps from forming.

3. Remove to a basin of icy water to cool completely, chill in fridge till ready to serve.

SAGO PUDDING

INGREDIENTS

120 g (4 oz) SANTAN instant coconut powder★
12 screw pine leaves

½ teaspoon salt | **A**
1 tablespoon sugar

285 g (10 oz) pearl sago

¼ teaspoon salt | **B**
3 tablespoons sugar

455 g (16 oz) palm sugar | **C**
155 g (5 oz) coarse sugar

METHOD

SANTAN milk:
1. Boil 570 ml (20 fl oz) water with 6 screw pine leaves for 5 minutes. Allow to cool. Whisk in SANTAN powder and add **A**.
2. Strain SANTAN milk and cool in fridge.

Pearl sago:
1. Soak pearl sago for 5 minutes. Drain well in colander.
2. Bring 625 ml (22 fl oz) water to boil in a saucepan. Lower heat, and pour in the pearl sago, stirring as you pour. Keep stirring till sago turns transparent.
3. Drain with a strainer and leave to stand under running tap for 3 minutes. Drain excess water and pour sago into a bowl. Add in **B** and stir well. Scoop into a well rinsed jelly mould to set. Chill in refrigerator.

Palm sugar syrup:
1. Boil **C** in 345 ml (12 fl oz) water. Cut 6 screw pine leaves into 1 in lengths and allow to boil together with the syrup for about 10–15 minutes or till mixture turns syrupy. Strain and allow to cool.

To serve:
Top chilled pudding with syrup and chilled SANTAN milk. Serve with a few ice chips.

★Equivalent to 4 lb white grated coconut.

SWEET RED BEAN AND LOTUS SEED SOUP

INGREDIENTS

258 g (9 oz) red beans, boiled in 570 ml (20 fl oz) water
1.7 litres (4 pints) water
½ piece dried orange peel, sliced thinly into shreds
225 g (8 oz) sugar
1 can lotus seeds in syrup
4 screw pine leaves, knotted

METHOD

1. Boil the red beans for ½ hour rapidly. Drain and rinse with cold water in a colander.
2. Put beans and the 1.7 litres water into a pressure cooker and boil for 45 minutes. Leave beans in cooker for ½ hour to release pressure.
3. Remove cover from cooker, pour in another 1 litre water, dried orange peel and screw pine leaves. Bring to a boil, stirring till beans become blended with liquid.
4. Reduce heat. Boil gently till soup thickens; add sugar and lotus seeds with syrup and continue boiling for ¾ hour. Keep stirring occasionally to prevent beans sticking at bottom of cooker. Serve hot.

Note:
Dried orange peel can be bought from Chinese medicine shops.

SWEET LOTUS SEED AND DRIED LONGAN SOUP

INGREDIENTS

455 g (16 oz) treated lotus seeds
85 g (3 oz) dried longans or 1 can sweet longans
905 ml (2 pints) water
4 screw pine leaves, knotted
Sugar to taste

METHOD

1. Cook treated lotus seeds in 250 ml (9 fl oz) water and 125 g (4 oz) sugar for 10 minutes.

2. Wash dried longans and drain immediately. Soak in 285 ml (10 fl oz) boiling water to allow to swell for ½ hour.

3. Boil sugar and screw pine leaves in water for 10 minutes over moderate heat. Remove leaves and add longans and water. Boil for another 2 minutes. Do not overboil or longan will lose its natural flavour.

4. Add lotus seeds and syrup or canned longans. Boil over gentle heat for 5 minutes. Remove from heat. Serve hot or chilled.

Cakes

Banana Cake

Butter Cake

Cheesecake

No Bake Lemon Cheesecake

Chocolate Chiffon Cake

Coffee Walnut Cake

Fruit Cake

Ginger Cake

Lemon Sponge Cake

Pandan Chiffon Cake

Pound Cake

Rose Marie Cake

Semolina Cake

Sponge Sandwich

Super Light Sponge Sandwich

Sultana Cake

Swiss Roll

Walnut Cake

White Christmas

Cheesecake

BANANA CAKE

455 g (16 oz) bananas
455 g (16 oz) butter
  4 tablespoons condensed milk
455 g (16 oz) castor sugar
  ½ teaspoon salt
  1 teaspoon banana essence
  1 teaspoon vanilla essence
  9 eggs
340 g (12 oz) self-raising flour, sifted

METHOD

1. Mash bananas with a fork.
2. Cream butter, condensed milk and half of the sugar for 5 minutes. Add salt, banana essence and vanilla essence.
3. In a clean mixing bowl, whisk eggs with the rest of the sugar till thick and creamy.
4. Fold in one cup of the egg mixture to the creamed butter till well mixed. Add the rest of the egg mixture, mashed bananas and lastly the flour, stirring as lightly as possible.
5. Pour into a greased cake tin. Bake in oven at 150°C (300°F) or Regulo 4 for 1–1¼ hours.

BUTTER CREAM

For a 20 cm (8 in) cake:
115 g (4 oz) butter
  55 g (2 oz) sifted icing sugar
  2 teaspoons rum
  ½ teaspoon vanilla essence
  2 egg yolks

1. Place all the ingredients in a dry mixing bowl.
2. Beat at moderate speed for about 7–8 minutes till mixture turns to a smooth cream.
3. Chill in refrigerator until ready for icing and filling cake.

Note:
To make coffee-flavoured butter cream, dissolve 2 tablespoonfuls of 'instant' coffee powder in 2 tablespoonfuls of boiling water. Cool completely. For chocolate flavour, add 115 g (4 oz) plain chocolate, grated. Beat into the creamed butter, continue beating for 1–2 minutes till well blended. Chill.

BUTTER CAKE

INGREDIENTS

310 g (11 oz) flour
 10 egg whites
310 g (11 oz) sugar
  2 teaspoons baking powder
 10 egg yolks, lightly beaten
455 g (16 oz) butter
  6 tablespoons condensed milk
  2 drops almond essence
  2 teaspoons vanilla essence
  2 teaspoons brandy

METHOD

1. Sift flour twice.
2. Beat egg whites, sugar and baking powder till thick. Add the beaten egg yolks, a little at a time, and continue beating till thick and creamy. Remove to a basin.
3. Place butter and condensed milk in a mixing bowl. Beat till well blended, about 5 minutes. Add almond and vanilla essence and brandy. Beat till blended.
4. Add one cup of egg mixture and mix thoroughly. Fold in flour lightly with the rest of the beaten egg mixture. Pour batter into a greased cake tin and bake in moderate oven at 175°C (350°F) or Regulo 6 for 10 minutes. Reduce heat to 135°C (275°F) or Regulo 3 and bake for further 45–50 minutes or till done. Turn cake on to a cake rack.

To make Rich Marble Cake:
1. Set aside one-third of the cake mixture in a bowl. Sift 2 tablespoons cocoa and stir lightly into the mixture.
2. Pour and spread half of the white batter into a greased cake tin.
3. Place and space out small heaps of the cocoa mixture over batter in tin.
4. Add the rest of the white cake mixture to cover the cocoa mixture completely. Bake as for Butter Cake.

CHEESECAKE

INGREDIENTS

170 g (6 oz) digestive biscuits
55 g (2 oz) butter
3 tablespoons canned syrup
30 g gelatine
1 small can evaporated milk, chilled
455 g (16 oz) cottage cheese
115 g (4 oz) castor sugar
35 ml (1 fl oz) double cream

METHOD

1. Lightly grease a 24 cm (10 in) deep cake tin with a removable base.

2. Crush biscuits till fine. Melt butter in a saucepan, and stir in crushed biscuits. Press the mixture in the base and side of tin. Leave to set in fridge till well chilled.

3. Place 3 tablespoons of canned syrup in a saucepan and sprinkle on gelatine. Place over a pan of hot water over low heat and stir till dissolved.

4. Whisk chilled evaporated milk until thick. Set aside. Beat cottage cheese with the castor sugar till smooth and fold in the gelatine mixture and chilled milk. Leave mixture in a cool place until just to the point of setting (approximately ½ hour). Whisk double cream till thick, stir till well mixed and pour into tin. Chill till well set in fridge.

Note:
Use the syrup of canned peaches or pineapple. For added flavour, add bits of the canned fruit to cream cheese mixture just before chilling.

Decorate cheesecake with fruit slices.

For best results, leave cheesecake in fridge overnight.

NO BAKE LEMON CHEESECAKE

INGREDIENTS

1 packet digestive biscuits
1 tablespoon icing sugar
115 g (4 oz) melted butter, hot

Ingredients for filling:
1 tablespoon gelatine crystals
2 tablespoons hot water
115 ml (4 fl oz) boiling water
1 teaspoon lemon rind
1 tablespoon lemon juice
1 tin evaporated milk, chilled overnight
225 g (8 oz) Philadelphia cream cheese
5 tablespoons condensed milk

Ingredients for topping:
½ can sliced peaches
2 tablespoons gelatine crystals
55 ml (2 fl oz) boiling water

METHOD

1. Crush biscuits till fine; mix with icing sugar, add hot melted butter and stir till well mixed. Press biscuit mixture to bottom and sides of low cake tin. Chill for 2 hours.

2. Heat gelatine and water over low heat till dissolved. Combine gelatine solution with 115 ml boiling water, lemon rind and juice. Set aside.

3. Whip chilled evaporated milk till thick, remove to a bowl. Add cream cheese to condensed milk and stir till combined.

4. Mix together gelatine mixture, whipped evaporated milk and cream cheese mixture. Beat till mixture is well combined and smooth.

5. Pour filling into biscuit crust in tin and decorate with sliced peaches. Dissolve 2 tablespoons gelatine in water over low heat. Allow to cool for a while and pour over peaches. Chill overnight to set.

Note:
Pour boiled gelatine over peaches when gelatine is about to set.

CHOCOLATE CHIFFON CAKE

INGREDIENTS

200 g (7 oz) flour
  4 level teaspoons baking powder   **A**
  1 level teaspoon fine salt

 55 g (2 oz) cocoa
  2 tablespoons 'instant' coffee powder   **B**
225 ml (8 fl oz) boiling water

370 g (13 oz) castor sugar
170 ml (6 fl oz) corn oil
  8 egg yolks
  1 teaspoon vanilla essence
  9 egg whites
  1 teaspoon sugar
  1 teaspoon cream of tartar

METHOD

1. Sift **A** together.
2. Blend **B** and let cool.
3. Place sifted flour and sugar in a mixing bowl. Make a well in the centre.
4. Pour oil, egg yolks, vanilla essence and cooled cocoa mixture into the well. Blend and beat slowly till smooth (5 minutes).
5. In a separate bowl, whisk egg whites with 1 teaspoon sugar and 1 teaspoon cream of tartar till very stiff (20 minutes).
6. Fold the egg white mixture lightly into the beaten mixture till well blended.
7. Place in an ungreased tube cake tin. Bake in a hot oven at 205°C (400°F) or Regulo 8 for ½ hour. Reduce heat to 175°C (350°F) or Regulo 6 and bake for another ¾–1 hour. The cake should spring back when lightly touched.
8. Invert cake and allow to cool before removing from pan.

Note:
Sift in the cream of tartar to the egg whites while whisking to mix it evenly. Pre-heat oven before use.

COFFEE WALNUT CAKE

INGREDIENTS

255 g (9 oz) flour
  1 teaspoon baking powder
 ½ teaspoon salt
170 g (6 oz) chopped walnuts
225 g (8 oz) butter
200 g (7 oz) sugar
  5 eggs

2 tablespoons 'instant' coffee powder mixes
  with 1 tablespoon hot water
3 tablespoons evaporated milk mixed with   **A**
  3 tablespoons water

  1 teaspoon vanilla essence

METHOD

1. Grease and flour cake tin.
2. Sift flour, baking powder and salt into a basin. Add the chopped walnuts. Set aside.
3. Beat butter and sugar till light and creamy. Add eggs, one at a time, beating well after each egg.
4. Mix **A** in a cup.
5. Divide flour into three portions and fold each portion one at a time into the creamed butter mixture. Lastly, add **A** and the vanilla essence. Mix lightly.
6. Pour batter into cake tin and bake in slow oven at 165°C (325°F) or Regulo 5 for 1–1½ hours or until cake is done. Leave cake in tin for 5 minutes to cool on a cooling rack.

FRUIT CAKE
(CHRISTMAS CAKE)

INGREDIENTS

285 g (10 oz) flour
  1 teaspoon salt   **A**
  2 teaspoons mixed spice★

225 g (8 oz) currants
225 g (8 oz) sultanas
225 g (8 oz) raisins
115 g (4 oz) candied peel   **B**
115 g (4 oz) almonds
115 g (4 oz) glace cherries

  3 tablespoons sugar
  2 tablespoons water
  6 tablespoons evaporated milk
225 g (8 oz) butter
175 g (6 oz) sugar
  5 eggs, lightly beaten
  1 teaspoon vanilla essence
  4 tablespoons brandy

METHOD

1. Sift **A** together. Chop **B** into small pieces.

2. Rub sifted flour into the chopped ingredients. Set aside.

3. Grease an 18 cm (7 in) square cake tin. Line with greaseproof paper at base and sides. Grease paper.

4. Caramelize the sugar and water to a dark brown. Add the evaporated milk and stir over a low heat to dissolve the caramel. Cool in refrigerator.

5. Cream butter and sugar till light. Add beaten eggs a little each time and beat till well blended.

6. Add the vanilla essence, caramel and 2 tablespoons of the flour to the egg mixture. Beat lightly till well blended.

7. Fold in the remaining flour-fruit mixture and the brandy. Stir well.

8. Pour batter into cake tin and bake in oven at 175°C (350°F) or Regulo 6 for 1–1¼ hours or till cake is done. Leave cake to cool in tin before turning out on to a cake rack.

★*See page 199.*

GINGER CAKE

INGREDIENTS

  4 egg yolks
 85 g (3 oz) sugar
 85 g (3 oz) butter
 55 ml (2 fl oz) black treacle
  4 egg whites with 1 teaspoon sugar
 ½ teaspoon cream of tartar

140 g (5 oz) flour
  2 teaspoons ginger powder
  ½ teaspoon mixed spice★   **A**
  1 teaspoon bicarbonate of soda

  1 tablespoon brandy or rum
 55 ml (2 fl oz) evaporated milk

METHOD

1. Grease and flour a cake or loaf tin. Pre-heat oven to 190°C (375°F) or Regulo 7.

2. Beat egg yolks with sugar till very thick and creamy.

3. Heat butter till almost boiling point, and add slowly to the beaten egg yolk. Pour in the black treacle and beat to blend.

4. Whisk egg whites with sugar till frothy. Sift in cream of tartar and continue whisking until mixture becomes stiff and can hold its shape.

5. Sift **A** together three times. Combine and fold in the egg white mixture, egg yolk mixture, brandy and milk. Mix well.

6. Pour into cake tin and bake in moderate oven at 175°C (350°F) or Regulo 6 for 20 minutes. Reduce oven heat to 135°C (275°F) or Regulo 3 for another 20 minutes or until cake springs back when pressed with finger. Remove and turn cake over on to rack to cool for 15 minutes.

★*See page 199.*

LEMON SPONGE CAKE

INGREDIENTS

12 eggs
1 cup castor sugar
1½ cups flour
115 g (4 oz) butter, melted and warmed
1 teaspoon vanilla essence
½ teaspoon fresh lemon juice
½ teaspoon cream of tartar

METHOD

1. Pre-heat oven to 205°C (400°F). Separate egg yolks from whites.

2. Beat egg yolks and sugar till creamy. Add flour and butter, stir till well blended. Add vanilla essence, lemon juice and mix well. Set aside.

3. Beat egg whites till frothy. Sieve in the cream of tartar and beat till stiff but not dry.

4. Pour in the egg yolk mixture and fold lightly into egg whites till well blended. Pour into an ungreased chiffon cake pan.

5. Bake for 10 minutes at 205°C for 10 minutes. Reduce heat to 177°C (335°F) and bake till cake is done (approximately 25–30 minutes). Test when cake leaves side of pan; cake should spring back when pressed gently with finger.

6. Remove cake from oven; invert pan and leave to cool for 10 minutes before taking out from pan.

PANDAN CHIFFON CAKE

INGREDIENTS

455 g (1 lb) grated coconut, white
9 egg whites
1 rounded teaspoon cream of tartar

2 tablespoons screw pine juice, from 12 screw pine leaves
1 teaspoon green food colouring

8 egg yolks
255 g (9 oz) castor sugar   } **A**
170 ml (6 fl oz) corn oil
1 teaspoon vanilla essence

140 g (5 oz) 'Softasilk' or 'Silksifted' flour   } *sifted*
2 heaped teaspoons baking powder   *twice*
½ teaspoon fine salt

METHOD

1. Pre-heat oven to 170°C (350°F).

2. Squeeze coconut for 170 ml (6 fl oz) No. 1 milk. Cook over low heat till it boils and thickens like cream, stirring all the time. Cool.

3. Beat egg white till frothy, sieve the cream of tartar on to egg white and continue beating till very stiff but not dry. Set aside.

4. Combine **A** in a bowl and beat lightly.

5. Put flour in a mixing bowl. Make a well in centre, and pour in **A**. Bring in flour from sides and beat with batter beater till smooth.

6. Add the screw pine juice, green food colouring and coconut cream. Stir till blended.

7. Fold in one-third of the egg white to the egg mixture and blend well. Then add the rest of the egg white and fold in lightly with rubber spatula till well blended.

8. Pour into an ungreased 25 cm × 10 cm (10 in × 4 in) chiffon cake tin and bake for 45–50 minutes or till cake springs back when pressed with finger. Remove from oven, invert cake tin and leave for ½ hour before transferring to a wire rack to cool.

Pandan Chiffon Cake

POUND CAKE

INGREDIENTS

225 g (8 oz) butter
  1 teaspoon vanilla essence
  3 drops almond essence
  6 egg yolks
225 g (8 oz) sugar
  6 egg whites beaten with 1 teaspoon sugar

170 g (6 oz) flour ⎤
¼ teaspoon salt ⎦ **A**

METHOD

1. Cream butter till fluffy. Add vanilla and almond essence to blend.
2. Beat egg yolks and sugar till thick.
3. Whisk egg whites with 1 teaspoon sugar till stiff.
4. Sift **A** together. Mix with egg yolks and creamed butter. Fold in the egg whites and mix thoroughly.
5. Pour cake mixture into a greased cake tin and bake in slow oven at 150°C (300°F) or Regulo 4 for 1–1¼ hours. Turn on to a rack to cool.

SEMOLINA CAKE

INGREDIENTS

455 g (16 oz) butter
225 g (8 oz) semolina
 12 egg yolks
  5 egg whites
255 g (9 oz) sugar
140 g (5 oz) flour
 ½ teaspoon mixed spice*

 4 tablespoons brandy ⎤
 3 drops almond essence ⎟
 1 teaspoon vanilla essence ⎟ **A**
 3 drops rose essence ⎦

225 g (8 oz) almonds, chopped coarsely

ROSE MARIE CAKE

INGREDIENTS

 20 egg yolks
170 g (6 oz) sugar
340 g (12 oz) butter
  1 teaspoon vanilla essence
  6 egg whites beaten with 1 tablespoon sugar

 85 g (3 oz) flour ⎤
170 g (6 oz) Marie biscuits, finely pounded ⎟
  and sifted ⎟ **A**
1½ teaspoons baking powder ⎟
 ½ teaspoon mixed spice* ⎦

METHOD

1. Beat egg yolks with 85 g (3 oz) of the sugar till thick and creamy.
2. Cream butter with the remaining sugar till fluffy. Beat in the vanilla essence.
3. In a clean and dry bowl, whisk egg whites and 1 tablespoon sugar till stiff.
4. Sift **A**. Fold the sifted ingredients, egg yolks and whites into the creamed mixture.
5. Pour mixture into a greased cake tin and bake in oven at 150°C (300°F) or Regulo 4 for 15 minutes. Reduce heat to 135°C and bake for another ¾–1 hour.

METHOD

1. Beat butter for 15 minutes; add the semolina and continue beating for another 10 minutes. Leave in bowl to stand for 4 hours.
2. Beat egg yolks, whites and half of the sugar together till creamy. Add the rest of the sugar and beat till very thick.
3. Sift flour and mixed spice twice.
4. Mix creamed butter and semolina with 225 ml (8 fl oz) of the egg mixture and **A** till well blended. Then fold in the flour and the chopped almonds alternately with the rest of the egg mixture.
5. Pour into a greased tin and bake in a very slow oven at 135°C (275°F) or Regulo 3 for 1–1½ hours.

*See "Mixed Spice" on page 199.

SPONGE SANDWICH

INGREDIENTS

12 egg yolks
200 g (7 oz) castor sugar
 5 egg whites
140 g (5 oz) butter

140 g (5 oz) flour | *sifted*
 1 teaspoon baking powder | *together*

 2 teaspoons brandy
 1 teaspoon vanilla essence
   Apricot jam, warmed

METHOD

1. Pre-heat oven to 190°C (375°F).

2. Brush two 20 cm (8 in) sandwich tins with butter and dust with flour.

3. Beat yolks with three-quarters of the sugar till thick and creamy.

4. In a dry clean bowl, beat egg whites with the rest of the sugar till stiff.

5. Bring the butter to a boil in a saucepan.

6. Fold egg white and flour, in parts, to the yolks adding brandy, vanilla essence and the boiling butter gradually. Stir lightly till well blended. Pour batter into two sandwich tins and bake till golden brown for about 20–25 minutes or till done.

7. Turn cake over and whilst still hot spread the warmed jam to sandwich cakes.

Note:
Level the cake batter in tin and with back of spoon make a slight dent in middle of cake so that cake will be level after baking.

SUPER LIGHT SPONGE SANDWICH

INGREDIENTS

 5 eggs and 2 egg yolks
225 g (8 oz) castor sugar

 30 g (1 oz) or 2 tablespoons butter |
 55 ml (2 fl oz) or 4 tablespoons boiling | **A**
   water |
   Pinch of salt |

140 g (5 oz) self-raising flour, sifted twice

METHOD

1. Grease and dust with flour three 20 cm (8 in) round sandwich tins.

2. Pre-heat oven to 165°C (325°F).

3. Beat eggs and sugar till thick and creamy, about 15–20 minutes.

4. Put **A** in a small saucepan and bring to the boil. Pour gradually into the egg mixture and beat lightly. Add small amounts of flour and fold it in.

5. Pour batter into tins and bake for 25–30 minutes or till cake springs back when pressed lightly with finger. Bake to a light golden colour.

6. Remove from oven, loosen cake by scraping sides of cake tin with a knife and turn over on to a wire rack immediately. Turn over once more to let cake cool.

7. Sandwich cake with warmed apricot jam, butter cream or whipped cream as desired.

Butter cream filling:
 2 small egg yolks
 85 g (3 oz) icing sugar
 1 tablespoon rum *or* 1 teaspoon vanilla essence
170 g (6 oz) unsalted butter

Beat all ingredients over moderate speed for 5 minutes.

SULTANA CAKE

INGREDIENTS

3 tablespoons brandy
400 g (14 oz) sultanas

255 g (9 oz) plain flour ⎤ *sifted*
 55 g (2 oz) self-raising flour ⎟ *together*
 Pinch of salt ⎦

115 g (4 oz) chopped almonds
225 g (8 oz) butter, semi-frozen
200 g (7 oz) castor sugar
 5 eggs
 2 teaspoons vanilla essence
 6 tablespoons fresh milk
10 whole almonds, halved

METHOD

1. Sprinkle the brandy over the sultanas and mix well. Leave to soak for 1 hour. Rub in 1 cup of the sifted flour and set aside. Mix 3 tablespoons of the flour with the chopped almonds.

2. Beat butter and sugar together till light and creamy. Add eggs one at a time, beat for about 5 minutes for each egg. Beat five more minutes after the last egg. Add the vanilla essence and 3 tablespoons of the milk and beat till just blended.

3. Fold in the rest of the flour with the rest of the milk, the sultanas, and the chopped almonds. Using a spatula, mix batter by folding from bottom of bowl till evenly mixed.

4. Grease and line cake tin with greaseproof paper. Pour the mixture into tin and bake in moderate oven 135°C (275°F) for 1½–1¾ hours or till done. Leave in tin for ½ hour before turning out on to a wire rack to cool. Keep cake for at least a day or two before serving.

Note:
Bake cake for 10 minutes before placing the halved almonds on top to prevent them sinking into cake. Continue baking till cooked.

SWISS ROLL

INGREDIENTS

200 g (7 oz) sugar
 8 eggs
2½ tablespoons evaporated milk
 1 teaspoon vanilla essence
130 g (4½ oz) flour

METHOD

1. Grease and flour two Swiss roll tins.

2. Beat sugar and eggs till very thick and creamy. Add evaporated milk and vanilla essence. Beat till well blended.

3. Fold flour lightly into egg mixture. Pour cake mixture into tins. Bake in a hot oven at 205°C (400°F) or Regulo 8 for 7 minutes.

4. Place cakes on a damp towel and roll using the towel. Leave for 1 minute, unroll and spread with jam. Roll again. Cool before cutting into pieces.

WALNUT CAKE

INGREDIENTS

115 g (4 oz) self-raising flour ⎤ **A**
 55 g (2 oz) plain flour ⎦

4 tablespoons evaporated milk ⎤ **B**
4 tablespoons milk ⎦

140 g (5 oz) butter
170 g (6 oz) fine sugar
 3 egg whites and 1 egg yolk
170 g (6 oz) finely chopped walnuts

METHOD

1. Cream butter and sugar till light and fluffy.

2. Add eggs, one at a time, beating well.

3. Sift **A** together. Mix **B** together.

4. Fold the flour, milk and walnuts lightly into the egg mixture.

5. Bake in a moderate oven at 175°C (350°F) or Regulo 6 for 20–30 minutes.

WHITE CHRISTMAS
(MIXED FRUIT AND COCONUT
CANDY BARS)

INGREDIENTS

250 g (9 oz) icing sugar, sifted
250 g (9 oz) full cream milk powder, sifted
250 g (9 oz) desiccated coconut, toasted lightly
250 g (9 oz) mixed fruit
  2 cups rice crispies
 65 g (2½ oz) walnuts, chopped coarsely
 65 g (2½ oz) toasted almonds, chopped
   coarsely

A

250 g copha★
  1 teaspoon vanilla essence

METHOD

1. Stir **A** in a mixing bowl to mix evenly.

2. Heat copha in a heavy bottomed pan till it melts. Add vanilla essence. Pour copha mixture into **A** and stir till well combined.

3. Pour mixture into a lightly greased 25 × 20 cm (10 × 8 in) baking tray or glass baking dish. Press top of mixture to smoothen till firm. Chill in refrigerator for two hours before cutting into fingers. Store in refrigerator.

Note:
★*Copha is solid cream of coconut available in specialty supermarkets.*

Biscuits, Cookies and Pastries

Special Almond Biscuits

Almond Raisin Rock Cookies

Cat's Tongues

Cheese Cookies

Chocolate Eclairs/Cream Puffs

Custard Tartlets

Fruit Scones

Melting Moments

Pineapple-Shaped Tarts

Pineapple 'Open' Tarts

Sponge Fingers

Spritches Butter Biscuits

Sujee Biscuits

Sweet Corn Fritters

Selection of cookies with Cheese Cookies
(middle) and Sugee Biscuits (in canister and foreground)

SPECIAL ALMOND BISCUITS

INGREDIENTS

680 g (24 oz) plain flour
170 g (6 oz) icing sugar
455 g (16 oz) butter, chilled in refrigerator
  3 egg yolks, lightly beaten with 1 teaspoon vanilla essence
  1 egg and 1 yolk, lightly beaten
115 g (4 oz) almonds, blanched and chopped coarsely

METHOD

1. Sift flour and icing sugar into a basin.
2. Rub butter into the flour till mixture resembles breadcrumbs. Pour the beaten egg yolks into the flour mixture. Mix lightly to form a soft dough. Chill in refrigerator for ½ hour.
3. Knead dough very lightly. Roll out to 0.5 cm (¼ in) thickness on a lightly floured board or marble table top.
4. Using a fancy cutter, cut dough and place on greased baking trays. Glaze with beaten egg and sprinkle top with chopped almonds. Bake in moderate oven at 150°C (300°F) or Regulo 4 for 20 minutes. Cool on a rack and keep in an airtight container.

Note:
Divide dough into three or four portions. Flatten the dough with palm of hand before rolling out to cut. Lift dough gently with a spatula and space apart on baking trays.

ALMOND RAISIN ROCK COOKIES

INGREDIENTS

225 g (8 oz) self-raising flour
  ½ teaspoon mixed spice★ (optional)
  Pinch of salt
  2 teaspoons baking powder
85 g (3 oz) butter, chilled
115 g (4 oz) sugar
55 g (2 oz) chopped almonds, roasted
55 g (2 oz) raisins
  2 eggs lightly beaten with 1 teaspoon vanilla essence

METHOD

1. Sift the spice, salt and baking powder into a bowl.
2. Rub butter into flour mixture till it resembles breadcrumbs.
3. Combine the flour, sugar, almonds, raisins and the beaten eggs to form a soft dough. Do not rub or knead.
4. Space dough out in small heaps on a greased tray and bake in a moderate oven at 150°C (300°F) or Regulo 4 for 20–25 minutes until brown.
5. Cool on a wire tray.

★See "Mixed Spice" on page 199.

CAT'S TONGUES

INGREDIENTS

455 g (16 oz) flour
  2 teaspoons baking powder
455 g (16 oz) butter
455 g (16 oz) sugar
  2 teaspoons vanilla essence
12 egg whites beaten with 1 teaspoon sugar

METHOD

1. Grease baking trays evenly with butter.

2. Sift flour and baking powder.

3. Beat butter and sugar till light and creamy. Add vanilla essence and beat till well blended.

4. In a very dry and clean bowl, beat egg whites and sugar till stiff, but not dry.

5. Fold one-quarter of the egg whites lightly into the creamed mixture. Fold (in three parts) the flour, and the rest of the egg whites lightly into the creamed mixture.

6. Scoop batter into an icing tube with a plain 1.3 cm icing nozzle. Press batter out in small heaps or in 5 cm lengths, 2.5 cm apart, on to greased trays.

7. Bake in oven at 150°C (300°F) or Regulo 4 for 20–25 minutes till pale brown. Remove from oven, take biscuits off trays immediately to cool on rack for 5 minutes. Keep in airtight containers immediately when cool.

Note:
Remove cat's tongues immediately from tray to cake rack after taking them out of the oven. Place them flat on a cake rack to prevent them from curling.

CHEESE COOKIES

INGREDIENTS

  1 tablespoon castor sugar
225 g (8 oz) self-raising flour
¼ teaspoon pepper
¼ teaspoon chilli powder (optional)
225 g (8 oz) butter, chilled
225 g (8 oz) cheese (preferably fully matured), grated
115 g (4 oz) desiccated coconut for rolling cookies

METHOD

1. Sift all dry ingredients into a mixing bowl; add butter, mix with fingertips to resemble breadcrumbs. Add cheese to flour mixture and knead lightly to form a dough. Chill in refrigerator for ½ hour.

2. Divide dough into 4 parts. Roll each part into thin logs and cut into equal pieces the size of a candlenut.

3. Spread the desiccated coconut onto a tray; roll cheese balls in desiccated coconut and space balls well apart on biscuit trays. Use a fork to flatten ball slightly and to form a pattern. Bake in moderate oven, 135°C (275°F), for 25–30 minutes till pale brown. Cool on cake rack before storing in an airtight container.

Note:
Cheese cookies should be very pale in colour but crunchy right through.

CHOCOLATE ECLAIRS/ CREAM PUFFS

INGREDIENTS

Choux Pastry:
170 g (6 oz) flour
  1 teaspoon baking powder
115 g (4 oz) butter
285 ml (10 fl oz) water
  5 eggs

METHOD

1. Pre-heat oven to 230°C (450°F) or Regulo 10.
2. Sift flour and baking powder.
3. Bring butter and water to the boil in a pan.
4. Stir in the sifted flour all at once and cook till mixture is smooth and leaves sides of pan.
5. Remove from heat and cool in mixing bowl. Beat in eggs, one at a time, till smooth and shiny.
6. Place cooked mixture in piping tube and press batter out in small heaps on a well-greased tray.
7. Bake in a hot oven at 230°C (450°F) or Regulo 10 for 15 minutes. Reduce heat to 175°C (350°F) or Regulo 6 and bake for another 15 minutes till golden brown.
8. Cook on cake rack. Split puffs at sides and fill with custard cream.

INGREDIENTS

Filling:
  3 eggs
115 g (4 oz) sugar
  3 tablespoons flour, heaped
  1 teaspoon custard powder

225 ml (8 fl oz) evaporated milk | **A**
225 ml (8 fl oz) water

  2 tablespoons condensed milk
  1 teaspoon butter
  1 teaspoon vanilla essence

METHOD

1. Beat eggs, sugar, flour and custard powder together in a heavy-bottomed saucepan.
2. Bring **A** to near boiling point.
3. Pour condensed and hot milk gradually into egg mixture. Cook mixture over a low heat, stirring continuously till mixture is thick.
4. Remove from heat. Stir in the butter and vanilla essence. Cool before filling.

For chocolate eclairs:
1. Pre-heat oven to 205°C (400°F) or Regulo 8.
2. Using a large plain piping tube, pipe the Choux pastry into 7.5 cm (3 in) lengths on a lightly greased baking tray.
3. Bake for 20–25 minutes until golden brown.
4. Slit each eclair horizontally. Then leave to cool on a wire rack.
5. When thoroughly cold, fill with custard cream and coat the top with chocolate butter icing. (See recipe)

CHOCOLATE BUTTER ICING

INGREDIENTS

55 g (2 oz) plain chocolate, grated
½ teaspoon 'instant' coffee powder
  1 tablespoon rum
55 g (2 oz) butter

METHOD

1. Stir grated chocolate, 'instant' coffee powder and rum in a bowl over saucepan of simmering water till chocolate turns into a smooth cream. Remove and set aside to cool.
2. Beat butter, adding the melted chocolate till mixture is of spreading consistency.
3. Spread on top of eclairs.

CUSTARD TARTLETS

Pastry:
225 g (8 oz) flour
  A pinch of salt
  2 tablespoons icing sugar
170 g (6 oz) butter
  1 egg, separated
4–5 tablespoons iced water

1. Sift flour, salt and icing sugar together.
2. Rub butter lightly into sifted flour till mixture resembles breadcrumbs.
3. Add egg yolk and water to form a dough.
4. Chill dough in refrigerator for 1/2 hour. Roll dough out thinly and cut to line greased patty tins. Prick pastry with fork and brush with egg white.
5. Bake 'blind' in hot oven at 150°C (300°F) or Regulo 4 for 10 minutes.
6. Remove from oven and fill with custard.

Note:
To bake 'blind' is to bake unfilled pastry shells.

Custard:
  4 eggs
  2 tablespoons condensed milk
    A pinch of salt
225 ml (8 fl oz) evaporated milk
340 ml (12 fl oz) water
  55 g (2 oz) sugar
  1 teaspoon vanilla essence
    Grated nutmeg

1. Beat eggs, condensed milk and salt lightly in a bowl.
2. Heat evaporated milk with water and sugar. Pour gradually into the egg mixture. Add vanilla essence and strain. Spoon custard into pastry cases.
3. Sprinkle with grated nutmeg and bake in oven at 150°C (300°F) or Regulo 4 for 20–25 minutes or until custard is firm.

FRUIT SCONES

INGREDIENTS

  1 egg, lightly beaten
    Pinch of salt
  1 cup milk
  2 cups self-raising flour
1/2 cup sugar
1/2 cup sultanas
  2 tablespoons lemon peel
100 g (3 1/2 oz) butter

METHOD

1. Pre-heat oven to 175°C (350°F). Mix egg, salt and milk in a bowl.
2. Combine flour, sugar and fruits in a mixing bowl and rub in butter.
3. Pour the egg mixture gradually into the flour mixture to form a soft dough.
4. Dust top and bottom of dough with a generous portion of flour. Put between pieces of wax paper and roll lightly till 2 cm thick. Cut with scone cutter and place in a sandwich tin to bake for 15–20 minutes or till done. Serve hot with butter and jam.

MELTING MOMENTS

INGREDIENTS

455 g (16 oz) self-raising flour
225 g (8 oz) coarse sugar
225 g (8 oz) butter
  2 eggs
115 g (4 oz) cherries, diced

METHOD

1. Mix flour, sugar, butter and eggs in a large basin.
2. Mix lightly with fingertips to form a soft dough.
3. Place portions (each the size of a hazel nut) of the biscuit mixture on a greased baking sheet. Top each with a piece of cherry. Bake in oven at 150°C (300°F) or Regulo 4 till light golden brown for about 20–30 minutes. Cool on rack before storing in an airtight container.

PINEAPPLE-SHAPED TARTS

INGREDIENTS

565 g (20 oz) flour
  2 teaspoons baking powder | **A**

340 g (12 oz) butter, chilled

  2 tablespoons castor sugar
  3 egg yolks
  1 teaspoon vanilla essence
  3 drops of yellow food colouring | **B**
½ teaspoon salt
  8 tablespoons boiling water

  Flour for dusting
  Cloves

METHOD

Glaze:
Beat 1 egg and 1 yolk with 2 drops of yellow food colouring.

1. Sift **A** into a basin.
2. Rub butter lightly into flour with tips of fingers till mixture resembles breadcrumbs.
3. Beat **B** lightly in a bowl.
4. Pour egg mixture into the flour mixture. Add boiling water and mix with both hands to form a pastry dough.
5. Chill in refrigerator for ½ hour.

To shape the tarts:
1. Divide pastry into two or three parts. Place each part on a well-floured board or marble table top. Knead for a moment till smooth. Flatten pastry with palm of hand and dust with flour. Roll pastry out to 0.5 cm (0.2 in) thickness.
2. Cut pastry pieces with an oval pastry cutter.
3. Place a piece of pineapple jam on one half of the pastry and fold the other half over it. Press the edges together, using finger and thumb. Roll tart so that one end is tapered. Insert a clove (without pit) at the broad end, to resemble a pineapple stalk.

4. Using a small pair of scissors, snip tiny 'v' shapes on the front half of the tart. Snip in rows.

5. Place tarts on greased trays, leaving space for expansion. Glaze and bake in oven at 175°C (350°F) or Regulo 6 for 10 minutes. Reduce heat to 150°C (300°F) or Regulo 4 and continue baking for another 15–20 minutes, till light brown.

Pineapple filling (to be made the day before):
6 pineapples, preferably Mauritian
Coarse sugar (See note below)
3 cloves
1 piece 5 cm (2 in) cinnamon stick
3 segments of star anise

1. Remove skin and 'eye' from pineapples.

2. Grate pineapples coarsely. Use muslin to squeeze out juice from pineapples. Do not squeeze too dry. Chop grated pineapples till fine. (Wear rubber gloves)

3. Place chopped pineapples, sugar, cloves, cinnamon and star anise in a heavy-bottomed aluminium saucepan.

4. Cook over moderate heat till almost dry (about 1 hour). Continue cooking over a low heat, till mixture is thick. Keep stirring all the while.

5. Cool. Store overnight in refrigerator.

6. Make into long rolls of 2.5 cm (1 in) diameter and cut into 1 cm (1½ in) pieces. Roll each piece to resemble a quail's egg.

7. Place jam pieces on a tray to chill in refrigerator till ready for use.

Note:
Amount of sugar should be exactly the same as amount of pineapple e.g. 1 cup sugar to 1 cup pineapple.

PINEAPPLE 'OPEN' TARTS

INGREDIENTS

680 g (1½ lb) flour
  1 teaspoon fine salt
  2 tablespoons fine sugar
455 g (1 lb) butter
  1 egg

55 ml (2 fl oz) iced water   ⎫
2 teaspoons vanilla essence   **A** *mixed together*
3 drops of yellow food colouring ⎭

METHOD

1. Sift flour with salt and sugar.
2. Rub butter into flour till mixture resembles breadcrumbs.
3. Beat egg lightly, add to the flour. Add Ingredients **A** to form a pastry dough. Chill for ½ hour.
4. Roll pastry to 0.5 cm thickness on a floured board or marble table top.
5. Cut with a special tart cutter.
6. Fill tarts with pineapple filling.
7. Pinch a small neat frill or pattern around the edge of tart. Cut thin strips from left-over pastry to decorate top.
8. Place tarts on a greased tray and bake in a hot oven at 175°C (350°F) or Regulo 6 for 15 minutes.
9. Reduce heat and bake for another 10-15 minutes till light brown.
10. Turn tarts out to cool on a wire rack before storing in an airtight container.

Note:
Use special brass pincers to pinch frill for tart. For pineapple filling see Pineapple-Shaped Tarts

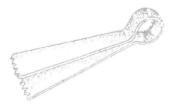

SPONGE FINGERS

INGREDIENTS

Butter for greasing
Flour for dusting
  4 egg yolks
115 g (4 oz) sugar
  1 teaspoon vanilla essence
  4 egg whites
A pinch of salt
  2 teaspoons sugar
  85 g (3 oz) 'Softasilk' flour
  85 g (3 oz) sugar, to sprinkle over sponge fingers

METHOD

1. Grease trays with butter; dust with flour.
2. Beat egg yolks and 115 g sugar till very thick and creamy. Add vanilla essence, beat till very well blended.
3. Beat egg whites till frothy; add the salt and 2 teaspoons sugar and continue beating till mixture is stiff, but not dry.
4. Lightly fold in one-third of the egg white mixture to the egg yolk mixture. Sift in one-third of the flour and stir very lightly to blend well. Repeat the process twice with the rest of the flour and the egg white and egg yolk mixture.
5. Spoon batter into an icing tube. Squeeze on to prepared greased trays to form finger shapes 10 cm (4 in) long and 2.5 cm (1 in) wide. Place sponge fingers 2.5 cm apart to prevent them from sticking to one another whilst being baked.
6. Sprinkle sugar over fingers and bake in oven at 150°C (300°F) or Regulo 4 for 20–25 minutes till light brown.
7. Remove fingers immediately from baking trays after taking them out of the oven. Place on cake rack to cool. Keep in an airtight container.

SPRITCHES BUTTER BISCUITS

INGREDIENTS

910 g (32 oz) plain flour
455 g (16 oz) cornflour
455 g (16 oz) butter
455 g (16 oz) icing sugar
  8 egg yolks
  2 teaspoons vanilla essence
  4 egg whites and 1 teaspoon sugar

METHOD

1. Sift the two types of flour together into a basin.
2. Beat butter, sugar and egg yolks to a cream. Add vanila essence and mix.
3. In a separate bowl, whisk the egg whites with 1 teaspoon sugar until thick.
4. Mix the creamed butter mixture with the flour and the whisked egg whites to form soft dough.
5. Press dough through biscuit pump using any design. Space biscuits out on a greased tin and bake in moderate oven at 150°C (300°F) or Regulo 4 for 25–30 minutes, or till light golden brown. Cool on rack before storing in an airtight container.

Note:
Beat egg whites in a very clean and dry mixing bowl.

SUJEE BISCUITS

INGREDIENTS

455 g (16 oz) ghee
340 g (12 oz) icing sugar
795 g (1³/₄ lb) plain flour

METHOD

1. Cream ghee and sugar for 5 minutes, add flour and knead into a soft dough. Leave covered for 4 hours.
2. Pre-heat oven at 120°C (250°F).
3. Divide dough in 4 parts. Shape each part into a roll and cut each roll into 50 pieces, the size of a marble. Press each piece lightly, put on a greased baking tin spaced well apart and bake in a moderate oven for 20–25 minutes. Cool on a wire rack and keep in an airtight container.

Note:
Bake biscuits to a pale cream to get the buttery taste of ghee. This recipe makes 200 biscuits.

SWEET CORN FRITTERS

INGREDIENTS

2 egg yolks	
1 small can whole sweet corn	
55 g (2 oz) breadcrumbs	
Pinch of salt	**A**
Dash of pepper	
1 teaspoon baking powder	
2 egg whites	

METHOD

1. Mix **A** in a bowl.
2. Whip egg whites till stiff. Fold in the sweet corn mixture. Leave to stand for ¹/₂ hour.
3. Drop spoonfuls of fritter batter into hot oil to deep-fry till golden brown or pour batter thinly into a frying pan and fry as for pancake.

List of some ingredients

ENGLISH	MALAY	CHINESE
agar-agar	agar-agar	石花菜
alkaline water (clear)	ayer abu (puteh)	白鹼水
alkaline water (yellow)	ayer abu (kuning)	黃鹼水
anchovies	ikan bilis	江魚仔
aniseed	jintan manis	大茴香
basil leaf	daun kemangi	羅勒菜
bean sprouts	towgay	豆芽
bird's eye chilli	chilli padi	指天椒
borax	tingkal	硼砂
cabbage	kobis	包菜
candlenut	buah keras	馬加拉
cardamom	buah pelaga	豆蔻
cashew nut	biji gajus	檳如果
Chinese celery	seladeri	芹菜
Chinese mustard greens	sawi	菜心
Chinese parsley	pasli	芫荽菜
Chinese turnip	bangkuang	蕪菁
chives	kuchai	韮菜
cinnamon bark	kayu manis	桂皮
cloud ear fungus	chendawan kering	木耳
clove	bunga chengkeh	丁香
coriander leaf	daun ketumbar	香菜
coriander seed	ketumbar	香菜子
cray fish	udang katak	蝦婆
crispy Chinese cruller	yu char kway	油條
cumin seed	jintan puteh	小茴香
curry leaf	daun kari	咖哩葉
cuttlefish	sotong karang	墨斗
dorab	parang-parang	西刀
dried bean curd wrapper	tauhu kering	大腐皮
dried chillies	chilli kering	辣椒乾
dried tamarind slice	kulit assam	羅望片
fennel seed	jintan hitam	茴香子
fenugreek	halba	茴香花
five-spice powder	serbok lima rempah	五香粉
flat rice noodles	kwayteow	粿條
fried spongy bean curd	tauhu bakar	豆腐泡
galangal	lengkuas	藍薑
garlic	bawang puteh	蒜
ginger	halia	薑
gingko nut	peck kway	白果
glutinous rice	pulot	糯米
gold-banded scad	selar kuning	君冷
granulated sugar	gula pasir	砂糖
green beans	kachang hijau	綠豆
green bean flour	tepong hoen kwe	綠豆粉
grouper	kerapu	石斑魚
Indonesian black nuts	buah keluak	巴克拉
lemon grass	serai	香茅
lime leaf	daun limau purot	檸檬葉
lime paste	kapor	石灰乳
local lemon	limau nipis	星檸檬
local lime	limau kesturi	酸柑
mint leaf	daun pudina	薄荷葉
monosodium glutamate	serbok perasa	味精
mustard seed	biji sawi	芥辣子
nutmeg	buah pala	荳蔻
onion	bawang besar	洋葱
palm sugar	gula melaka	椰糖
peppercorn	biji lada	胡椒子
phaeomaria	bunga kantan	香花
polygonum	daun kesom	古蒿葉
pomfret	bawal tambak	島鯧
poppy seed	biji kas-kas	罌粟子
prawn paste	petis	蝦膏
preserved bean curd	tauhu asin	腐乳
preserved soya bean	taucheo	豆醬

ENGLISH	MALAY	CHINESE
red beans	kachang merah	紅豆
red snapper	ikan merah	紅雞
rice noodle	kway teow	粿條
rice vermicelli	bee hoon	米粉
rock sugar	gula batu	冰糖
saffron	safron	黃薑色
sago flour	tepong sago	西米粉
salted plum	plam asin	鹹梅
salted radish	lobak asin	菜脯
screw pine leaf	daun pandan	香葉
sesame seed	bijian	胡麻子
shallot	bawang merah kechil	葱頭
shark	yu	沙魚
shrimp paste	belachan	馬來羹
snapper	ikan tanda	記魚
soya bean	kachang soya	黃豆
soya bean cake	tauhu keping	豆腐乾
soya bean strip	tauhu kering	腐竹
soya sauce	kichap	醬油
spanish mackerel	ikan tenggiri	鯖魚
spring onion	daun bawang	葱
star anise	bunga lawang	八角
star fruit	belimbing	羊肚
sweet red sauce	kichap manis merah	海鮮醬
sweet thick black sauce	kichap pekat manis	甜醬
tamarind	assam	羅望子
threadfin	kurau	午魚
transparent bean vermicelli	tang hoon	粉絲
turmeric	kunyit	黃薑
turmeric leaf	daun kunyit	黃薑葉
water chestnut	sengkuang China	馬啼
water convolvulus	kangkong	旱菜
wet rice flour	tepong beras basah	濕米粉(占)
white bean curd (soft)	tauhu	豆腐
white radish	lobak puteh	蘿蔔
wolf herring	ikan parang	西刀魚
yeast	ragi	酵母
yellow noodle	mee	麵

Kitchen Equipment

Aluminium frying pans:
Suitable for deep-frying as they retain a steady heat and give food a nice golden brown colour. Frying chilli paste in an aluminium pan will give the mixture a natural bright colour whereas an iron wok (kuali) will turn it darkish and may give it a slight taste of iron.

Aluminium saucepan:
The heavy flat-bottomed pan is the best buy. It is suitable for both the electric or gas stove. Food is cooked easily without burning. A thin saucepan will buckle when it is overheated and will not be in contact with the electric hot plate.

Enamel saucepan:
Enamel saucepans are more suitable for soups and certain types of food that contain acid like tamarind or vinegar. Chipped enamelware is vulnerable to rust.

Iron wok (kuali):
Most Chinese prefer the iron wok to the aluminium one chiefly because the iron wok can retain extreme heat before the other ingredients are added. Ingredients will cook in a shorter time, keep their taste, and retain their crispness. The most important point to remember is that fried food and pounded ingredients will not stick to the bottom of the wok when it is well heated.

To season an iron wok:
Boil some grated coconut and water till dry [the water should fill up three-quarters of the wok.] Stir occasionally till the coconut turns black, approximately 3–4 hours.
Daily care: Do not use any detergent. Wipe wok well after each wash. If it is to be stored for a long period, grease wok lightly to prevent rust.

Stainless steel pans:
Stainless steel pans look attractive and are easily cleaned, but do not heat evenly. Food burns easily, too.

Copper pans:
Copper pans are rarely used in Asian recipes. For instance, salted mustard turns a very bright green colour when boiled in a copper pan. They are very rarely used, also, as they are very expensive.

Non-stick pans:
There are many brands of non-stick pans to select from. Choose carefully. Whenever possible, buy the best quality products as they are the cheapest in the long run.
Some points to remember when using non-stick pans:
1. Non-stick pans are ideal for frying fish and soft soya bean cake. In a non-stick pan, food that is to be braised or simmered needs less liquid. Food does not burn easily in a non-stick pan nor does the gravy evaporate as fast as in an ordinary pan.
2. The Teflon in a non-stick pan should not be heated through. If this happens, then the pan would lose its non-stick qualities. Since stir-frying requires that it is done over a high heat, do not stir-fry in a non-stick pan. It is always best to stir-fry in an iron wok.
3. Do not use the non-stick pan as a steamer, since this will again damage the Teflon, making the pan less likely to be non-stick.
4. Never use a metal slice on a non-stick pan.
5. Always pour in the oil or gravy first before putting on the heat.

China clay pot:
Braising and stewing of chicken and pork are usually done in the China clay pot. It simmers food very nicely without burning and has a lower rate of evaporation than other saucepans. It also retains any special flavour of the food and is widely used in Chinese homes. It is also used to cook rice and porridge. Buy one with a smooth, glazed finish.

Pounder (pestle and mortar):
Insist on local granite which is white with black/grey spots. To season the pounder, grind a small handful of fine sea sand in the mortar until both the pestle and mortar are reasonably smooth.

INDEX